BEING A SPERM DONOR

Fertility, Reproduction and Sexuality

GENERAL EDITORS:

Soraya Tremayne, Founding Director, Fertility and Reproduction Studies Group and Research Associate, Institute of Social and Cultural Anthropology, University of Oxford.

Marcia C. Inhorn, William K. Lanman, Jr. Professor of Anthropology and International Affairs, Yale University.

Philip Kreager, Director, Fertility and Reproduction Studies Group, and Research Associate, Institute of Social and Cultural Anthropology and Institute of Human Sciences, University of Oxford.

For a full volume listing please see back matter.

BEING A SPERM DONOR
MASCULINITY, SEXUALITY, AND BIOSOCIALITY IN DENMARK

Sebastian Mohr

berghahn
NEW YORK · OXFORD
www.berghahnbooks.com

First published in 2018 by

Berghahn Books

www.berghahnbooks.com

© 2018, 2020 Sebastian Mohr
First paperback edition published in 2020

Library of Congress Cataloging-in-Publication Data

Names: Mohr, Sebastian, author.
Title: Being a Sperm Donor: Masculinity, Sexuality, and Biosociality in
Denmark / Sebastian Mohr.
Description: New York: Berghahn Books, 2018. | Series: Fertility,
Reproduction and Sexuality; Volume 40 | Includes bibliographical
references and index.
Identifiers: LCCN 2018016346 (print) | LCCN 2018017006 (ebook) |
ISBN 9781785339479 (eBook) | ISBN 9781785339462 (hardback:
alk. paper)
Subjects: LCSH: Sperm donors—Denmark. | Artificial insemination,
Human—Social aspects—Denmark. | Masculinity—Denmark. |
Sex—Denmark.
Classification: LCC HQ761 (ebook) | LCC HQ761 .M64 2018 (print) |
DDC 362.17/8309489—dc23
LC record available at https://lccn.loc.gov/2018016346

British Library Cataloguing in Publication Data

A catalogue record for this book is available from the British Library.

ISBN 978-1-78533-946-2 hardback
ISBN 978-1-78920-812-2 paperback
ISBN 978-1-78533-947-9 ebook

To those men who make a difference with every donation.

CONTENTS

ACKNOWLEDGMENTS

While ethnographic fieldwork and writing can feel lonesome at times, ethnographic research and analysis are never solitary events. That is why I want to thank the following people:

I am indebted to the men who shared their stories with me. Without their commitment to the research endeavor, these insights into being sperm donors would have never been possible. Given that many of the donors I talked to considered insights into the lives of sperm donors valuable, I hope that this book lives up to their idea of a nuanced account of what it means to donate semen. Equally important was the cooperation of sperm banks and clinical research centers and the willingness of lab technicians, donor coordinators, physicians, and receptionists to let me be part of their working lives. I am thankful for their help.

As this book is the product of many years of work, there are a number of colleagues who have made a difference in how it took shape. During my years as a PhD student at the University of Copenhagen, colleagues at the Center for Medical Science and Technology Studies and the Section for Health Services Research influenced my thinking. Thank you for all your help and support. I especially want to thank Klaus Hoeyer and Ayo Wahlberg for guiding me through my fieldwork, analysis, and writing. I also want to thank Elizabeth Roberts and Eric Plemons for sparring with me during my time at the Department of Anthropology at the University of Michigan. A thank you to Bob Simpson, Lynn Morgan, Linda Layne, Stine Adrian, and Charlotte Kroløkke for their encouragement during my research. A special thank you to my committee members, Marcia Inhorn, Tine Tjørnhøj-Thomsen, and Mette Nordahl Svendsen, for their valuable feedback.

After finishing my PhD, I had the privilege of joining the Department of Educational Sociology at the Danish School of Education,

Aarhus University. While I certainly have learned a lot from all my colleagues at the department, I want to thank especially Marianne Hoeyen, Ning de Coninck-Smith, Christian Sandbjerg Hansen, Jonas Lieberkind, Charlotte Mathiassen, and Matti Weisdorf for inspiring conversations, new ideas, and feedback. During the same years, I had the honor to join a network of scholars working on the global histories of IVF headed by Sarah Franklin and Marcia Inhorn. I want to thank everyone in that network for inviting me in and helping me to develop my work. Part of this book was written during a visit at the Department of European Ethnology at Humboldt University in Berlin. I want to thank the department for its hospitality and Beate Binder and Maren Heibges as well as the members of the research laboratory GenderQueer for their support, feedback, and inspiration.

Much of the analysis offered in this book developed due to feedback from colleagues and scholars at conferences and workshops. Without being able to account for every single presentation that I have given since the beginning of my research, I nevertheless want to thank those colleagues and scholars who took their time to offer comments, questions, and feedback. Especially I want to thank colleagues in the Sexuality Research Network of the European Sociological Association and colleagues from the European Association of Social Anthropologists and the American Anthropological Association who have been so kind to offer comments and help following presentations at (bi)annual meetings.

The research for this book was funded by the Danish Council for Independent Research. Some publications coming out of this research prior to this book were important for the development of my thinking. They were central in helping me figure out how best to understand Danish sperm donors' lives analytically. Because the help of anonymous reviewers and, in some cases, the teamwork with co-authors was important for those publications, and thus for this book, I want to account for them here: Sebastian Mohr and Klaus Høyer, "Den gode sædcelle . . . En antropologisk analyse af arbejdet med sædkvalitet," *Kultur og klasse* 40, no. 113 (2012): 45–61; Sebastian Mohr, "Beyond Motivation: On What It Means to Be a Sperm Donor in Denmark," *Anthropology & Medicine* 21, no. 2 (2014): 162–173; Sebastian Mohr, "Living Kinship Trouble: Danish Sperm Donors' Narratives of Relatedness," *Medical Anthropology* 34, no. 5 (2015): 470–484; Sebastian Mohr, "Containing Sperm—Managing Legitimacy: Lust, Disgust, and Hybridity at Danish Sperm Banks," *Journal of Contemporary Ethnography* 45, no. 3 (2016): 319–342; Sebastian Mohr, "Donating Semen in Denmark," in *The Routledge Handbook of*

Medical Anthropology, ed. Lenore Manderson, Elizabeth Cartwright, and Anita Hardon (New York: Routledge, 2016); Susanna Graham, Sebastian Mohr, and Kate Bourne, "Regulating the 'Good' Donor: The Expectations and Experiences of Sperm Donors in Denmark and Victoria, Australia," in *Regulating Reproductive Donation,* ed. Susan Golombok, Rosamund Scott, John B. Appleby, Martin Richards, and Stephen Wilkinson (Cambridge: Cambridge University Press, 2016); Sebastian Mohr and Lene Koch, "Transforming Social Contracts: The Social and Cultural History of IVF in Denmark," *Reproductive Biomedicine & Society Online* 2 (2016): 88–96; Sebastian Mohr and Andrea Vetter, "Eindringliche Begegnungen: von körperlichem Erleben und Feldforschung," in *Kulturen der Sinne: Zugänge zur Sensualität der sozialen Welt,* ed. Karl Braun, Claus-Marco Dietrich, Thomas Hengartner, and Bernhard Tschofen (Würzburg: Königshausen & Neumann, 2017).

I also want to thank Berghahn for making this book possible and the three anonymous reviewers for their critique, feedback, and encouragement. Thank you also to Charlotte Mosedale and Margit Siri Midjord for helping me with the English language.

Last but not least, I want to thank all those people in my life who have been there for me as dear colleagues and friends: Karen Dam Nielsen, Marie-Louise Holm, Henrik Andersen, Jesper Urban, Aco Atanasovski, Christian Matheis, Sebastian Gastes, and Martin Lenhard. Thank you for being there. I want to thank my parents, Beate and Wolfgang Mohr, for all their support. You are the heroes of my life. Finally, thank you, Lasse, for making my world the wonderful place it is—all because of you. I love you.

INTRODUCTION
BEING A SPERM DONOR

S perm donation is probably one of reproductive biomedicine's most long-standing endeavors. On official record since at least the middle of the eighteenth century (Ombelet and Robays 2010), the practice of collecting semen in a container through masturbation for purposes of artificial insemination has been around for about 250 years. Together with donor insemination, it has ever since functioned as a low-tech solution for childlessness and infertility requiring no laboratory or clinical equipment. Having a man willing and able to masturbate into a container, a woman wanting to undergo insemination, and a person prepared to carry out the insemination procedure is all that is required, and while today's sperm donation and donor insemination involve semen collection and testing at sperm banks and insemination procedures at either a clinic or at home with specialized insemination kits, sperm donation and donor insemination can also be carried out using everyday objects such as cups and turkey basters.

The relatively ready availability of donor semen and sperm donation's low-tech status are certainly part of what made it into a viable success. At the same time, however, sperm donation is also reproductive biomedicine's stepchild, so to say, since the use of donor semen in reproductive biomedicine goes against at least three long-standing Euro-American social taboos: masturbation, infidelity, and multilineal kinship. It is sperm donation's reliance on men masturbating in order to produce semen, its invocation of infidel relations between sperm donor and donor semen recipient, and its disturbance of bilineal kinship that stir moral concerns about the use of donor semen in reproductive biomedicine. The development of, for example, in vitro fertilization (IVF) and intracytoplasmic sperm injection (ICSI) as well as efforts to produce artificial sperm cells

(Medrano et al. 2016) could all be understood as attempts to do away with the need for donor semen and thus bar reproductive bio-medicine against the social interventions that sperm donation and donor insemination carry with them (Mohr and Høyer 2012).

This history of technical simplicity on the one hand and moral complicacy on the other has left a mark on sperm donation as we find it today. While working procedures at sperm banks certainly have changed since the first successful use of frozen human semen for conception in 1953 (Sherman 1980), mostly due to changing regulations for and the commercialization of sperm banking (Barney 2005; Daniels and Golden 2004; Richards 2008), ways of assessing semen quality and determining the fitness of sperm cells today are remarkably similar to biomedical classifications of semen developed during and after World War II (Heinitz and Roscher 2010; Kampf 2013; Swanson 2012). And while acceptability of multilineal kin-ship has increased and the role of social media and readily available genetic testing have made a difference in how moral concerns about the use of donor semen are articulated, the continuous problemati-zations of donor-offspring relations, lesbian and single mothers by choice, and not least sperm donors themselves are all mirroring con-cerns already voiced about the use of donor semen in the first part of the twentieth century (Mohr and Koch 2016).

It is in this sense that sperm donation is (extra)ordinary: while it has been practiced for over 250 years, it still stirs moral concerns, and while it is of concern for the larger public and lawmakers as well as recipients of donor semen and sperm donors, it is also prob-ably one of reproductive biomedicine's most continuously practiced effort to overcome infertility. When considering sperm donation's (extra)ordinariness in these terms, it is quite surprising that knowl-edge about and scholarly insights into the everyday of sperm dona-tion are rather scarce. While there certainly is not a lack of scholarly efforts to investigate why men would want to donate semen (Mohr 2014; Van den Broeck et al. 2013) or media coverage of the so-called secret world of sperm banking (Klotz and Mohr 2015; Mohr 2013; Schneider 2010; Thomson 2008), insights into what sperm dona-tion means as an everyday endeavor are limited. This lack of un-derstanding of the social dynamics of sperm donation is even more surprising when considering the remarkable and far-reaching social consequences that sperm donation has. Most obviously, sperm do-nation challenges dominant conceptions of parenthood, family, and kinship, which are based on bilineal descent (tracing one's ances-try through one's mother's and father's [biogenetic] lineage) and a congruence of biogenetic and social connections. While 250 years of sperm donation certainly have not destabilized the stronghold of such heteronormative understandings of kinship in Euro-American societies, the fact that men have donated their semen to people with whom they have no social relations and the circumstance that couples and single women have been willing to accept their semen in an effort to have children either without biogenetic connections to the father or with no father at all suggest that ways of being a family and living kinship do not always necessarily take the forms prescribed by legal texts, social norms, and cultural traditions (Klotz 2014; Mohr 2015; Nordqvist 2013). Donor-sibling, dibbling, and donor-conceived individual are just three of the terms that have made their way into contemporary kinship vocabulary due to the prevalence of sperm donation, and sperm donation has also fostered the emergence of new forms of sociality and relatedness, such as international networks of families and individuals connected biogenetically through one sperm donor. In addition, sperm donation touches directly on issues of intimacy, gender, and sexuality, opening avenues in which questions of identity and selfhood have to be confronted (Almeling 2011; Graham 2012; Layne 2013; Mohr 2014, 2016b).

In this book, I am concerned with this (extra)ordinariness of sperm donation. I offer insights into the everyday of donating semen by focusing in on the men who provide the substance that makes sperm donation and donor insemination possible in the first place. While the success of sperm donation as a commercial, social, and cultural endeavor throughout its 250 years of history fundamentally depended on men's willingness to continuously commit themselves to providing their semen, these men often go unnoticed when scholars turn their attention to the social and cultural consequences of reproductive biomedicine (but see Almeling 2006, 2007, 2009, 2011; Baumeister-Frenzel et al. 2010; Kirkman 2004; Kirkman et al. 2014; Riggs 2008, 2009; Riggs and Russell 2011; Riggs and Scholz 2011; Speirs 2007, 2012; Steiner 2006). In this book, however, men's experiences with donating semen and reflections on being a sperm donor are the focal point. Based on ethnographic fieldwork at Danish sperm banks and interviews with men who donate their semen in Denmark, I attend to the (extra)ordinariness of sperm donation by looking at men's encounters with the practical matters when donating semen and men's contemplations of the moral dimensions of being a sperm donor.

The point of departure for this book is the argument that being a sperm donor in contemporary Denmark represents a microcosmos of what it means to be a man in a biomedical day and age. Put dif-ferently, insights into the everyday of being a sperm donor provide us with an understanding of how biosociality (Rabinow 1996) plays out in men's gendered and sexualed[1] lives. Not only is Denmark a country with a relatively high societal acceptance of reproductive biomedicine as a legitimate way of conceiving children and a coun-try guaranteeing relatively easy and state-financed access to repro-ductive health services for its citizens (Adrian 2015; Larsen 2015; Mohr and Koch 2016), but Danish sperm banks have also been drivers of the expansion of reproductive health services, not only in Denmark and in Europe but internationally, with sperm banks and fertility clinics offering customer-centered services early on and actively working toward a political and social acceptance of sperm donation and donor insemination (Adrian 2006, 2010, 2015). Den-mark is the country in Europe with the most treatment cycles of both donor insemination and in vitro fertilization on average per capita annually (Calhaz-Jorge et al. 2017; Präg and Mills 2017). Be-tween 8 and 9 percent of all children born every year are conceived with the help of reproductive biomedicine (Fertilitetsselskab 2017), making it hard for people in Denmark not to know someone either conceived with or having used reproductive technologies, especially considering that Denmark's population is only about 5.6 million. In-clusive legislation guaranteeing access to reproductive technologies also for lesbian and single women and tax-financed public health services covering a large extent of the costs involved in conceiving children via assisted reproduction are important parts of Denmark's biosocial (extra)ordinariness. Since the founding of the first Danish sperm bank in 1967 and the birth of the first Danish child conceived with the help of in vitro fertilization in 1983, Denmark has thus transformed from being a society "concerned about the social con-sequences of reproductive technologies to a moral collective charac-terized by a shared sense of responsibility for Denmark's procreative future" (Mohr and Koch 2016: 90).

This development fundamentally relied on Danish men wanting to donate their semen. The successful recruitment of donors by Dan-ish sperm banks helped to secure a supply of semen that was neces-sary for the expansive use of reproductive technologies, especially donor insemination and in vitro fertilization. What is more, the in-ternational success of Danish sperm banks since the beginning of the 1990s brought Danish sperm donors international attention as part of a global brand of Nordic fertility providers (Kroløkke 2009) adver-tising to fulfill the promise of reproductive futurity (Edelman 2004;

Mohr 2010, 2016a). While there are no exact numbers for how many sperm donors there are in Denmark, a well-informed estimate of how many men have donated semen at a Danish sperm bank at some point in their life since the 1950s (when experiments with freezing semen for purposes of insemination started at Frederiksberg Hospital) would be between twenty-five thousand and thirty-five thousand. Even though a committee on donor insemination commissioned by the Danish Ministry of Justice had already called for the establishment of a central sperm donor register in 1953 (Justitsministeriet 1953), no such register was ever established and thus information about sperm donors is mostly in the hands of sperm banks. Currently, there are four registered sperm banks in Denmark that supply semen for donor insemination (Sundhedsstyrelsen 2015). The largest sperm banks advertise with the availability of semen from three hundred to one thousand men on their webpages and, besides Denmark, export donor semen to international destinations with most of these exports going to countries within the European Union (Sundhedsstyrelsen 2014). In addition, Danish sperm banks have subsidiary locations in other countries from which they recruit sperm donors locally and distribute donor semen worldwide. In 2016, the two largest Danish sperm banks had a combined gross profit (the difference between the revenue from sales and the costs of producing goods/services) of about 94 million Danish krone, roughly 13 million euros (Proff.dk 2017).

All of this requires men's willingness to be sperm donors. The success of Danish sperm banking as a global endeavor relies on men accepting the biomedical regulation of their daily lives and routines: they need to be comfortable with being screened and tested and having their medical, genetic, and personal history evaluated and judged. They need to consent to an invasion of their intimate spaces of self and accept control over their orgasmic functioning. They need to render their bodily and affective boundaries vulnerable and agree to being tapped for blood and provide urine and semen samples on demand as well as having the medical gaze intrude on their body and self-image. They need to tolerate the objectification of their semen and having it assessed in terms of biomedical classifications and valued in terms of monetary compensation. They need to provide personal information to be made available in databases on sperm banks' websites that they have no control over, and they need to endure the moral challenges of being a sperm donor in relation to lovers, partners, families, friends, colleagues, children, donor-conceived individuals, recipients of donor semen, and not least the general public. Most of all, they need to be willing to accept all of this continuously for the years that they are actively donating semen, if not even for the rest of their lives.

Contrary to what some people might assume, being a sperm donor has no expiration date. Contracts with sperm banks, changing legal regulations, moral obligations to loved ones, and biogenetic connections to donor-conceived individuals require a lifetime commitment to being a sperm donor. The ever-present potential of donor-conceived individuals contacting men after they stopped donating semen twenty years ago, no matter whether they donated anonymously or not, probably captures best what a lifetime commitment as a sperm donor entails. The use of social media and genetic testing by donor-conceived individuals to find the men who provided the semen for their conception has made this an even more likely event (Klotz and Mohr 2015). Also, changes in legislation in regard to donor-conceived individuals' rights to have access to donor-identifying information with consequences for the men who were promised lifelong anonymity when they began donating semen, as is the case in Australia (Graham, Mohr, and Bourne 2016), mean a lifetime commitment as a sperm donor. In addition, contracts and regulations bind sperm donors to continuously update their contact information so as to be available for potentially necessary medical and genetic testing, and, probably most profoundly, men's self-perceptions and ways of being a man are persistently changed by the biomedical and organizational logic of institutionalized sperm donation programs (Almeling 2006, 2009; Mohr 2014, 2016a, 2016b; Riggs 2009; Riggs and Scholz 2011).

It is in this sense that sperm donors' lives are a microcosmos of what it means to be a man in a biomedical day and age. Sperm donors not only commit themselves to donate semen two or three times a week for two, three, four, or even more years; rather, they live the biosociality of masculine selves, intimate experiences, and social relations. Living a life as a sperm donor means not only enduring continued testing and evaluation of your health status, your bodily fluids, and your lifestyle choices; it also means thinking of yourself and your social relations in terms of biosociality, that is, the embeddedness of the self and its constituting social relations in "a variety of biopolitical practices and discourses" (Rabinow 1996: 98). In other words, sperm donors are not simply men that donate semen; sperm donors are biosocial selves whose gendered, sexualed, and moral constitution is profoundly intertwined with contemporary (reproductive) biomedicine and its sociocultural and not least political dimensions.

This book provides an understanding of biosocial subjectivation—the persistent invocation of the subject in terms of biomedical registers and biopolitical valuations—by exploring sperm donors' intimate spaces of gender and sexuality as they are interpellated by reproductive biomedicine. The argument that I make throughout the book is rather straightforward: reproductive biomedicine opens up for the performativity of gender as a lustful experience of the self, something that I call the enticement of gender, and thus binds men to biopolitical objectives. The enticement of gender describes situations or processes of being affected in a way that incites an excitement about, a pleasure of, and/or a desire for gender normativity. It is a way of embodying the world in and through a gendered praxis that makes that praxis more desirable and alluring than other possible ways of en*gendering* the world. For sperm donors this means that donating semen is about more than only providing semen samples for donor insemination. It is about biomedically mediated spaces of the self, which provide for the possibility of enjoying the performativity of gender. Sperm donors remake themselves as men through sperm donation; their biosocial selves are continuously reconstituted in sperm donation practices through the alluring power of gender that entices men to remake themselves as gendered subjects.

I will lay out the conceptual pathways of this argument in chapter 1 and thus invite readers interested in the theoretical underpinning of what I term biosocial subjectivation and the enticement of gender to proceed to that chapter before reading the rest of the book. In the remainder of this introduction, I will provide insights into the ethnographic and empirical background of this book and give an outlook on how the nuances of sperm donors' biosocial subjectivation are explored in the different chapters.

The Ethnography of Sperm Donors' Lives

Following the everyday lives of sperm donors is not a straightforward task. While my ideal research design would have included "hanging out" with sperm donors or at least being able to engage them in continuous conversations about the ordinariness of being a sperm donor, it was clear from my own experiences and those of other researchers that men who donate semen are not necessarily seeking engagements with ethnographers beyond the duration of one interview. In spite of donating semen being an ordinary part of their lives, the ordinariness of being a sperm donor does not include the interrogating presence of an ethnographer. As I will show in more detail in chapter 5, biosocial subjectivation might be said to have its limits, and having an ethnographer intrude into the ordinariness of sperm donor selfhood is one of them. Getting insights into the ordinariness of being a sperm donor thus required a different approach than simply hanging out with sperm donors.

My fieldwork began in the beginning of 2011 and lasted until the end of the summer of 2013. It included participant observation at three sperm banks in Denmark and the United States and at one clinical research and treatment center for male infertility in Denmark, interviews with twenty-three men who donated their semen at Danish sperm banks, interviews with three men who donated semen as part of informal donor insemination, interviews with two men who donated semen for a research project, one interview with a man who had been rejected as a sperm donor, interviews and informal conversations with sperm bank staff and with scientists working with spermatozoa, and participant observation at courses on reproductive biology and spermatogenesis. In addition, I systematically followed media coverage of sperm donation in Denmark throughout my fieldwork and went to public engagement events on sperm donation and male infertility, attended to legal documents regulating sperm donation in Denmark, read biological and andrological literature on semen, sperm cells, and sperm cell development, and not least involved myself with popular culture artifacts of sperm donation, such as movies, documentaries, artwork, and books—in short, I tried to make sperm donation a part of my daily life.

Based on previous experiences of trying to recruit sperm donors for interviews in Germany (Knecht et al. 2010), I was aware that the best chance of meeting men who donate semen was to collaborate with sperm banks. While private inquiries to interview men on their experiences as sperm donors might easily be viewed as dubious, inquiries that are approved by sperm banks are likely to be seen as respectable since they reach men through sperm banks' official communication channels. Therefore, I formulated an email that was sent out to active sperm donors by the sperm banks that I collaborated with. This email contained information about my project and a link to my project home page from which men could write to me via a contact field. A total of forty men replied, over twice as many as I had hoped for in my most optimistic estimates, since experience from other qualitative research on sperm donors shows that recruitment of sperm donors in larger numbers is difficult (Almeling 2011; Kirkman 2004; Riggs 2009; Speirs 2012; Steiner 2006). Of course, the men did not reply all at once but rather continuously throughout the duration of my fieldwork. As some men did not come to agreed interviews and others did not reply to emails or simply contacted me too late in my fieldwork, I was not able to interview all forty men who had contacted me initially.

Those interviewees who donated semen as part of informal donor insemination arrangements rather than at sperm banks contacted me after I had registered on a website that served as a forum for women looking for donor semen on the one hand and men offering their semen on the other. Through participant observation at a clinical treatment and research center for male infertility, I got to know two men who donated semen to a research project at the center, and the only rejected donor I was able to interview contacted me following an email he had received from one of the sperm banks informing him about my project.

Not of Danish origin, I had moved to Denmark a year before my fieldwork started as part of an attempt to receive funding for my research. I had visited Danish sperm banks once before during a graduate student research project in cultural anthropology at Humboldt University on sperm donation and donor insemination in Germany (Knecht et al. 2010). While I was fluent in Danish by the time I started fieldwork, it still took some time to understand the subtleties of engaging in conversations about topics considered private, if not even taboo, by the majority of Danes. When embarking on fieldwork at the beginning of 2011, I thus not only encountered terms and concepts that were foreign to me since they were part of the scientific language and logic of reproductive biomedicine and andrology, but also because they referred to a "whole way of life" (Williams 2011), which was in some aspects different from my upbringing in Germany. For example, the linguistic nuances that men employed to talk about masturbation were not always obvious to me during conversations, but only after interviews had been transcribed. In other instances, men's dialects proved quite difficult to understand, and I felt rather inadequate during one interview in particular, since I constantly had to ask the interviewee to repeat what he had just said. Acknowledging these limitations, conducting interviews with men in English was never a consideration. While all men were able to communicate in English—being a Danish sperm donor requires men to fill out most information about themselves in English since sperm banks target an international group of customers—having to talk about their experiences in English would certainly not have produced the same kind of familiar linguistic space for them. As donors repeatedly remarked during interviews, having to fill out sperm banks' forms and answer personal questions for donor profiles in English limited their possibility to express themselves.

Between the initial contact with donors and then actually meeting them, a couple of weeks or even months went by. I arranged interviews with donors so that they could fit them into their schedules, and interviews took place either at the men's homes, in hotel rooms, in my office, at restaurants, at sperm banks, or via telephone or internet. When planning the interviews, I thought of them as conversations between men about what it means to be a sperm donor with a focus on four topics: being a sperm donor, donating semen, relatedness, and semen and sexual practices. The topic *being a sperm donor* was supposed to address more general questions, for example, when, how, and why men became sperm donors and how they dealt with being a donor as part of their daily social life. Under the headline *donating semen,* I concentrated on men's specific experiences at the sperm bank and their evaluations of encounters with staff, the various procedures and examinations, as well as the atmosphere at the sperm banks and especially the donor rooms. Questions regarding the topic *relatedness* addressed men's thoughts on connections to donor-conceived individuals and recipients, while questions on *semen and sexual practices* explored men's sexual life and their understandings of and knowledge about semen. Even though each topic would address different issues, aspects of a specific topic also appeared throughout the rest of the interview. For example, I would ask about masturbation and men's sexual habits when talking about their experiences at sperm banks, while also posing similar questions when talking about their sexual life in general. Questions as to how men would define a family would appear under the topic *being a sperm donor* as well as when talking about connections to recipients and donor-conceived individuals. This deliberate decision on my behalf, to repeat topics and questions, was a way of securing that interviewees as well as I would have a chance to reflect on central dimensions of being a sperm donor throughout the whole interview and as the narrative itself progressed, thereby producing a *thick description* (Geertz 2000) of particular experiences and reflections.

The men that I had a chance to talk to about their experiences of being a sperm donor came from very different backgrounds. The youngest sperm donor was eighteen years old and had just started donating semen. The oldest was thirty-nine and had more than five years of experience as a sperm donor. Only about a third of the men were still students in a variety of disciplines—pedagogy, psychology, medicine, biology, engineering, political science—while the rest of them (besides one who was unemployed at the time of the interview) were full-time employees or entrepreneurs in a range of fields: physiotherapy, mechanics, personal coaching, finance, logistics, landscaping, IT services, sales, graphic design, transportation, law enforcement, communications, and business consultancy. About half of the men were still single, with the other half either in a relationship or married. Accordingly, a little bit more than half did not have children, while the rest had one child or more. As was to be expected, the vast majority of the men self-identified as heterosexual, although three men stated bisexual interests. All but one donor were Danish citizens and white, and the majority of them were also registered organ and blood donors.

Men's interest in participating in my research was often grounded in a sense of responsibility in regard to being a sperm donor. By participating in interviews about what it means to be a sperm donor, men saw an opportunity to contribute to knowledge about sperm donors and therewith to a better understanding of sperm donation from their point of view, a result of biosocial subjectivation and its implications, as I would argue. In this sense, participating in research about donors was honorable and connected to core biopolitical values. The men deemed knowledge about sperm donors especially important with regard to recipients and donor-conceived individuals, since it, in their eyes, provides recipients and their children with information about otherwise unknown men. In addition, men clearly regarded participation in my research as an opportunity to reflect on their engagements as sperm donors. During interviews, I often felt as if the men took a reflective position on becoming a sperm donor or used me to inquire about legal contexts or to hear more about the experiences of other interviewees. Using the interview as a reflective space, the men often did so out of curiosity. In some cases, however, they also used the interview to reconsider their decision to become a sperm donor. One donor, for example, seemed rather unsure about whether he was engaging in something that he could stand for at the end of the interview. He worried about future repercussions, which he currently could not anticipate, something that I call the limits of biosocial subjectivation and that I will explore in more detail in chapter 5. The majority of donors, however, did construct a narrative that presented them as confident about the fundamental goodness of being a sperm donor, a narrative reflecting the lived ordinariness of biosociality and the implications of biosocial subjectivation for donors' daily lives. This was the case for William, for example, in his twenties and a donor for just about a year when I met him:

> I think this (research on semen quality) is really interesting, also be-
> cause my training deals a lot with physics and chemistry and the like,
> so I think that all of this is really interesting. When I began as a donor,
> I went into a clothing store and bought a bunch of loose boxer shorts
> [laughing], and basically changed my wardrobe. I had a lot of tight
> underwear, but threw them out. They were too old and used and
> instead I only bought loose boxer shorts. And I also stopped using
> my laptop on my lap and instead started to put a pillow underneath
> it. Sometimes, I have to use a car a lot when I am at work and there
> I have stopped using the heater, because, some of the things I read
> dealt with taxi drivers and truckers. They are supposed to have really,
> really bad (semen quality) since they sit down all day. I think this is
> all very interesting and I began to be curious about this part of the
> body, how the genes work and how they are influenced and all that.

Yet such narratives about the ordinariness of being a sperm donor could not stand alone, so I conducted participant observation at
three sperm banks and one clinical treatment and research center
for male infertility to get a better understanding of the daily life at a
sperm bank. I would start participant observation at each field site
when the laboratory opened, which was usually at around 8:00 A.M.
The first day at a particular site always began by me introducing
myself to the staff if they had not already met me at previous meetings, and being given a short tour of the premises by a staff member.
I would thereafter join technicians working at the lab, observe their
working practices, and ask questions about the procedures in general without focusing on particular details. After the first day at the
laboratory, I would divide my second day at each field site into focused observations. This meant that after having observed the general working process at the lab on the first day, on the second day
I would specifically focus on certain procedures and observe them
repeatedly to understand the intricacies of working with semen. On
the third day, I would usually change location and attend more to
the reception desk and waiting area for sperm donors. Here, sperm
donor conduct and interactions between donors and staff were most
important. At one sperm bank, I was allowed to assist with checking in donors when they came in to drop off a sample. Afraid at first
that I would not be able to do the work properly, while at the same
time trying to be a good ethnographer and record every detail of the
work as well as my interactions with donors, I valued that particular

experience later on, since it provided me with an understanding of the interactions between staff and sperm donors.

On the fourth day, I would return to the lab and introduce my video camera. While staff had been informed by me of the fact that I would be using video as part of my observations, the moment of introducing the camera was always a delicate one. The presence of the camera was emphasized in instances where I had to carry it myself, since the lab did not allow for a good full-shot angle without also filming arriving donors, something that I did not want to do, as none of the potential donors had given permission to be filmed. Taking photographs was a less disturbing practice. In comparison to filming at the lab, taking photos of working procedures was regarded as a legitimate, if not even legitimizing, practice by lab technicians, since technicians saw photographs as a more accurate way of capturing what their work encompasses.

I also drew maps of locales and sketched the interior of laboratories. Mapping the spatial organization of sperm banks and especially laboratories was first and foremost a way for me to understand how the lab was positioned as part of the overall premises. The location of a specific lab was of particular importance for how work at that lab was carried out, and what spatial encounters sperm donors had to navigate while being at the sperm bank. Due to certain time dynamics at sperm banks, characterized by peak and off-peak hours, not all days were filled with activity. At each sperm bank, donors would come in at certain hours, and the donor traffic determined the amount of work in the lab. During peak hours with many donors, the work pace at the laboratory would be hastened, while during off-peak hours, with none or only very few donors, moments occurred in which literally nothing happened. Sometimes, I would use these moments to experiment with my senses. I would for example deliberately close my eyes and focus only on the things that I could hear. At other times, I would concentrate on the smell in the lab and the olfactory dimensions of particular working procedures. I noticed a particular laboratory smell during my first week of participant observation. It was a very subtle sour smell, hardly noticeable. At first, I thought that this smell was the result of my own body odors due to perspiration. But then I encountered a similar odor at other sperm banks. Intrigued, I asked lab technicians whether they could smell this particular odor as well. After I had described the odor, they explained to me that it actually came from semen samples and would normally blend in with other olfactory dimensions at the lab. These dimensions are important both for sperm donors and for staff at the lab, since they are decisive for whether sperm donors feel comfortable at the sperm bank, and since they can intervene in working practices at the lab (Mohr 2016a).

Besides the laboratories and the registration desks of sperm banks, two other spaces were central during participant observation: donor candidate interviews and physical examinations of sperm donors. Donor candidate interviews are scheduled with men that have applied to become a sperm donor and whose initial semen sample passed quality requirements. These interviews are usually carried out by personnel who manage donor contacts or, if the interviews coincide with a physical exam, by a physician and are used to assess whether an applicant can be admitted as a donor. As I will argue in the first chapter, these interviews represent more than just a biomedical assessment. They can also be understood as rites of passage into sperm donor subjectivity and thus form an important part of biosocial subjectivation. Physical exams are recurring features of being a sperm donor and thus perpetuate the making of biosocial subjects. Throughout these exams, donors are checked by a physician at the sperm bank on a regular basis, a legal requirement in order to release semen samples from quarantine.

For me to be allowed to sit in on donor candidate interviews, the staff member in charge of conducting these interviews would inform the men scheduled to be interviewed during a particular week of my presence and ask them whether I could join the interview. Before each interview, I would introduce myself to the donor candidates and ask them one more time for permission to be present. This particular dynamic probably did not leave any room for the men to deny my presence, yet any other way of getting access to these interviews would have been neither feasible nor permissible. During the interviews, I would usually not participate in the ongoing conversation. Recording the interview's progression as well as its content in my fieldnotes, I took the position of a silent observer. After each interview, I would discuss certain parts of it with the staff member who conducted the interview, and then write a full-length protocol based on my notes. During some of the interviews, however, I became directly involved in the conversation between the staff member and the donor candidate. Sometimes, the staff member would approach me directly with questions regarding my expertise on sperm donation, such as regulation or experiences of other donors. At other times, donor candidates would ask me questions with regard to, for example, donor anonymity or semen quality measurements. In some cases, I would just jump into the conversation when, for example, I had the impression that staff members lacked crucial information, such as knowledge about donor-conceived individuals. I would then advise donor candidates to search the internet for documentaries dealing with donor-conceived individuals or point out sites such as the Donor Sibling Registry (DSR). These kinds of interventions on my side were intended to assist either staff members or donor candidates with information and reflection on certain issues deemed important by them in deciding whether to become a sperm donor. However, whether they were helpful to either party involved in these situations, I cannot say.

Physical examinations of donors were carried out by a physician. All these physicians were male, whereas personnel conducting donor candidate interviews were all female. The gendered space of the physical exam was dominated by the authority of the physician, as opposed to donor candidate interviews, in which the female staff member's authority was sometimes challenged by men. Initially expecting to record the progression of these physical exams in a similar fashion as with donor candidate interviews, I realized during the first examination that the exposure of the donor body during the exam installed a feeling of shame in me and in the men being examined. Looking at the naked men seemed inappropriate to me, and thus observation in these instances was characterized by me looking down and only listening to what was being said. The limits of biosocial subjectivation were clearest in these cases; a dynamic also echoed by sperm donors during interviews by pointing out that they would probably stop donating semen if more intrusive exams would take place. I will return to the sense of shame involved in these exams and the limits of biosocial subjectivation in chapter 5.

The Nuances of Sperm Donors' Biosocial Subjectivation

The remainder of this book is dedicated to exploring the nuances of sperm donors' biosocial subjectivation. Each chapter will attend to a particular facet of what it means to live the ordinariness of biosociality as a sperm donor in Denmark, and thus each chapter will provide insights into what it means to be a man in a biomedical day and age. What makes sperm donors interesting epistemologically speaking is the circumstance that their daily life weaves together the gendered and sexualed norms of contemporary social life in an era of (reproductive) biomedicine in a seemingly unproblematic fashion. Sperm donors are biosocial subjects not because they are sick (though they potentially might be), but because they are assessed to be just perfect in terms of biomedical registers and biopolitical valuations. Unlike infertile men who do not produce good enough semen (Bell 2016; Birenbaum-Carmeli and Inhorn 2009; Goldberg 2010; Inhorn et al. 2009) or impotent men who have difficulties achieving erections (Riska 2010; Wentzell 2013b; Zhang 2015), sperm donors live up to the normative expectations that men are met with in contemporary biosociality: they performatively enact reproductive masculinity each time they produce a semen sample, and they do so one, two, or even three times a week as part of a strict ejaculatory regimen.

Chapters 1 to 5 will explore how sperm donors come into being as biosocial subjects in four different ways through the enticement of gender. Chapter 1 will provide the conceptual pathways through which to understand biosocial subjectivation and the enticement of gender. Chapters 2, 3, and 4 are concerned with the making of bio-social subjects through the enticement of gender in a pleasurable sense, and chapter 5 is concerned with the limits of biosocial subjec-tivation and thus how the displeasure of gender normativity marks the regulatory and normative boundaries of biosociality.

Chapter 1, *Becoming a Sperm Donor*, lays out the conceptual path-ways of the argument that being a sperm donor can be understood as a process of biosocial subjectivation that happens through the en-ticement of gender. In laying out these pathways, I will interweave ethnographic observations and sperm donors' personal narratives with anthropological and sociological discussions of biosociality, bio-medicalization, and biological citizenship, on the one hand, and with queer-feminist discussions of gender and sexuality, on the other.

In chapter 2, entitled *Regimes of Living*, I will look at sperm do-nors' contemplations about the morality of donating semen. Sperm donors find themselves in a moral landscape that heralds invest-ments into human reproduction on the one hand while stigmatizing and tabooing their contributions on the other. What is of interest here is thus how sperm donors construct ways of being in the world that align their decision to donate semen with their gendered moral self-perceptions, thereby (re)creating regimes of living that allow them to live life ethically. Sperm donors emerge here as biosocial subjects by taking acceptable and not least recognizable positions in terms of gender and morality, such as the loving son, the caring fa-ther, or the responsible husband, thereby (re)making themselves as gendered subjects of a particular moral order.

Chapter 3 is entitled *Affective Investments* and deals with sperm donors' experiences of masturbating at sperm banks. While sperm donors' affective investments are most of the time taken for granted and not discussed, they are important to consider analytically if biosocial subjectivation through the enticement of gender is to be understood properly. Considering masturbation as important in its own right, I attend to the making of sperm donors as biosocial subjects through their affective investments when producing semen samples. What is in focus here is how men performatively (re)constitute their gendered and sexualed subjectivity in terms of biomedical registers and biopolitical valuations through masturbation. Learning to be affected in particular ways, men know how to excite and stimulate themselves in order to produce semen samples on demand, incorporating control regimes as part of their performativity of gender.

Chapter 4 has the title *Biosocial Relatedness* and deals with how sperm donors relate to loved ones and family members as well as donor-conceived individuals and recipients of donor semen. Unpacking biosocial subjectivation as a matter of relatedness, the chapter explores what kind of responsibilities come with relating and being connected to other people through the use of reproductive technologies. While laws regulating sperm donation in Denmark and contractual obligations provide a context in which men determine what their responsibilities are as sperm donors, they are also faced with a context in which they need to determine themselves what being a responsible sperm donor might mean. Navigating the terrain of biosocial relatedness, sperm donors (re)make themselves as men through the enticement of gender as responsibility. Claiming positions as responsible men, sperm donors become biosocial subjects through the performativity of gender as responsibility.

In chapter 5, entitled *The Limits of Biosocial Subjectivation,* I explore the instances in which the making of sperm donors as biosocial subjects through the enticement of gender reaches its limitations. In these instances, the limits of biosocial subjectivity are marked by male shame, situations in which men's gender performativity becomes unpleasant and thus threatens their continuous commitment as sperm donors. While generally accepted, medical exams, atmospheres in donor rooms, and confrontations with the moral complexities of being a sperm donor can also require affective investments from sperm donors that they regard as unacceptable transgressions of their intimate spaces of self, and these kinds of affective investments therefore lead men to reconsider whether being a sperm donor is such a good thing after all. Being a sperm donor and becoming a biosocial subject is not a given and requires work, and chapter 5 thus explores the limits of the making of biosociality.

Finally, in *Conclusion: Biosocial Subjectivation Reconsidered*, I formulate suggestions for how insights into the (extra)ordinary lives of Danish sperm donors might be useful in different scholarly and professional fields. Reflecting on the book's main argument and analytical points, I consider how the book's contribution may make a difference in scholarship on biosociality, for queer and feminist thinking of gender, in anthropological and sociological discussions of kinship and relatedness, and, not least, for the practical matters of running a sperm bank or working with sperm donors.

Note

1. The term "sexualed" refers "to generic meanings and activities in relation to sexuality" (Hearn 2014: 402) in the same sense that the term "gendered" connotes meanings related to gender.

Chapter 1

BECOMING A SPERM DONOR
CONCEPTUAL PATHWAYS

B efore men are accepted as sperm donors by Danish sperm banks, they have to undergo various tests. Among those are, of course, assessments of semen quality but also blood and genetic tests, physical exams, and not least evaluations of their personal integrity through a series of interrelated interviews. While these tests and personal meetings serve the purpose of reassuring sperm banks that a sperm donor candidate will comply with what is expected of him and that he exhibits the responsibility that is deemed necessary in order to be a sperm donor (Graham, Mohr, and Bourne 2016; Mohr 2010), going through these tests and evaluations might also be understood as a more formal process of initiation into becoming a sperm donor and thereby an important part of biosocial subjectivation. Understood as a rite of passage in Arnold van Gennep's sense of a set of practices that ensures the successful change of a person's affiliation and belonging (Van Gennep 2004), this initial testing and evaluation could be comprehended as calling the biosocial self into being. It is at this stage before actually being accepted as a sperm donor that men might be thought of as undergoing a transformation of their sense of self, identification, and belonging.

To give you an idea of what this process looks like and to provide you with ethnographic grounding for the conceptual pathways that will follow, I want to present you with a rather lengthy note from my fieldwork at Danish sperm banks describing a meeting between a donor coordinator and a sperm donor candidate. These meetings take place before men are accepted as sperm donors and represent formal interviews during which men have to answer questions in regard to their medical and genetic history, and during which staff tests men's commitment to being a sperm donor. What is of importance here are the ways in which the biosocial self is called into being during these interviews—a careful and continuous invocation of the subject in terms of biomedical registers and biopolitical valuations:

Stine, the donor coordinator, sits at the table across from Jonas, a donor-candidate in his early twenties. Jonas had been called in for an interview because his initial semen sample had passed the required threshold for semen quality. As with all other donor applicants, his ejaculate needed to have a sperm count of at least 200 million sperm cells per milliliter, since it is not very likely that enough sperm cells will survive the freezing process at a sperm count lower than that, as I have been repeatedly told by laboratory staff. While these technical details are not necessarily part of conversations between staff and donor-candidates, the awareness that only a few men's semen samples make the grade certainly is.

Stine tells Jonas that his first semen sample had turned out to be of good quality; a piece of information that Jonas accepts with visible appreciation saying: "That is great!" Stine starts the question and answer section of the interview with an inquiry about Jonas' educational background. Jonas tells her that he is currently working as a volunteer in a social work project after having finished his so-called *studentereksamen,* a formal secondary school degree giving access to university education, and that he has applied for a business administration program at a local university. Going through the questionnaire, which Jonas had filled out before the interview, item by item, Stine moves on to Jonas' eye color. Jonas leans in over the table and Stine checks the color of his eyes. "You have green eyes! That is very rare," she exclaims.

Moving further in the questionnaire, Stine then asks about sexually transmitted diseases: "You state here that you have had chlamydia. Is that correct?" "Yes," says Jonas, explaining that that had been the result of teenage carefreeness. Not probing his explanation any further, Stine moves on to Jonas' visits to foreign countries. As certain destinations are categorized as having higher rates of infectious diseases, especially sexually transmittable ones, men who travel frequently to these destinations are thought to be at risk of exposure and thus make rather unreliable candidates. "I have been in Greenland and in New Zealand," says Jonas, locations which do not spark a reaction from Stine.

She then wants to know whether Jonas wants to be an anonymous or non-anonymous donor. "Originally, I had thought about being anonymous but now I think I want to be an open donor," Jonas explains. Stine then provides more details about the open donor program, pointing out that the children conceived with his semen would be able to contact him when they are eighteen years of age, a situation which could potentially be uncomfortable, she adds. "What does that contact look like," asks Jonas now seemingly less sure about his decision than just a moment ago. Stine answers with an explanation that I have heard her giving also to other donor applicants in similar situations: "Well, what the contact looks like really depends on how the children and the individual donor handle the situation." In a more reassuring tone, she then adds: "But the contact would be arranged through us," to which Jonas obviously relieved replies: "Oh, okay, it is just one contact."

Without dwelling any further on the subject of possible contact to donor-conceived individuals, Stine moves on to elaborate on the more practical arrangements, which Jonas has to adhere to as a sperm donor: he would have to respect a period of abstinence of last at least forty-eight hours in between semen samples. However, he would be able to donate whenever he pleases during business hours as long as he donates at least once a week or four times within one month. In case he wants to go on vacation, he should inform the staff so that they know not to expect any samples from him during that time. He would also have to supply blood samples on a regular basis so that his semen samples can be released from quarantine. Blood samples would be taken every three months. For each semen sample, he would get 300 Danish krone (about 40 euros), 200 whenever he stops by to provide a sample and the rest once the samples have been approved and released through blood tests. Should the blood tests show any irregularities, he would be contacted: "If there is anything out of the ordinary, we will let you know." Stine then explains what Jonas would be tested for: HIV, HTVL (human T-lymphotropic virus), hepatitis, syphilis, gonorrhea and "of course also chlamydia, which you already have experience with." They would also do a full karyotype, Stine continues, and they would specifically test for cystic fibrosis.

Jonas' only reactions throughout all of these elaborations are an occasional "Yes" or "That's fine," reactions that I have seen most other donor-candidates exhibit as well. Stine then mentions the donor profile and the extended information that Jonas needs to supply so that future customers can get an idea of what kind of man he is, and lets him know that he can fill out that specific paperwork at home. "And make sure that you save all your health and medical information since we will be asking for it again." As a donor Jonas would have to regularly answer questions about his health and medical status: "We are evaluating you as a donor at all times." Stine then turns to Jonas' family medical history: "I am assuming that you are well and healthy," she wants to know. "There has never been anything wrong with me," Jonas replies. He adds that his sister is overweight. Stine wants to know by how much. He explains that his sister would not have any problems in her daily life; she would just weigh more than other people. Jonas answers all of Stine's questions in regard to his family members' individual medical history and possible causes of death with the help of a piece of paper that contains information about his relatives and which he must have prepared at home on the computer and then printed out to take with him to the interview. He looks at this piece of paper again and again and then checks what Stine enters into her computer by looking at the screen in front of him and Stine. Jonas mentions that his mother has an allergy: "But neither my sister nor I have had any symptoms," he reassures Stine. His uncle has had heart problems: "But he was a drug and alcohol addict, so this was clearly due to his lifestyle," Jonas explains and adds that a genetic test which his mother has had done revealed that this heart problem was not hereditary. "It could very well be that our geneticist will want to know more about this," Stine says. "That is absolutely fine," Jonas answers.

At the end of the family medical history, Stine goes over each of Jonas' answers one more time to make sure that all the information she entered into her computer is correct. Once this is done, Jonas folds the piece of paper he has been using to answer all the questions and puts it back into his pocket. Stine then takes two pictures of Jonas, one from the front and one from the side, which would be used in case staff would have to match Jonas phenotypically to the partner of a future customer. A test for whether Jonas is colorblind is next. With the help of a small book that contains images consisting of different colored dots representing lines, figures, and numbers, Stine asks Jonas to identify the specific representation on each page. Jonas is apparently not colorblind since he gives only right answers.

Finally, Stine reminds Jonas that it would be his responsibility to declare the compensation he receives for his semen samples to the tax authorities. Jonas nods and then signs a form declaring that he has received this information. He also signs all of the other paperwork: consent forms, the contractual agreement, and release forms. At the end of the interview, Stine says to Jonas that she will be in touch with him once the geneticist has gone through all of his medical information and once the semen sample he has delivered today has been assessed: "And in case it shouldn't be as good as the first one, you will hear from us."

While these interviews can vary in length, and even though their details might change depending on the individual donor applicant's history and the questions he has, the above fieldnote nevertheless shows what such first encounters between men applying to be a sperm donor and staff interviewing them usually look like. I provided this rather lengthy fieldnote because these first encounters give an understanding of what men who become sperm donors face for the rest of their lives: a continuous process of biosocial subjectivation, that is, the careful and persistent invocation of their subjectivity in terms of biomedical registers and biopolitical valuations. As becomes clear in the meeting between Stine and Jonas, it is not so much Jonas's possible interests in computer games, art history, or horseback riding or his potential melancholic or cheerful selfperception that are of interest, but rather biomedical registers such as his infection status, his disease history, and his genetic makeup. It is through registers such as these that Jonas becomes a recognizable subject at the sperm bank, someone who is identifiable within the organizational and biomedical logic of contemporary reproductive medicine.

These kinds of registers are certainly not the only ones at play when becoming a sperm donor. However, they definitely determine whether a man can become a sperm donor in the first place, and whether he is allowed to continue to donate semen for a longer period of time. As Stine points out to Jonas during the interview, he will be continuously evaluated as a sperm donor, among other things by means of blood and genetic tests, assessments of his semen quality, regular medical exams, and recurring checks of his medical history, with the measurable results of these tests providing the evidence base for the continuous evaluation of Jonas's performance as a sperm donor. What is more, the importance of biomedical knowledge about Jonas and the need to carry out tests of his biomedical condition are connected to the invocation of his subjectivity in terms of biopolitical valuations. Providing access to his bodily fluids, his medical history, and his genetic makeup are regarded as necessary steps if the protection of life—the children conceived with the help of Jonas's semen—is to be guaranteed, and it is Jonas's willingness to participate in the protection of life—by signing consent and release forms—that is seen as an expression of his commitment to the value of reproduction. As a sperm donor Jonas is expected to take responsibility for his actions—sticking to the abstinence period, staying away from risky behavior, and living a healthy life—thereby signaling his commitment to the value of life itself (Rose 2001).

Understanding this first encounter between men who want to become sperm donors and staff at Danish sperm banks as a rite of passage into sperm donor selfhood and thus as an important part of biosocial subjectivation, I am building on insights into processes of subjectivation and the formation of subjects in biomedical contexts within feminism (Franklin 1997; Martin 2001; Rapp 1999), medical anthropology (Heath, Rapp, and Taussig 2004; Petryna 2002; Rabinow 1996), medical sociology (Conrad 1992; Rosenfeld and Faircloth 2006; Zola 1972), and science and technology studies (Clarke et al. 2003; Hoeyer 2013; Rose 2007) as they have developed since the 1970s. While it will be impossible to cover the vast literature on what could be summarized as biosocial subjectivation or biosocial subjects, I nevertheless want to retrace how I understand biosocial subjectivation by laying out some of this literature in more detail. Following these attempts to map how I think of biosocial subjectivation, I want to bring this scholarship on biosociality into discussion with theories of gender and sexuality in order to explicate what I mean by the enticement of gender, what it has to do with biosocial subjectivation, and how it plays out in the lives of Danish sperm donors.

Biosocial Subjectivation

Within ethnographic scholarship the idea of biosociality developed at the end of the 1980s and the beginning of the 1990s, a time when molecular genetics and reproductive biomedicine had made their way into public consciousness as medical technologies with the possibility of altering the course of life itself (Flower and Heath 1993; Franklin and McNeil 1988; Rabinow 1994; Rapp 1988). This was a time when the use of reproductive biomedicine was still framed as a novel approach to building a family (Edwards et al. 1993; Strathern 1992) and when the ready availability of personal genetic testing (Klotz 2016; Palsson 2012; Richards 2010) had not yet become an ordinary part of people's identities and social relations. When biosociality made its debut as a conceptual term in the writing of Paul Rabinow (Rabinow 1996), scholarly discussions concerned the potential of medico-technological developments to do away with onto-epistemological truth claims such as nature being the unaltered opposite sphere of culture and human social relations representing a naturally gendered and sexualed order of the world (Haraway 1991; Latour 1993; Strathern 1995). While Paul Rabinow was thus surely not the first to invoke the idea of a possible new way of living due to developments in science and technology, he did offer a conceptual term—biosociality—that captured both the societal and cultural changes in light of these medico-technological advancements as well as their repercussions for how people would come to understand themselves and their social relations.

In his well-known essay "Artificiality and Enlightenment: From Sociobiology to Biosociality," first published in 1992, Rabinow makes the argument that molecular genetics will reshape society in a fundamental way by becoming part of "the social fabric at the micro level" and by giving rise to "a circulation network of identity terms and restriction loci" (Rabinow 1996: 98–99). In this society, sociality would no longer be a representation of nature (sociobiology), but rather sociality would itself be an ordering dimension of nature; that is, nature would be remade through sociality (biosociality), and biosociality would become "a prime locus of identity—a biologicalization of identity . . . understood as inherently manipulable and re-formable" (Rabinow 1999: 13). Developing his argument through a discussion of the Human Genome Initiative, Rabinow suggests that biosociality would constitute itself through, for example, groups of people developing social collectives around certain genetic conditions, a way of socializing based on an awareness of the social potency of biological states and on a will to act on this awareness (e.g., Finkler 2000; Gibbon 2007; Gibbon and Novas 2008; Trundle and Scott 2013). Influenced by Michel Foucault's idea of biopower (Foucault 1990), Rabinow offers the term biosociality "as an initial attempt at framing the issues of a re-problematization of 'life'" (Rabinow 2008: 188), a perspective that focuses on a new form of power "that exerts a positive influence on life, that endeavors to administer, optimize, and multiply it, subjecting it to precise controls and comprehensive regulations" (Foucault 1990: 137). From such a perspective, contemporary sociality becomes understandable both in terms of its biomedical registers and biopolitical valuations and in terms of its particular mode of subjectivation, that is, the making of subjects committed to an improvement of life and health on behalf of themselves, those whom they associate with, and not least the social body as a whole. This mode of subjectivation is central to the workings of biopower since it exerts its efficacy by bringing individuals "to work on themselves, under certain forms of authority, in relation [to] truth discourses, by means of practices of the self, [and] in the name of . . . life or health" (Rabinow and Rose 2006: 197).

Following Rabinow's initial use of biosociality, a concept that he never intended to describe a universal truth (Rabinow 2008), a number of terms appeared within anthropology, sociology, and Science and Technology Studies that in one way or another capture similar dimensions of what Rabinow alluded to with biosociality:

bioidentity (Waldby et al. 2004), genetic citizenship (Heath, Rapp, and Taussig 2004), biological citizenship (Petryna 2002; Rose and Novas 2005), biomedicalization (Clarke et al. 2010; Clarke et al. 2003), bio-objectification (Vermeulen, Tamminen, and Webster 2012), bioconstitutionalism (Jasanoff 2011), and the biofinancial subject (French and Kneale 2012) only to name a few. While each of these terms has its own specific origin and analytical focus, what they have in common with the concept of biosociality is an interest in the dynamics of biopower in contemporary society as Foucault initially developed it and, as a result, also an interest in the ramifications of biopower for the development of individual and collective identity. I want to go into detail with two of these terms—biomedicalization and biological citizenship—since they lend themselves for a further elaboration of what I mean by biosocial subjectivation.

While biomedicalization as a term had already made its debut at the end of the 1980s and the beginning of the 1990s (Cohen 1993; Estes and Binney 1989; Vertinsky 1991), conceptually it was more fully developed by Adele Clarke and colleagues at the beginning of the 2000s (Clarke and Olesen 1999; Clarke et al. 2003). Biomedicalization describes "the transformations of both the human and the nonhuman made possible by . . . technoscientific innovations" understood as "multisited, multidirectional processes of medicalization" (Clarke et al. 2003: 162). What comes into focus here is biomedicine's role as an institution of social control and regulation as well as its potential to transform contemporary sociality and processes of identity formation. In light of the importance of biomedicine and biotechnology in contemporary society, Clarke and colleagues offer biomedicalization as a reformulation of the medicalization thesis as it has developed within medical sociology since the early 1970s (Conrad 1975; Zola 1972). Medicalization describes the processes by which social phenomena are understood, defined, and treated as problems in need of medical attention. Even though medicalization is more often than not used as a descriptive term for the (negatively positioned) extension of medicine's power in all of social life, the original proposition of medicalization as an analytical pathway in medical sociology encompassed both the authoritative incorporation of social issues under the umbrella of medical responsibility and the willingness of individuals and society to expand medical expertise on everyday life. In his now classical text on medicine as an institution of social control, Irving Zola writes that the "'medicalizing of society' is as much a result of medicine's potential as it is of society's wish for medicine to use that potential" (Zola 1972: 500).

In the original conceptualization of medicalization, the expansion of medical influence was thus not conceived of as being only the result of authoritative power, but rather as a consequence of a dispersion of medical potentiality as part of (self-)governance.

This notion of dispersing medical potentiality is important for an understanding of biosocial subjectivation. Whereas much of the literature on biomedicalization tends to focus on the negative effects of medicalization and is inclined to draw a picture of an all-encompassing medical jurisdiction over contemporary sociality (Brubaker and Dillaway 2009; Rafalovich 2013), it is important to recognize that biomedicalization is never complete and that medicalizing dynamics are very likely to be accompanied by demedicalizing counter currents (Conrad 1992, 2007). Moreover, biomedicalization is not inherently negative as some of the literature seems to suggest, nor does it only work through a top-down power model. Rather, biomedicalization is probably most likely to be effective when it incites new kinds of agencies within individuals and provides them with new possibilities to take on authoritative positions in their own life courses (Earp, Sandberg, and Savulescu 2015; Petersen, Nørgaard, and Traulsen 2015), since that is what biopower is all about, namely, the incitement to discourse as Michel Foucault termed it and not the subordination to it. In this sense, then, the production of what Clarke and colleagues call technoscientific identities, that is, identities "produced through the application of sciences and technologies to our bodies" (Clarke et al. 2003: 182), rests on the performative effects of biosocial subjectivation—the continuous invocation of a subject position through an incitement to discourse in terms of biomedical registers and biopolitical valuations.

Similar points are made in the literature on biological citizenship as it emerged at the beginning of the 2000s (Novas and Rose 2000; Petryna 2002, 2004; Rose 2001, 2007; Rose and Novas 2005). In her ethnography of nuclear disaster survival in Ukraine, Adriana Petryna coins the term biological citizenship to describe the mobilization of Ukrainian Chernobyl survivors around "radiation-induced injuries" reflecting "a massive demand for but [simultaneously also] selective access to a form of social welfare based on medical, scientific, and legal criteria that both acknowledge biological injury and compensate for it" (Petryna 2002: 5–6). In the aftermath of the nuclear havoc of 1986, Chernobyl survivors had to develop a biomedical literacy that enabled them to make welfare claims and thereby secure their survival. As Petryna explores in her ethnography, knowledge about biological conditions relating to radiation damages and expertise in

medical diagnoses and treatments as well as persistence in claiming access to these treatments were fundamentally important for
people's lives, since it was only those knowledgeable enough about
their nuclear-biological states that could successfully navigate the
medico-bureaucratic network relating to the Chernobyl disaster.
In other words, citizens configured themselves first and foremost
in biological terms that could be recognized in the state-organized
compensation schemes and had to develop forms of citizen activism—either individually or collectively—that secured them access
to welfare payments and services.

This interlinking of biological awareness and citizen activism
configures also in the conceptualization of biological citizenship as
Nikolas Rose and Carlos Novas develop it. Primarily drawing from
examples within the context of genetic testing and counseling, the
forms of citizenship they see emerging in contemporary society are
demanding active biological citizens that "engage in a constant work
of self-evaluation and the modulation of conduct, lifestyle, and drug
regime, in response to the changing requirements of the susceptible
body" (Rose 2007: 161). Part of this active biological citizenship is
a collectivizing dimension that leads people to come together in social groups and communities forged around biomedical awareness
about conditions such as bipolar disorder or Huntington's disease
(Novas and Rose 2000; Rose and Novas 2005). Here forms of citizenship emerge that center around the kinds of responsibilities that
a biopolitical invocation of life demands, namely, citizens who make
decisions and conduct their life in "light of knowledge of his or her
present and future biomedical make-up" (Rose and Novas 2005:
451).

While this form of biological citizen activism is less important for
sperm donors—men who donate semen in Denmark do not organize
politically in order to make citizenship claims or claims to belong to
a particular social group in need of state acknowledgement and support—the underlying societal current inherent to it—invoking biomedical registers such as genetic makeup and biopolitical valuations
such as responsibilities due to one's genetic makeup—certainly is.
What is important for sperm donors' biosocial subjectivation is not
so much the political efficacy that can potentially emerge from biosocial subjectivation, but rather the ordinariness in which the invocation of a subject in terms of biomedical registers and biopolitical
valuations becomes an unquestioned part of sperm donors' daily life
and self-conduct. Sperm donors are not biosocial subjects because
of their political activism or their attempts to get together in sperm

donor communities. Sperm donors are biosocial subjects simply because they live the ordinariness of biopolitical responsibility.

There is vocabulary in the work of Adriana Petryna and Nikolas Rose and Carlos Novas that brings me even closer to the sense of ordinariness to which I am referring here. Whereas Rose and Novas explicitly develop a term that tries to capture the potency of biosocial subjectivation in its ordinary sense, something they call somatic individuals or somatic selves, Petryna alludes to a broader notion of common sense when describing how states of suffering experienced by Chernobyl survivors become ordinary parts of everyday life (Petryna 2004). This notion of a new common sense that people develop in a historical and societal context in which biomedical registers create recognizable subjects encompasses both the intellectual level of being knowledgeable about biological states as well as developing a sense of self in these terms and, moreover, a form of embodiment that makes biosociality part of who one is: "a common sense that is enacted by sufferers themselves in ways that can promote protection as well as intensify new kinds of vulnerability in domestic, scientific, and bureaucratic spheres" (Petryna 2004: 265). Rose and Novas understand this kind of common sense that people inhabit both on an intellectual level and through forms of embodiment as the somatization of personhood, that is, "ways of thinking about and acting upon human individuality in 'bodily' terms" (Novas and Rose 2000: 491). It is in this sense that biosocial subjectivation requires individuals to have an embodied sense of self that makes them feel themselves in terms of biomedical registers and biopolitical valuations. Danish sperm donors do not simply deliver semen samples that are tested and evaluated; they actually incorporate donating semen as part of who they are in terms of sperm counts, contractual obligations, and possible future responsibilities to donor-conceived individuals. Just as Chernobyl survivors in Petryna's invocation of a common sense enact who they are by being citizens recognizable due to certain biological conditions, sperm donors are somatic selves that embody the biopolitical logics inherent to sperm donation.

These notions of a common sense and of a somatic self are important components of biosocial subjectivation, because they provide a central link between biopolitics on the one hand and people's sense of self and being on the other. Only when bodily, emotive, and affective dimensions of the self are interpellated by biomedical registers and biopolitical valuations does biosociality turn into the ordinary foundation of being in the world. In other words, biosocial subjects do not simply represent the normative logics of (reproductive) biomedicine; rather, they *are* biosociality in the sense that they think and feel in terms of as well as are made up of biomedical registers and biopolitical valuations. In her seminal essay on situated knowledges, Donna Haraway suggests thinking of the production of postmodern bodies in terms of what she calls, with reference to Katie King, the apparatus of bodily production (Haraway 1988). This apparatus of bodily production can be understood as a matrix of the intersections "of biological research and writing, medical and other business practices, and technology" that generates bodies (Haraway 1988: 596), and it is within this matrix or apparatus that biosocial subjectivation might be said to take place, since biosocial subjects are made in the fleshy bodily sense of being in the world and not simply as intellectual entities. Sperm donors and their bodies are produced through biosocial subjectivation. They come into being through a continuous invocation of an embodied subject in terms of biomedical registers and biopolitical valuations.

These considerations of how biosocial subjectivation might take form mirror discussions within anthropology and sociology about how culture or sociality makes its way into the identificatory and bodily makeup of people, and how identities and bodies might speak back, so to say, to the structuring moments of communal life. Clifford Geertz's well known idea of culture being a self-spun web of significance (Geertz 2000) or Pierre Bourdieu's influential notion of a practical sense and the incorporation of social life into people's habitus (Bourdieu 1990) are just two examples of an array of conceptualizations within social and cultural theory that attempt to grasp the interplay between human existence and personhood on the one hand and the performative effects of culture or sociality on the other. Within anthropological, sociological, and Science and Technology Studies scholarship discussing biosociality, similar considerations are made with particular emphasis on the reworking of the long-standing divide between the social and the biological (Ingold and Palsson 2013; Meloni, Williams, and Martin 2016; Schramm, Skinner, and Rottenburg 2012). Whereas I share the willingness to undo the opposition between what has been called nature-culture, the experiences of sperm donors warrant a slightly different attention. Rather than focusing on the revolutionary political moment of biosociality as represented in the attempt to undo the (fictitious) foundations of modernity (Latour 1993), I want to attend to the commonsensical dimensions of biosociality as described above. Sperm donors live biosociality in their everyday lives; they remake the boundary between the social and the biological in who they are, and it is precisely this ordinariness of biosociality in sperm donors' lives that is epistemologically relevant here.

In their conceptual note on how to think the interplay between the social and natural in people's everyday lives, Clara Han and Veena Das suggest thinking of the integration of the social into the natural and the natural into the social in people's lives in terms of Ludwig Wittgenstein's *Lebensform* or form of life (Han and Das 2015). While Han and Das develop Wittgenstein's notion of Lebensform in order to point to the fragility in everyday life "that comes from the ever-present possibility that the fine alignment between [the social and the natural] will be lost" (Han and Das 2015: 30) and use it as an epistemological device that allows for the exploration of "the ways in which identity and existence are tied to each other" (Han and Das 2015: 9), I want to hold on to the notion of Lebensform as the unquestioned ways of doing things that make up life and render it meaningful while simultaneously not being explainable. Sperm donors might be able to articulate a motivation for why they donate semen, as an endless array of studies into sperm donors' motives attests (Mohr 2014; Van den Broeck et al. 2013), yet the sedimentation of biosocial reality in their lives and the form of common sense or form of life that comes with it is not necessarily something that can be intellectualized and articulated but is nevertheless important for who they are.

Stephen Collier and Andrew Lakoff offer the concept *regimes of living* in order to capture this dynamic between biosocial ways of being in the world and their accessibility for intellectual reasoning (Collier and Lakoff 2005). Precisely occupied with offering a conceptual term that captures forms of life in a biomedical day and age, Collier and Lakoff understand regimes of living as "a situated form of moral reasoning" (Collier and Lakoff 2005: 23), as "situated configurations of normative, technical, and political elements that are brought into alignment" thereby providing "possible means . . . for organizing, reasoning about, and living 'ethically'" (Collier and Lakoff 2005: 31). Sperm donors' lives might be understood in this way in the sense that they donate semen on a regular basis for a number of years without necessarily questioning the goodness of the act. As becomes clear when listening to men talk about their experiences of donating semen and their contemplations about being a sperm donor, delivering semen samples twice or three times a week and therewith contributing to the conception of new human life is very likely to be bound up with men's sense of moral reasoning, how different these may be, of feeling that being a sperm donor is the right form of life. The regimes of living in which biosocial subjectivation takes place as a continuous invocation of the subject in terms of biomedical registers and biopolitical valuations are aligned configurations in which men's gendered and sexualed sense of self and their moral positioning come together so as to enable their continuous commitment to the biopolitical objective of contemporary reproductive biomedicine. But how might we think of the interplay between biosocial subjectivation and men's gendered and sexualed sense of self? I will consider this question in the next section by elaborating what I call the enticement of gender and how it plays out in the lives of Danish sperm donors.

The Enticement of Gender

One question I continuously faced from colleagues and friends during my fieldwork on Danish sperm donors' experiences was why men would want to donate semen when their sexual conduct is regulated (Mohr 2010), they are likely to experience transgressions of personal boundaries (Mohr 2016a), they are confronted with moral dilemmas (Mohr 2014), and they have to negotiate troubled kinship relations as the result of being a sperm donor (Mohr 2015). While I for a long time did not attend to the epistemological insight that this seeming paradox holds, it seems ever more important when considering the process of biosocial subjectivation as I have just laid out in the previous section. If Foucault's argument that biopower incites to discourse rather than subordinating us to it is to be taken seriously and if biosociality's commonsensical regimes of living and their embodied dimensions are to be of relevance analytically, then surely there would have to be other dynamics at play in sperm donors' persistent commitment than only the subjugating dimensions of the regulatory and normative scripts of morality, kinship, gender, and sexuality as they enfold into one another as part of sperm donation. If being a sperm donor was only about subjugating formal and informal types of regulation (Graham, Mohr, and Bourne 2016), then surely fewer men would commit to it. But since there are men who donate semen and since sperm donation in Denmark has been a successful endeavor due to their commitment, men's experiences of being a sperm donor need to encompass qualitatively other dimensions than only those that an anthropological and sociological interest in the subjugating force of regulatory and normative dimensions of sociality can allude to.

The argument that I make throughout the book aims at addressing those dimensions of sperm donors' biosocial subjectivation that cannot be captured by an analytics of biopolitics, reproductive biomedicine, gender, and sexuality that regards them first and foremost as arenas of power in and through which human behavior and people's sense of being in the world are regulated, controlled, and sanctioned in a subjugating sense. The experiences of men who donate semen in Denmark beg us to also look at a sense of enjoyment and fulfillment that biosocial subjectivation entails; the making of gendered subjects in the biomedically mediated spaces of self that sperm donation provides. What I call the enticement of gender could be understood as an incitement to gender as praxis through the lustful experience of the normatively gendered self enabled by sperm donation. It describes ways of being affected that entice men to remake themselves as gendered subjects in and through their engagements as sperm donors. It is a way of embodying biosociality that centers on the enjoyment of the performativity of gender normativity, the continuous making of the gendered self. Sperm donors remake themselves as men through sperm donation; their biosocial selves are continuously reconstituted in sperm donation practices through the alluring power of gender that entices men to remake themselves as gendered subjects. For an ethnographic elaboration of this understanding of the enticement of gender, consider the following description of my meeting with Elias, a single man in his early thirties who had been donating semen for about two years when I met him:

Elias lives in a rather large apartment building facing a road with heavy traffic. To get to his apartment I had to take an elevator to one of the top floors. When Elias opened the door, I was taken aback by the amount of clutter in his apartment and the impression of untidiness. However, I reckoned that this might just as well be part of his youthful bachelor carefreeness and hedonism. After escorting a friend out of his apartment, Elias asked me to sit down on one of the sofas in the living room. Just as the rest of the apartment, the sofa I sat down on was partly covered in pieces of clothing some of which I removed before sitting down. Elias sat down on the sofa across from me and we began our conversation about his experiences as a sperm donor.

While Elias had been donating semen for about two years, his visits to the sperm bank are not as frequent as those of other sperm donors. Considering that most donors donate once or twice a week, Elias does not necessarily stick to such a rigid schedule, and as Elias told me, there was also a good reason for that: his semen quality would fluctuate quite a lot so that a fairly large amount of his semen samples would not pass quality assessments. This meant that the period of abstinence in between ejaculations which Elias has to adhere to in order for samples to pass assessments is longer than the usual forty-eight hours. Elias' experiences of donating semen are simultaneously influenced by his difficulties to reach an orgasm at the sperm bank. As he told me, he would have to concentrate in order to reach an orgasm: "You know this (masturbating at the sperm bank) is not really because of fun since I know that everything will be spoiled by this stupid tiny cup. You need to hit it and all of that. It is not jacking off in order to release tension [*det er jo ikke en spiller for at lette trykket*], it is a duty."

Elias talked about himself as a man confident about his sexual performance and alluring qualities in regard to women. According to his depictions of himself during our conversation, Elias enjoys the company of women regularly in order to still his sexual lust, and the focal point for him during these encounters would be to pleasure the women he is with, to satisfy them sexually. In order to be able to pleasure women sexually, he had started to practice tantric sex, which requires him to control his orgasms in order to extend the period of sexual excitement and pleasure for both him and his sex partners. He had started with tantric sex when he was younger and not yet able to control his orgasms: "I just wanted to learn how to do it. I thought, if this exists then I have to know how to do it. When I was younger, during my teenage years and at the beginning of my twenties, I came a lot faster. But after I had been in a longer relationship I learned how to control it." Because of the extended abstinence period in between ejaculations, Elias' possibilities to have sex depend on his ability to control his orgasms. Tantric sex provides him with the opportunity to abstain from ejaculation while simultaneously still having sex and, most importantly for him, being able to pleasure the women he is with: "I have had some of my best orgasms by myself. The last 20 seconds of having sex, you know when you come, those are not important for me. It is more about this kind of intimacy, that there is this other person, and I really enjoy seeing her completely climaxing and saying: stop, stop, stop. And then we lay there and cuddle for a bit. That is a lot more rewarding for me."

What is striking in Elias's story is his commitment to being a sperm donor even though that masturbating at the sperm bank does not seem fun for him, nor does he receive a lot of compensation for his efforts since many of his semen samples do not pass quality assessments. Nevertheless, he sticks to being a sperm donor. Without being able to apply the usual explanations for why men would want to donate semen—earning money while simultaneously enjoying sexual excitement—a different experiential dimension needs to be considered if Elias's commitment as a sperm donor has to be properly understood analytically. I am suggesting framing Elias's and other men's experiences of being a sperm donor in terms of the enticement of gender. While Elias does not seem to receive any immediate pleasure when masturbating at the sperm bank and while his financial compensation for his semen samples is less than what sperm donors usually receive, Elias seems to be able to enjoy the performativity of gender enabled through sperm donation. For Elias being a sperm donor seems not to be so much about the immediacy of sexual pleasure (although some men do position their experience at the sperm bank as pleasurable) or the financial compensation he receives. Rather, being a sperm donor for him seems to be about the continuous performativity of gender. Being a sperm donor enables him to experience himself as a man who knows how to control his orgasms, and thus a man who knows how to pleasure women over and over again. A period of abstinence of more than forty-eight hours requires him to master tantric sex since he has to abstain from ejaculating, a continuous incitement to gender as praxis that gives him the possibility to remake himself into the gendered subject he desires to be. Thus, it might be said that it is not despite the regulatory scripts in place in sperm donation that Elias is a sperm donor but because of them. Being a sperm donor is one way in which Elias performatively (re)constitutes his masculinity. It is the enticement of gender made possible through sperm donation that commits him to the biosocial life of a sperm donor.

This experiential dimension of the enticement of gender somehow stands in contrast to how gender and sexuality have been theorized in large parts of feminism and queer theory. Just as there seems to be a tendency within medical anthropology and sociology and Science and Technology Studies to regard (reproductive) biomedicine and its biopolitical momentum as a somehow corrupting force leading to bioeconomics (Rose 2001) and the production of biovalue (Waldby 2002) and ultimately aimed at bio-objectification (Vermeulen, Tamminen, and Webster 2012) and commodification of the human body (Sharp 2000; Scheper-Hughes and Wacquant 2006), an argument that has been convincingly contested (Birch and Tyfield 2012; Hoeyer 2009, 2010, 2013), a large part of feminist and queer theorizing seems to have been focused on gender and sexuality as arenas of a subordinating or subjugating rather than an inciting and enticing form of power. While I do want to hold on to an analytics of gender and sexuality as restrictive regimes and as violently enforced norms, in light of the biosociality of sperm donors' lives, I also want to consider those dimensions of gender normativity and sexuality that are enabling, lustful, and enticing; dimensions that might be just as important for the reproduction of gender and sexuality as continuously pivotal categories of social differentiation as their restraining and violent aspects are. In other words, if gender is a norm "that only persists as a norm to the extent that it is acted out in social practice" (Butler 2004: 48), then it must (re)constitute itself also by other means than only through the subordination of willful subjects (Ahmed 2014).

My point of departure for this conceptual exercise is queer-feminist scholarship on the interplay between gender and sexuality. While it would be an impossible exercise to want to map the breadth of this scholarship, I nevertheless want to point to some parts of it that formed my thinking of sperm donors' engagements with biomedically mediated spaces of self, the point of this being to conceptualize biosocial subjectivation as a gendered and sexualed process of becoming a subject.

There have been numerous conceptualizations of how to think of gender ever since gender made its way into the standard vocabulary of not only feminists and queer scholars but also mainstream anthropologists and sociologists. A grammatical term before becoming a centerpiece of contemporary cultural and social theorizing, a scholarly interest in gender as a social relation nevertheless arose earlier than that. Marianne Weber (Weber 1919) and Georg Simmel (Simmel 1985), for example, were already discussing the social dynamics of gender at the end of the nineteenth and the beginning of the twentieth century. They were debating whether or not women and men were *wesensgleich*, that is, essentially the same in nature, and whether they therefore should be treated as equals or not (Gilcher-Holey 2004). Around the same time that Simone de Beauvoir published *The Second Sex* a few decades later in 1949 (Beauvoir 1972), and therewith opened a path for the distinction between sex and gender that would become so important for feminism (Butler 1986), John Money, clinical psychologist and sexologist, introduced gender as part of a clinical treatment regime for the intersex (Germon 2009; Goldie 2014). Interested in how well intersex individuals would adjust to their normatively assigned sex, he offered gender as a conceptual term to discuss the femininity and masculinity of individuals who did not fit a sex dichotomy. He can thus be understood as formulating the idea of gendered subjectivation independent from an individual's sex. This conceptual innovation notwithstanding, as a part of Money's clinical treatment regime gender violently imposed a heteronormative order onto intersex individuals by forcing them to be so-called unambiguous men and women who were supposed to exhibit heterosexual desire.

The structural violence of gender behind such rigid clinical treatment regimes would become the center point of much of feminist theorizing. Separating sex from gender enabled feminist sociologists and anthropologists to attend to gender as a socializing force that leads to social inequality. Here, gender describes a set of relationships that establishes a hierarchal social space in which women (and men) are subject to masculine domination, an argument that can be found in Sherry Ortner's essay about the universal devaluation of women (Ortner 1972) but that also echoes in later theories of gender, such as Sylvia Walby's notion of *patriarchy* (Walby 1989), Raewyn Connell's terms *gender regime* and *hegemonic masculinity* (Carrigan, Connell, and Lee 1985; Connell 1987) or even Pierre Bourdieu's *masculine domination* (Bourdieu 2001). What is of concern here is how power is implicated in the (sexual) relations between women and men and how socialization and subjectivation processes contribute to the reproduction of these relations.

Even though Gayle Rubin can be said to generally subscribe to this understanding of gender as a social relation of domination in her influential essay "The Traffic in Women" from 1975 (Rubin 1975), she can also be read to open up for a slightly different argument about how the interplay between gender and sexuality works. Interested in why women are the object of male oppression, Rubin's analysis points to the centrality of sexuality in the regulation of gender relations, a thought she develops more fully in her essay "Thinking Sex" a few years later in which she is concerned with the politics of sexuality (Rubin 1984). According to Rubin's initial analysis, forced heterosexuality is at the base of the gender hierarchy as we know it and functions as what she calls *a sex/gender system* in which gender is regulated through its implication into "a set of arrangements by which society transforms biological sexuality into products of human activity, and in which these transformed sexual needs are satisfied." (Rubin 2011: 34).

While Rubin's analysis could be read as part of an argumentative tradition within feminism that focuses on gender's subjugating dynamics, reading her conceptualization of the sex/gender system through the experiences of Danish sperm donors enables a different reading as well. Rubin's analysis clearly points to the power of forced heterosexuality to (re)constitute hierarchal gender relations. Yet it also opens an analytics interested in the ways in which a sex/

gender system is part of how individuals learn to be affected in ways so that a specific arrangement of the sex/gender system—call that a praxis—makes more sense to and is more desirable for them than other possible arrangements. In other words, if gender is part of an arrangement in which sexual needs are satisfied, then qualitatively gender is also very likely to be linked to incitement and enticement. And if gender is connected to incitement and enticement, then it is also likely to offer a space in which the self can remake itself as a specific gendered and sexualed subject.

A similar thought can be found in Michel Foucault's work even though gender as a term had not made it into Foucault's vocabulary just yet when he published the first part of his *History of Sexuality* in the middle of the 1970s (Foucault 1990). Heralded for his development of the term biopower and less for his conceptualizations of sexuality in much of the anthropological and sociological scholarship concerned with (reproductive) biomedicine, his notion of sexuality as an ordering dimension of social life can be read as containing the idea of gender as an enticing praxis. Foucault conceived of sexuality as a *dispositif* (dispositive): "a great surface network in which the stimulation of bodies, the intensification of pleasures, the incitement to discourse, the formation of special knowledges, the strengthening of controls and resistances, are linked to one another, in accordance with a few major strategies of knowledge and power" (Foucault 1990: 105–106). What Foucault offers here is to think of sexuality as a force that binds us together, much like a sex/gender system, sexuality as an organizing principle of lived reality. Whereas the regulation of gendered subjects and their relations to one another through subjugating forms of knowledge and discourse is without doubt important in this surface network as Foucault terms it, so also are the stimulation of bodies and the intensification of pleasures. In other words, sexuality becomes understandable as a regulative force that works through enticement and that thus makes for pleasurable experiences of the world by providing the possibility for a continuous remaking of the gendered and sexualed subject.

Even though Foucault seems to have a very specific sexual subject in mind, namely, one that comes into being through an internalization of knowledge/power/discourse and that, as a result, seeks the truth of sex in itself, the lived realities of Danish sperm donors seem not necessarily to be about such truth-seeking in sex. Rather, sperm donors might be said to seek spaces in which they can enjoy the performativity of gender. What seems to be at work in the biosocial subjectivation of sperm donors is the stimulation of bodies and the intensification of pleasures made possible through being a sperm donor, the biomedically regulated spaces of the gendered self that sperm donation provides, the enticement of gender as an instance of subjectivation that teaches men to be affected in a way that commits them to gender as praxis by ways of excitement, pleasure, and desire.

This notion of gender as an enticing praxis might also be said to emerge in Judith Butler's work on gender performativity (Butler 1990, 1993), Candace West and Don Zimmerman's concept *doing gender* (West and Zimmerman 1987; West and Zimmerman 2009), and in Raewyn Connell's conceptualization of masculinity as patterns of practice (Connell 1985, 1987, 1995; Connell and Messerschmidt 2005). Whereas Connell and West and Zimmerman offer their concepts of gender as part of a critique of the then prevalent sex role model within sociology, Judith Butler develops her thinking of gender performativity as a critical reflection on feminism's grounding in a sex-gender divide. In *Gender Trouble*, published in 1990, Judith Butler invites us to think the underlying premises of feminist and gender theory anew and argues that it is this very separation of gender from sex that hinders feminism from intellectually investigating and politically intervening in the normative workings of gender. As she maintains, gender is the very premise of sex and not only its social and cultural expression, since unambiguous women and men, as John Money would have it, can only be identified as such when there are categories through which to identify them: "Because there is neither an essence that gender expresses or externalizes nor an objective ideal to which gender aspires, and because gender is not a fact, the various acts of gender create the idea of gender, and without those acts, there would be no gender at all" (Butler 1990: 140). What is important in Butler's conceptualization of gender performativity is what she terms the *heterosexual matrix*, a normative configuration of sexuality that scripts sexual desire to flow between women and men only, an idea that reflects Rubin's sex/gender system and Foucault's *dispositif*, as they all contain the idea of subjects learning to be affected in particular ways in order to be enticed by a specific gender praxis.

This idea of being enticed by a specific gender praxis is also reflected in Raewyn Connell's argument about how gender becomes effective as a social relation. While Connell's notion of a *gender regime* (Connell 1985) and the concept *hegemonic masculinity* (Carrigan, Connell, and Lee 1985; Connell 1987, 1995; Connell and Messerschmidt 2005) are first and foremost concerned with analytically grasping the persistence of patriarchal power relations and the global domination of men over women and other men, Connell also points to the pleasurable sides of gender normativity (Connell 2009). As she argues in relation to how gender becomes a social force to which people commit themselves in their daily life, for gender to be effective people undergo a process of embodied learning. In this process individuals actively appropriate gender norms and develop gender identities continuously as part of their daily life through pleasurable experiences of doing gender (right): "The pleasure involved in learning gender is to some extent a bodily pleasure, pleasure in the body's appearance and in the body's performance" (Connell 2009: 98).

Seen through the experiences of Danish sperm donors, gender performativity or doing gender right in this sense constitutes spaces of self in which sperm donors remake themselves as men. In these spaces, the idea and experience of gender is created through the various acts that men engage in, such as medical exams, blood and urine tests, waiting in line with other men for an available donor room, masturbation and ejaculation at the sperm bank, dropping off semen samples, and receiving monetary compensation. While these acts are performative in the sense that they create the idea of a particularly gendered subject—the sperm donor—through subjugating gender regimes or scripts, they are also performative in the sense that they entice men to do gender. They not only work through subjugation, but through the intensification of pleasures and the stimulation of bodies. They participate in making the gendered and sexualed subject through an invocation of it in terms of biomedical registers and biopolitical valuations, or, as Butler writes in *Senses of the Subject*: "Already undone, or undone from the start, we are formed, and as formed, we come to be always partially undone by what we come to sense and know" (Butler 2015: 11).

Being partially undone by what we come to sense and know is an important dimension of sperm donors' lives in that the enticement of gender as it happens through sperm donation is an instance in which men come to know, sense, and (partially) (un)do themselves as men in biomedical terms, an idea that reflects the interest of feminist ethnographic scholarship on reproductive biomedicine in the interplay between gender and reproductive biomedicine. Whereas early feminist scholars such as Lene Koch in Denmark (Koch 1989; Koch and Morgall 1987) or Emily Martin in the United States (Martin 2001) were primarily concerned with the medicalization of women's bodies, since, as Charis Thompson writes in her elegant overview of feminist theorizing of reproductive technologies, "pregnancy and childbirth had become mechanized and pathologized by a patriarchal and increasingly interventionist medical establishment" (Thompson 2005: 57), in the 1990s, feminist ethnographers following this work were beginning to address the intricacies of the interplay between gender as praxis on the one hand and reproductive biomedicine on the other in more detail. In Sarah Franklin's work on women undergoing IVF treatment in the United Kingdom, for example, the interplay between gender and medical technologies makes itself noticeable in the sense that women's identities are both threatened and empowered by IVF, remaking pregnancies into embodiments of hope, risk, and not least (failed) progress (Franklin 1997). Tine Tjørnhøj-Thomsen makes a similar argument in her work on infertility treatment in Denmark (Tjørnhøj-Thomsen 1999, 2009), where reproductive technologies become both instances of gender identity loss as well as enablers of membership in the gendered communities of parenthood. Cynthia Daniels and Lisa Jean Moore explore how the rise of the American sperm banking industry intersected with the medicalization of the male body and male reproduction (Daniels 1997, 2006; Daniels and Golden 2004; Daniels and Heidt-Forsythe 2012; Moore 2008; Moore and Durkin 2006; Moore and Schmidt 1999). The exposure of male infertility lead to a destabilization of traditional scripts for masculinity, while simultaneously reinstating common masculine stereotypes of virility and reproductive prowess. More recently, feminist ethnographic scholarship on the interplay between gender and (reproductive) biomedicine emphasizes (reproductive) biomedicine's transformative capacities regarding gender. Marcia Inhorn, for example, suggests the concept *emergent masculinities* in order to analytically approach men's engagements with reproductive technologies (Inhorn 2012), pointing to the (re)making of masculinities through medico-technologically infused and locally and historically situated embodied gender practices. In a similar vein, Emily Wentzell proposes the concept *composite masculinities* as a way to understand how men "construct and revise their gendered selfhood across time and context," weaving different (biomedical) elements "together into masculine selfhood" (Wentzell 2013b: 26).

These conceptualizations of biosocial gendered selfhood are important for the enticement of gender insofar as they offer to understand masculinity to be specific enactments and embodiments of gender as praxis through the subjectifying repertoires of medico-technological contexts. The experiences of Danish sperm donors might be understood in this way as their daily lives involve regimes of living that call on their gendered subjectivity in terms of biomedical registers and biopolitical valuations. When Elias and other donors stick to their abstinence period in order for their semen samples to pass quality assessments or when they answer biomedical questionnaires, they not only obey contractual obligations and biomedical logics. They also (re)make experiential spaces of the self in which they sense and enjoy themselves as specifically gendered subjects.

I already hinted at these kinds of experiential spaces, or what could be called the somatic, emotional, and/or affective dimensions of biosociality, in the previous section, and I want to return to them here since they are important to what I call the enticement of gender. The enticement of gender as a part of Danish sperm donors' biosocial subjectivation might be understood as a process of learning to be affected in certain ways so as to remake oneself as a gendered subject through a specific gender praxis. By becoming sperm donors, for example when donor candidates like Jonas are asked to represent themselves with the help of biomedical questionnaires as described earlier, men learn to be affected in such a way that specific forms of gender praxis—a specific sex/gender system, or a specific weaving together of masculine selfhood—seem more alluring than others; that is, being a sperm donor makes for gender performativity in terms of biomedical registers and biopolitical valuations. The spaces of gendered and sexualed selfhood that sperm donation opens up affect how men register themselves affectively. Encounters such as Jonas's interview or Elias's prolonged time of abstinence, but also medical exams, blood tests, or the atmosphere inside of donor rooms and having to carry one's own semen to the front desk of a laboratory, are all instances in which sperm donors come into being as gendered subjects through the encounters of bodies and materialities and the logics and politics of (reproductive) biomedicine, and, as such, these instances are pivotal in making them into gendered and sexualed biosocial subjects.

In her book *The Cultural Politics of Emotion*, Sarah Ahmed develops a similar idea of affective and emotional subjectivation by exploring what emotions do, and how emotions form individual and collective bodies (Ahmed 2012). Ahmed's conceptual starting point for this exploration is the argument that "bodily sensation, emotion and thought" cannot be separated from one another since they are not "'experienced' as distinct realms of human 'experience'" (Ahmed 2012: 6). As such, the affective dimensions of the making of subjects and bodies as Ahmed describes it are tied to a notion of political efficacy. This political efficacy keeps the violent history of nationalism, racism, sexism, and heteronormativity alive while also opening up for potential "different orientations to others" (Ahmed 2012: 202), understood as the possibility to relate differently to the exclusionary norms of sociality. Central to this argument is the idea that norms are sustained because we develop particular relations to them through emotions; that is, norms require emotional investments in order to be affective as part of social life, or as Ahmed writes in relation to injustice: "[i]njustice may work precisely through sustaining particular kinds of affective relations to social norms through what we do with our bodies [while] challenging social norms involves having a different affective relation to those norms, partly by 'feeling' their costs as a collective loss" (Ahmed 2012: 196). Whereas sperm donors do not necessarily defy gendered or sexualed norms and thus are not likely to be willful subjects in Ahmed's sense (Ahmed 2014), the idea of developing particular kinds of affective relations to norms and thus reproducing these norms is important to consider if the continuous commitment of sperm donors as the enticement of gender is to be understood properly. Sperm donors would analytically be misunderstood as political activists, as I have pointed out earlier. Rather, what makes their lives fascinating in an epistemological sense is the ordinariness in which they inhabit the gendered and sexualed norms of contemporary biosociality, that is, the ways in which they learned to be affected in order to invest in the affective relations that the gendered space of being a sperm donor affords.

It is in this sense that Ahmed's notion of emotional investments in norms, ways of learning to be affected, might be understood in relation to the experiences of sperm donors. The gender performativity that ensues as part of their biosocial subjectivation is epistemologically interesting, not because they revolt against gender as a norm, but because they do not. Sperm donors are not queer activists (although the men who have sex with men but still donate semen in spite of it being against regulations might be). They are men who can be said to be enticed by gender (which does not mean that queer activists are not enticed by gender). This enticement is individual in the sense that different men are likely to have different normative understandings of who they are as men, what they aspire to in terms of an ideal of masculinity, and thus what entices them as gendered subjects. Elias's rather traditional understanding of gender relations, for example, was not necessarily shared by other sperm donors I met during my fieldwork. Yet, at the same time, what was common across their different ways of doing gender was the circumstance that they all had to relate to themselves as men in terms of biomedical registers and biopolitical valuations. Being a sperm donor, they all had to face the biomedical measurements of their body and its substances, and they all had to make themselves available to evaluations of their biomedical fitness. For some men this means reappropriating forced abstinence as a form of tantric sex like Elias does, and for others it means buying new underwear that guarantees that testicles and thus sperm cells are not exposed to too much heat, and for still others it means thinking of their semen in terms of the monetary compensation they receive for good-quality samples. In whatever way sperm donors may be enticed as gendered subjects, their gender performativity will certainly be related to the biomedical registers and biopolitical valuations that being a sperm donor encompasses.

Continuing this line of thought, I want to end my conceptualization of the enticement of gender by considering what Nick Fox and Pam Alldred call the *sexuality-assemblage* (Alldred and Fox 2015; Fox and Alldred 2013). Building on affect theory in the tradition of Gilles Deleuze and Félix Guattari (Deleuze and Guattari 2013), Fox and Alldred suggest thinking of sexuality in terms of an assemblage, a configuration of "bodies, things, ideas and social institutions, which produces sexual (and other) capacities in bodies" through flows of affect and that "is productive of all phenomena associated with the physical and social manifestations of sex and sexuality" (Alldred and Fox 2015: 907–908). Mirroring earlier conceptualizations such as Rubin's *sex/gender system* or Foucault's *dispositif,* the notion of a sexuality assemblage also contains the idea that bodies are enticed and stimulated, that subjects learn to be affected in particular ways (even though the objective of assemblage thinking is to decenter the subject/individual from analysis), and that they are invested into particular kinds of affective relations so as to performatively (re)make themselves as specific gendered subjects. Applying the vocabulary of Deleuze and Guattari, Allred and Fox understand the (re)making of specific norms in relation to gender and sexuality as *territorializations* inside the sexuality assemblage, that is, normative codifications and categorizations of gender and sexuality, for example heteronormative masculinity and sexual identity.

While the notion of a sexuality assemblage is also grounded in a political impetus to overcome essentialism (something that does not necessarily best describe the lived experiences of sperm donors), the idea that subjects are constituted through flows of affect is valuable when trying to think how the enticement of gender works as part of biosocial subjectivation. In a sexuality assemblage, it is not so much the gendered and sexualed identifications of the individual sperm donor that are of interest. Rather, what is important is how the flows of affect are territorialized, that is, how they are codified or categorized through the encounters of bodies, materialities, logics, and politics in order for a particular kind of sexuality assemblage to take shape (something that might also be called a sex/gender system, a dispositif, a (hetero)sexual matrix, a weaving together of different elements into gendered selfhoods). In other words, whereas sperm donors might think of themselves as men in different ways, normatively speaking, the enticement of gender makes them into biosocial subjects by directing the flows of affect in one particular way through the invocation of their gendered and sexualed selves in terms of biomedical registers and biopolitical valuations. Thus, what makes sperm donors' biosocial subjectivation so successful and hence being a sperm donor such an ordinary feature of their life-worlds is the making of gendered and sexualed subjects through a territorialization of the flows of affect. The enticement of gender makes biosocial subjects through an incitement to gender as biosociality.

Chapter 2

REGIMES OF LIVING

DONATING SEMEN AND THE PLEASURE OF MORALITY

Malthe is a father of two and married. In his thirties, he had been donating semen for about five years when I met him, with an average of one to two semen samples per week. Donating semen had thus become a routine part of his life. As he told me during our interview, he would stop by the sperm bank on his way either to or from work. Malthe also talked about donating semen as a professional commitment to which he had no emotional attachment, comparing it with his job at a consultancy firm: "I am also a product at work. There I am supposed to sell myself and create a surplus value for my employer. So, I am a product because of my professional qualifications and my educational background. Here (as a sperm donor) I am a product because of a baby picture, a few physical characteristics, and a donor profile." However, his decision to become a sperm donor was nevertheless linked to emotional investments in parenthood. When he and his wife had tried to have their first child, they encountered problems. This led to a short involvement with infertility treatment, causing Malthe to feel the disappointment of potentially being unable to have children. Since that time, Malthe had been convinced that becoming a sperm donor was an inherently good decision, as it spares people from similar painful experiences. Framing his decision to become a sperm donor with an I-want-to-help narrative, Malthe invoked the image of the childless heterosexual couple in need of help, a well-known and accepted image among sperm banks and infertility clinics in and beyond Denmark. Yet while Malthe's decision to become a sperm donor can

certainly be positioned within the discursive framework put forth
by sperm banks and fertility clinics, Malthe's contemplations were
also more complex in the sense that his immediately sympathetic
gesture of wanting to help people was countered by his decision not
to tell his wife and children about it: "So, who knows about you donating semen?"—"I, the sperm bank, and now you." Immediately
taken aback by Malthe's decision to keep this to himself, I found
myself struggling to understand him. Is it morally permissible not to
tell one's life partner that one is donating semen? Or does one have
the right to keep this decision to oneself? Much of my conversation
with Malthe circled around the dynamic between these two positions, with me facing my own normative assumptions about what
is morally acceptable and what is not. Malthe was fully aware that
his decision not to tell his wife that he was donating semen positions him in a morally delegitimized space, primarily because of an
established norm that holds that (sexual) secrets are out of place in
a loving relationship. During our interview he referred to the moment when he would eventually have to tell his wife as a difficult
one. When explicating his decision not to tell his wife and children
about being a sperm donor, Malthe explained that his decision was
a way of protecting them:

> Telling my family about it would also be admitting that I have kept
> something secret [*hemmeligt*] from them for twenty or twenty-five
> years. I have kept it a secret because I know from myself that these
> thoughts pop up and follow you, and you look at stories about do-
> nor children from a different angle. I have made this choice, it is my
> choice that I have to live with these thoughts and I feel okay with
> them. But one could also experience these thoughts as something
> negative and as some kind of insecurity, and I did not want to force
> [*pådutte*] that kind of insecurity on my children: "I wonder if that boy
> from the other class actually is my biological brother"; "Dad, he looks
> a lot like you." If I had to tell my wife and my children at some point,
> if they had to find out that I kept something secret from them for
> twenty-five years, then my explanation to them would be that I have
> kept it a secret because I did not want to force this doubt upon them.
> And I still believe that that is the right thing to do. It could then very
> well be that they don't agree with me but at least it has been a very
> deliberate choice of mine for their sake.

While Malthe was convinced that not telling his wife and children
was the right decision for the time being, he was also aware that this
decision might have to be reevaluated later, when circumstances
have changed. When he and I were talking about the possibility of

donor-conceived individuals contacting him in twenty years' time, he said:

> The thing that I keep thinking about is what my reaction would be and how I would handle that situation in regard to my wife and my children. As I told you, I have kept this completely anonymous, so they don't know about it. If I were contacted by a donor child at some point I would find it to be too secretive not to tell them about it because at that point the whole thing would be a lot closer and it would be a very different situation (than it is now).

This chapter looks at the process of biosocial subjectivation by focusing on the moral reasoning around donating semen that Danish sperm donors engage in. The making of Danish sperm donors as biosocial subjects requires that men overcome possible moral inhibitions about sperm donation by aligning their individual convictions, societal attitudes toward sperm donation, and their practical engagements as sperm donors so that donating semen can be positioned as a morally acceptable part of their everyday life. As I will argue throughout this chapter, this alignment happens through the enticement of gender. In order to make donating semen a morally acceptable part of their everyday life, Danish sperm donors need to find a recognizable (to them) position in a gendered moral order that positions them as someone who does good, for example the loving son, the caring father, or the responsible husband. It is these gender subjectivities that form part of sperm donors' acceptance of the (im)morality of sperm donation. The ethnographic examples in this chapter thus connect my earlier discussion of biosociality as a form of life, a form of common sense, and a regime of living with Danish sperm donors' contemplations on the morality of donating semen by showing how they make it meaningful in a gendered moral sense. For biosocial subjectivation to be successful, Danish sperm donors engage in creating regimes of living, something that Stephen Collier and Andrew Lakoff define as situated forms of moral reasoning (Collier and Lakoff 2005). These regimes of living help sperm donors to align their own moral reasoning about donating semen with the biopolitical project of reproductive biomedicine. This alignment happens through the enticement of gender by inciting men to invest in a particular gendered moral order, and the moral reasoning behind this investment shall be the focal point of this chapter.

Malthe's decision not to tell his wife that he is a sperm donor is likely to provoke most people's moral consciousness. In fact, every person whom I told about Malthe reacted with disapproval. However, his degree of reflexivity while contemplating the morality of his decision makes it impossible to position him as irresponsible. Instead, Malthe's narrative makes being a sperm donor understandable as an ongoing process of coming to terms with the (im)morality of sperm donation, a process in which the decision to become a donor is continuously legitimized and reembedded in shifting claims about whether donating semen is permissible or not. Whereas some might claim that not telling his wife positions Malthe as someone who undermines trust as the basis of a marital relationship, Malthe's narrative positions his decision to keep it a secret as an act of care, a deliberate decision not to burden his wife and children. Moreover, Malthe's justification for keeping donating semen a secret is only morally acceptable for him now, and not in twenty years' time when possible donor-conceived individuals might contact him. At that point, not telling his wife and children would be unacceptable, as Malthe makes clear, since "the whole thing would be a lot closer." Thus, as Malthe laid out during our conversation, finding a moral ground for his decision demands engagements in situated forms of moral reasoning. Furthermore, these situated forms of moral reasoning are tied to Malthe's ways of being a man. When Malthe reasons whether or not it is permissible to keep donating semen a secret from his wife and children, he (re)makes himself not only as a good person but also as a good man. He situates himself in a specific gendered moral order that makes his decision understandable as the act of a caring husband and as the choice of a responsible father. In other words, in aligning his individual moral convictions with public attitudes about sperm donation and with his practical engagements as a sperm donor, Malthe engages in situated moral reasoning of a gendered order. Malthe's reasoning concerns not only his moral consciousness but also his gendered self. His moral positioning is incited by emotional investments in a particular gendered moral order through the love he feels for his wife and children. In this sense, keeping donating semen a secret makes Malthe a good husband and father, a gendered and sexualed position that situates Malthe not only in a moral terrain but also inside a specific set of gender and sexual relations.

Claiming Recognizable Positions
Inside a Gendered Moral Order

As is the case in other social and cultural contexts (Inhorn 2006; Kirkman 2004; Simpson 2004), sperm donation in Denmark is embedded in a moral landscape (Pálsson and HarÐardóttir 2002) in which donating semen is not necessarily regarded as an honorable thing to do. In fact, sperm donors might feel that they cannot talk to anyone about it because it is seen as a taboo topic, as shown by a survey conducted among Danish sperm donors (Bay et al. 2014). When asked to assess how open they are with other people about being sperm donors, the majority of men in this survey (74 percent) clearly state that they either have not talked about it with anyone or have talked about it only with a select group of individuals. In his interviews with sperm donors in Australia, Damien Riggs finds similar experiences (Riggs 2009, 2008; Riggs and Russell 2011; Riggs and Scholz 2011). As his work shows, sperm donors might face emotional distress because they experience sperm donation as being socially stigmatized, with no available positive identification models for men who donate semen. These kinds of experiences are reflected in the public portrayal of sperm donors as "public wankers" and irresponsible individuals (Klotz and Mohr 2015; Mohr 2013; Petersen 2013; Schneider 2010; Thomson 2008), images that are unlikely to encourage men to view sperm donation as a morally acceptable activity. Furthermore, sperm donors might also feel alienated and objectified, as Rene Almeling shows in her work on American egg and sperm donors (Almeling 2011), with monetary compensation leaving men feeling like commodities.

August was one of those men who expressed inhibitions about telling people that he is a sperm donor. As with the other men I interviewed, he had written to me following an email he had received from the sperm bank at which he donates. In his twenties when I met him, August was one of the younger donors that I talked to and fit the stereotype of a sperm donor in the sense that he was a student and positioned his decision to become a sperm donor as one based on monetary incentives. On average, he stopped by the sperm bank three times a week, which did not leave much room for a personal sex life, something August was very aware of. Having only been a sperm donor for approximately a year, he still seemed unsure about whether donating semen was really a good idea. On the one hand, August rationalized it as a win-win situation since it would help those in need of donor semen as well as providing him with extra cash. On the other hand, however, the idea of people knowing about him being a donor made him uneasy. When he and I were talking about whether being a sperm donor makes a difference to his daily life, he said:

I have been very careful about whom I tell (that I am a sperm donor). There was one episode where I was together with friends and some people from university who I did not know that well, and we were joking around, making jokes about sperm, and then a friend of mine shoved his elbow into me from the side and there I said "Can we talk about something else?" I mean, I know that we were just joking among friends, but this is something that I want to keep for myself. I don't want people to judge me and I don't know how people will react. I don't think people would judge me, but I just don't want people to know. They don't need to know, that's how I see it. Actually, afterwards they said that they were very sorry about what happened and that it of course was up to me whether I wanted to tell people or not.

Another man who expressed discomfort about being open about being a sperm donor was Oliver. Whereas August had difficulties finding the right words to express why he thinks no one should know about him being a sperm donor, Oliver was more vocal about why telling people made him uncomfortable. Oliver and I could not meet in person, as he travels a lot, and thus we talked via phone. In his twenties and single, Oliver had been a donor for less than a year when we met, and he donated semen twice a week. He described his motivation to become a sperm donor as a mixture of financial incentives, an evolutionarily determined male need to spread one's genes, and an interest in helping people. Oliver was also still a student, and his contemplations about the morality of sperm donation circled around the fact that it involves masturbation. When he and I were talking about how open he is with other people about being a sperm donor, Oliver said:

> I am open about it with my closest friends and we actually joke a lot about it together. But those people that I have told know very well to keep quiet about it. It is not something they are allowed to talk about with others. It is a rather private issue I think. Actually, this is totally ridiculous, but I think it has to do with the fact that I feel ashamed about it and I think that is about the fact that I have to masturbate. Even though it is a totally natural thing to do, I feel ashamed about it. Just like I feel ashamed about having to use a public restroom and that it smells in there when I have to use it. Everyone uses the toilet but we feel ashamed about it nonetheless. I feel the same way about this here (being a sperm donor). I know very well that it is absolutely normal but I don't feel that people should know that I go there (to the sperm bank) and masturbate in a room.

Both August's and Oliver's contemplations about their own inhibitions in telling people that they donate semen reveal a set of
moral questions that sperm donors are faced with: should people
have children with the help of donor semen? Is it okay that men
are compensated financially for providing semen samples? Does the
fact that sperm donation involves masturbation put sperm donors
in a questionable light? Can one be proud about being a sperm donor? Or should men keep donating semen a private matter? These
questions are not trivial ones. They touch the very heart of sperm
donors' subjectivity; the way in which a sperm donor positions himself in regard to them becomes a matter of personal integrity. The
condemnation of monetary compensation for one's bodily products,
such as is involved in discussions about the permissibility of sperm
donation (Almeling 2009; Daniels and Hall 1997; Mohr 2014) as
well as in the larger field of social science scholarship that judges
any kind of financial incentive for bodily donations as immoral (Hoeyer 2007), points to this dynamic. Another example is the moral
discourse about masturbation (Laqueur 2003; Rosewarne 2014;
Stengers and Neck 2001), which positions the masturbating individual as corrupt or at least dubious, something that is reflected in
August's and Oliver's reasoning but that is also part of regulating
sperm donor behavior more generally (Mohr 2010). Being a sperm
donor in Denmark thus means that men are likely to meet situations
in their daily life in which the moral permissibility of being a sperm
donor is questioned. As becomes clear in Malthe's, August's, and
Oliver's stories, men's moral reasoning in these instances involves
navigating through what they themselves might deem appropriate
but also what a larger public might think about sperm donation and
sperm donors. For Malthe, August, and Oliver, the decision not to
tell people about donating semen is a way of finding a ground from
which they can manage the tension between their personal engagements as sperm donors and the public assessment of their decision to
become sperm donors. They make themselves into biosocial subjects
by assuming a moral middle ground that allows them to be sperm
donors while also adhering to a more general assessment about the
(im)morality of sperm donation.

While men's decisions to become sperm donors are most commonly believed to be a matter of rational decision making and
thought to be motivated by clearly identifiable motivations (Mohr
2014; Van den Broeck et al. 2013), both August's and Oliver's stories as well as Malthe's complex dynamic of positioning himself as a
good husband and father allude to the fact that being a sperm donor

is likely to involve other dimensions than those we can capture in a survey, or even in interviews. Finding a moral ground from which to justify the decision to donate semen is a complex process that never really ends; men's reasoning about whether donating semen is morally justifiable will depend on the life situations in which they find themselves. For August and Oliver, being a sperm donor is a rather new experience. Both had been donating semen for less than a year and thus their contemplations about the morality of sperm donation very much revolved around questions of masturbation and the potential embarrassment attached to it, something that is not necessarily a matter of concern for men who have been donating semen for a longer period of time, like Malthe. For Malthe, the moral permissibility of being a sperm donor was rather connected to the interpersonal challenges of his decision not to tell his wife and children about it. In other words, how being a sperm donor is made meaningful in a moral sense is likely to shift throughout a sperm donor's life. Yet at the same time, these different forms of situated moral reasoning all seem to mobilize men's gendered subject positions: August's and Oliver's embarrassment about masturbation reflects concerns about appropriate gender performance, just as Malthe's invocation of the figure of the good husband and father reflects an attempt to performatively remake himself as a responsible man.

I want to go into more detail about these gendered dimensions of sperm donors' moral reasoning by unfolding three prominent figures among the sperm donors that I interviewed: the loving son, the caring father, and the responsible husband. The situated moral reasoning that these three figures involve can be understood in terms of the enticement of gender, since finding a moral ground as a sperm donor happens through the invocation of recognizable positions in a gendered moral order. As such, the enticement of gender enables men's biosocial subjectivation as sperm donors by providing a space in which they can morally justify their decision to donate semen through the assumption of acceptable gender subjectivities.

The Loving Son

The figure of the loving son describes strategies that legitimate being a sperm donor in a moral sense by assuming the role of a son, that is, a recognizable gendered position that situates men's practical engagements as sperm donors as part of an intergenerational relationship and thus a gendered moral order. As loving sons, men make their decisions as sperm donors meaningful due to the moral responsibility they feel in regard to their parents, a process of gender performativity in which reasoning about the (im)morality of certain decisions involves positioning oneself inside a particular set of gender and sexual relations.

This kind of moral reasoning can be seen, for example, in situations during interviews in which men discussed how they had communicated to their parents their decision to become a sperm donor. For August, for example, talking to his mother was an important part of feeling comfortable with being a sperm donor, because he felt that he needed to address her concerns about the implications of it. August's mother, like August himself had been, was concerned about large numbers of possible offspring, something that the two of them discussed during August's application process at the sperm bank. A part of this process, August needed to fill out a medical questionnaire that concerned his family medical history, which made it necessary for him to talk to his mother: "My mom was especially concerned that she would be grandmother to 100 children. So, I had to explain to her that these were not my children and that she would not meet them in the future. I don't really know what she had thought would happen, but once I had explained to her what this (being a sperm donor) actually means, she was relaxed about it." Whereas questionnaires about the medical history of a sperm donor's family are about finding possible diseases or genetic conditions sperm banks want to avoid, for sperm donors these questionnaires invoke personal relationships to parents and thus position them inside a specific gendered moral order that assigns responsibilities to them as sons. August's mother's concern about being the grandmother of 100 children assumes August's decision to become a sperm donor to also be about her possible gendered moral future in the sense that August's reproductive potential could install obligations upon her as a grandmother. August is thus forced to consider her concerns as part of his relationship to her as a son, making his decision not only a matter of feeling personally uncomfortable about having to masturbate, as we saw earlier, but also a matter of being a good son who respects his mother's concerns. The conversation between August and his mother happens within a moral order in which August and his mother are bound to one another through a set of particular gender and sexual relations, and, in effect, for August being a good sperm donor hence necessarily invokes the performativity of gender as a loving son who accepts his responsibilities in terms of a specific gendered moral order that positions sons as also always potential fathers already. The moral reasoning that sperm donors participate in when coming to terms with the (im)morality of donating semen situates them as gendered subjects. Gender entices sperm donors to remake themselves as biosocial subjects by assuming positions within a gendered moral order that are recognizable as acceptable gendered subject positions because they offer positive gender subjectivities, for example the loving son.

The invocation of the position of the loving son was particularly present in interviews with men like August who were younger, not in a long-term relationship or married, and without children, and who thus saw their primary moral obligations to be about their relations to parents, siblings, and other immediate family members instead of to possible partners, wives, and/or children. As described above, conversations between these donors and their family members provided a space in which men could situate their moral reasoning by reflecting on the pros and cons of being a sperm donor as well as the moral obligations bestowed upon them as sons. This kind of intellectualized moral reasoning characterized most sperm donors' accounts, probably in part also enforced through my methodical exercise of engaging men in conversations about being a sperm donor. Yet whereas the enticement of gender in terms of the loving son partly takes place through these intellectualized reflective spaces in which people can talk about sperm donation, the making of biosocial subjects through an incitement to gender in a moral sense is also likely to involve an embodied sense of gender subjectivity, a sense of feeling good about performatively remaking oneself as a gendered subject.

This dimension, of assuming a recognizable position as part of a gendered moral order in terms of the loving son, was visible in Chris's story. Chris was a donor in his twenties who, like August and Oliver, had only recently begun to donate semen. I met Chris during one of my final weeks of participant observation at Danish sperm banks. I had become aware of him because he had come into the sperm bank three times in that particular week—always at the same time, always with a charming smile on his face, and every time willing to engage in short conversations when checking in and when dropping off his semen sample. Curious about the very precise regularity of his visits to the sperm bank—especially when considering the forty-eight-hour abstinence rule—and his charming personality, I asked Elisabeth, the donor coordinator, about Chris's background. "He is a really nice guy," Elisabeth immediately said, and explained that Chris would drive all the way from a smaller town nearby, a trip that was likely to take him about forty-five minutes each way. Chris would work night shifts, go to the gym afterward, and would then stop by the sperm bank. What is more, he had very good semen quality. Chris's semen quality was exceptional in the sense that his samples usually allowed for the production of eight straws—thin plastic tubes with about half a milliliter of semen—whereas the average sample allowed for only three to four straws. Elisabeth had made a habit of telling men like Chris who had only recently started as donors that their semen samples were of good quality: "I think it is good to motivate them by telling them that they have good samples."

Since Chris had started donating, he had been a regular visitor at the sperm bank, with none of the irregularities that can cause difficulties for a donor coordinator, such as not showing up for appointments, missing abstinence periods, or forgetting medical checkups: "He is one of those guys whom you don't have to tell things twice. He always sticks to the rules." As her characterization of Chris reveals, Elisabeth was clearly fond of him. Yet her appreciation of his commitment as a donor was not purely due to the fact that he seemed perfectly responsible and thus a reliable semen provider, but rather because of the way in which Chris had made becoming a sperm donor meaningful in a moral sense. As Elisabeth continued her characterization of Chris, it was hard not to be emotionally touched by the circumstances that made up Chris's current life situation as she described it. Shortly before Chris had applied to become a sperm donor, both of his parents had passed away. His father had been diagnosed with a terminal illness and Chris and his mother were in the middle of coming to terms with this diagnosis when Chris's mother suddenly died without warning or prior illness. Chris and his father had been taken aback by the sudden passing of Chris's mother. While mourning her death, Chris's father died three weeks later. Elisabeth was convinced that Chris was still in the middle of working all these things out: "I think he works night shifts and works out so much at the gym in order to deal with his emotions and aggressions." Chris had also shown Elisabeth the tattoos that he had gotten in honor of his parents. "When I told him that he could start as a donor, he was so happy and really proud," Elisabeth told me, striking a winner's pose in order to convey Chris's reaction to the news of his acceptance. Chris was an only child and "it was important to his parents that he would have children someday," Elisabeth explained Chris's reasoning, clearly marking his motivation to become a sperm donor as noble. Shaking her head slightly, she then added: "But I feel so sorry for him sometimes!"

While Chris's story is certainly an exceptional one in the sense that I have not heard of similar personal investments in coming to terms with being a sperm donor from other men I have met during my fieldwork, his story is also exceptional in the sense that it captures so well the affective dimensions of the enticement of gender that are involved when men legitimate their decision to become sperm donors. The way that Chris remakes himself as the loving son by becoming a sperm donor clearly points to the emotional investments that the enticement of gender involves. As a way of mourning his parents' death, Chris assumes the recognizable gendered subject position of the loving son by becoming a sperm donor, allowing him to honor his parents' last wish, namely, to become grandparents. This situated moral reasoning is hardly the intellectualized rational discursivation of the pros and cons of sperm donation as it is important for men like August. Rather, Chris's situated moral reasoning reflects the affective investments in a particular gendered moral order that biosocial subjectivation requires. Honoring his parents' last wish, Chris not only assumes a gendered subject position that is recognizable for outsiders like Elisabeth and me. He also remakes himself as a particular gendered subject—the loving son—through an incitement to gender as an affective self-recognition. By becoming a sperm donor, Chris *is* the loving son, enabling him to inhabit the precise location of gender subjectivity that he deems appropriate for his relationship to his parents. The process of biosocial subjectivation that characterizes Chris's story thus clearly marks his situated moral reasoning as also a process of embodying gender subjectivity through becoming a sperm donor.

The Caring Father

Whereas the figure of the loving son positions sperm donors as recognizable gendered subjects through moral obligations they might feel toward their parents, situations in which sperm donors assume the role of the caring father position them as morally obligated to their children. Here the decision to become a sperm donor is negotiated through what they deem morally acceptable positions as fathers, a process of gendered becoming that allows men to be caring fathers and that thus enables them to experience themselves in concordance with what they think a caring father should be. In other words, the enticement of gender makes it possible for them to come to terms with the (im)morality of sperm donation by giving them the opportunity to experience themselves as fathers who care about their children.

Most men that I met talked about being sperm donors inside the rhetoric of reproductive heteronormativity. They saw their contribution as sperm donors in helping heterosexual couples have children while at the same time being aware that being a sperm donor also constitutes an intervention into heteronormative coupledom and parenthood. Accordingly, they did not regard the individuals being born as the result of their semen being used for donor insemination as their own children, but rather as a possible threat to their own current or possible future reproductive heteronormativity (Mohr 2015), something that I will return to in more detail in chapter 4. Talking about being a sperm donor inside the rhetoric of reproductive heteronormativity thus inevitably led donors to also consider their role as fathers even when they did not have children themselves.

This became particularly obvious in the story of Mathias. I met Mathias in his apartment after work. Mathias was in his twenties with no children, and had been a donor for about a year when he heard about my research project and contacted me. Self-employed in communications, he engages in an active lifestyle with regular soccer training and gym practice. His first encounter with the possibility of becoming a sperm donor took place when he and his long-term girlfriend were considering having children. While seemingly self-confident throughout the interview, he had nevertheless wondered at that time whether he had semen quality good enough to have children: "I had worried a bit at the time. I think that always happens, you know, when you're thinking about having kids then you also start wondering whether you can have kids in the first place. But this was nothing that bothered me big time or made me sleepless at night." When he found out that his semen quality was not just good but rather exceptional, Mathias became interested in becoming a sperm donor. His girlfriend, however, was not at ease with it at the time, and as a consequence Mathias refrained from signing up. Later on, when his girlfriend had accepted the idea, Mathias applied to become a sperm donor. His contemplations about whether or not sperm donation was a good thing thereby involved Mathias's reasoning about how being a sperm donor might impact his future family life. When talking about how long he would want to donate semen for, he said: "I think until I settle down and have my own family. I think when you reach that point then everything should be more about myself and my family. Should I nevertheless feel that I have extra energy [*overskud*] to continue, then it could also very well be that I go down there (to the sperm bank) once in a while." Invoking his ideal of a good life that included a nuclear family, owning a house, and having a successful career, Mathias clearly positioned himself as a father and husband who knows how to take care of his family. As such, for a caring father, donating semen would have to come second, since his obligations would require him to think of his family first: "When we have a house, and two children, and I have a job that keeps me even busier than I am now, and when we at the same time should be home with the kids in the evenings, then I would not be able to do all of this. It would be something that I would have to squeeze into my daily life because we would have small children, and then the whole thing would feel more like a duty rather than something that I do voluntarily." Thus, while Mathias did not have children at the time, he nevertheless invoked the figure of the caring father in order to reason about the permissibility of sperm donation. While being a sperm donor is acceptable when you do not have children, once reproductive heteronormativity materializes in nuclear family life, donating semen would no longer be permissible as it would diverge attention from the role of the caring father who spends his evenings at home with his children. By positioning himself in this particular way, Mathias assumes a position in a gendered moral order that is recognizable and acceptable for him and other people. Connecting his reasoning about sperm donation to the figure of the caring father, Mathias negotiates the (im)morality of sperm donation through the enticement of gender.

While being a caring father was an abstract future scenario (though nevertheless a pivotal one) when reasoning about the permissibility of sperm donation for donors like Mathias who did not have children of their own, for men who were fathers and sperm donors simultaneously, the role of the caring father was a continuous part of their practical engagement as sperm donors. Here, being a father provided the space for men's situated moral reasoning about sperm donation. As the introduction to this chapter shows, Malthe was one of the men who situated himself as a caring father. While his decision not to tell his wife and children about being sperm donor might provoke disapproval, in his reasoning, not telling his children protected them from having to live with the burden of knowing that there are other individuals out there who are genetically connected to their father, an awareness that Malthe understands as threatening to the mental well-being of his children. Not telling them was thus Malthe's way of helping them to grow up carefree. At the same time, however, Malthe lived with the consciousness that he was trying to protect his children, taking the burden on himself and thus in a very embodied sense making himself into a caring father by feeling the burden he was carrying for them. Making himself into a caring father required him to take on this burden and thus entailed an affective investment in that particular gendered subject position. How this burden played out in his moral reasoning became clear when we were talking about how he would tackle the situation of donor-conceived individuals contacting him in the future:

> I have thought about this for quite some time, not so much in regard to my relation (to the donor-conceived) because should I be contacted by a donor child once I am sixty, I am sure I will be able to handle it. But I thought a lot about a hypothetical example: imagine that my daughter finds a boyfriend, and imagine it turns out that this guy is a donor child, and, on top of that, imagine that he turns out to be my donor child. Now that would be a very, very awkward [*kejtet*] situation. You could say that this could happen without me actually knowing about it, but this was a situation which I have thought about a lot and which worried me quite a bit and which also filled me with negative thoughts.

As Malthe explains, he invested a lot of his time in thinking about what would happen should his daughter fall in love with a man who turns out to be conceived with the help of his semen. He positions this scenario as "very, very awkward" and also explains that the thought of this happening worries him and figures negatively in his life. Here, Malthe's decision to become a sperm donor is the object of moral reasoning by invoking his relation to his daughter and thereby simultaneously his obligations toward her. Exclaiming that the incest scenario filled him "with negative thoughts," Malthe verbalizes the weight of the burden that he carries as a sperm donor, a weight that also makes him into a caring father since not being concerned would position him as not caring about his children. Constructing the scenario of his daughter falling in love with her half-brother is of course a well-known cultural theme, yet it is nevertheless a pivotal one for Malthe because it helps to actualize his position as a caring father. Feeling the negative consequences that such a scenario might have for his daughter, Malthe inhabits the gender subjectivity that the figure of the caring father for him is all about. It acts as a recognizable position in a gendered moral order that helps Malthe to find grounds from which to reason about his decision to become a sperm donor. While his concerns about this scenario certainly actualize as negative thoughts, as Malthe frames it, it is nevertheless also an enticement of gender in the sense that the actualization of worrying about the well-being of his daughter also provides him with the experience of himself as a caring father, an experience that proves to him that he *is* the caring father he wants to be.

Assuming the position of the caring father is an important part of Danish sperm donors' moral reasoning. Independent of whether sperm donors actually have children of their own, men both with and without children positioned themselves as caring fathers. While this position is a hypothetical one for those who are yet not fathers, the invocation of the caring father as a future scenario was nevertheless pivotal for them in order to make decisions about the permissibility of sperm donation. Positioning themselves as always already potential fathers, these donors negotiated under which conditions donating semen is acceptable and under which it is not by actively taking a position within a gendered moral order. This positioning within the framework of reproductive heteronormativity takes on very tangible dimensions for those donors who are already fathers. For them, the position of the caring father was an actual experience of being a sperm donor. Their moral reasoning about sperm donation involved the continuous actualization of being the caring father through emotional investments in this gendered subject position. They continuously reasoned about the moral status of sperm donation by embodying the role of the caring father, that is, the enticement of gender enabled the moral reasoning that biosociality demands from them. Positioning themselves as caring fathers, Danish sperm donors assume a recognizable and acceptable position and thus are able to experience themselves as consistent with what they deem a caring father to be. It is this experience of positive gender subjectivity that allows them to come to terms with the (im)morality of sperm donation.

The Responsible Husband

The position of the responsible husband figured in sperm donors' reasoning about the (im)morality of sperm donation in instances in which being a donor was contextualized as part of the obligations men felt they had in regard to their wives, life partners, or girl-friends. Thus, while the two previous figures—the loving son and the caring father—both involved men's obligations due to intergen-erational kinship relations, something I will return to in chapter 4, assuming the position of the responsible husband allowed sperm donors to reason about the permissibility of sperm donation by in-voking their obligations as sexual and romantic partners of women. The moral reasoning that this positioning enables therefore involves the enticement of gender in terms of experiencing oneself as a man who knows how to sexually satisfy women as well as a man who assumes responsibility for the woman he loves.

Elias's story, as described in chapter 1, could be seen as an exam-ple of how sperm donors assume the position of a man who knows how to sexually satisfy women. While Elias might be categorized as being far away from living a responsible life—his sexist world view and hedonistic escapades are certainly open to different in-terpretations—he nevertheless assumed a recognizable and in parts acceptable gendered subject position in the sense that his conduct toward women was centered on providing them with sexual plea-sure. Being a sperm donor allowed him to assume that position, since the ejaculatory regimen to which sperm donors are subjected enabled him to practice tantric sex and thus satisfy women sexually by putting his orgasmic experience second to that of the women he is with. William, in his twenties and in a long-term heterosex-ual relationship with no children, was another donor who reasoned about being a sperm donor in terms of his intimate and sexual obli-gations to his girlfriend. I met William in his apartment. While Wil-liam went to college and training to become an engineer, he also worked alongside his studies and was very keen on advancing in life. This included his relationship with his girlfriend, with whom he had been together for a number of years at the time. He had heard about becoming a sperm donor from some of his friends at college, and felt that if they were sperm donors, surely he could be too. At the time, he had not told his girlfriend about it, and this resulted in a dispute when she found out by chance that he had applied to become a donor. As William told me, she had been very upset, and this had been the moment at which he realized that being a sperm donor also had implications in regard to her. As a consequence, Wil-liam did not follow through with his application at the time, which was his way of making it up to her. About a year later, it was actually William's girlfriend who brought up the possibility of him becoming a sperm donor again:

We were sitting on her balcony and the sun was shining and we were having some beers when I talked about wanting to move to a different place. I was living together with some roommates but was tired of it and really wanted to move. But I didn't have the money. I work a lot on the side and also during summer vacations but it just didn't add up. And while we were drinking beer it was her who brought it up again: why don't you become a sperm donor? So, it was actually her who brought it up the second time around. However, I could also sense that she was a bit tired of it, but, you know, she also knew that that would be a big help for me economically.

Since then, William and his girlfriend have had an agreement in place: he is allowed to donate semen as long as it does not interfere with their intimacy and sex life. Talking about how often William donates semen—on average three times a week—and reasoning about the influence this has on his sex life, he said:

I want to stop at some point because the biggest price you pay is, and as a guy I can tell you this, you are really restricted by the fact that you have to go down there and have to ejaculate [*at have udløsning*] and that there should be forty-eight hours in between. I don't live with my girlfriend, but that doesn't mean that you don't miss this freedom, you know, you can't fall asleep at night or whatever, and then this becomes the biggest sacrifice. Sometimes, I also think about this when I am with my girlfriend. It is just really hard to avoid those kinds of thoughts, you know, thinking about the money and then wondering if it is worth it. But as soon as I get these thoughts, I try to suppress them. Sometimes, though, I can't help it; you can't always stop yourself from being aware of it. But in a strange way, somehow I think all of this has also been good for our sex life. I mean, we have been together for almost four years and somehow, when I have to wait a little longer, in that way that has been good for us. But it is nevertheless a small sacrifice. Sometimes, I have money on my mind. You're thinking: oops, there you go, 300 crowns.

Being aware that his girlfriend has difficult feelings in regard to him being a sperm donor, William constantly tries to minimize the influence it has on his intimate life with her. However, as a sperm donor he also needs to plan his sex life in order to be able to donate semen three times a week, a difficult exercise that sometimes forces him to make excuses for abstaining from sex. Knowing that his girlfriend would be upset if he were to say that he cannot have sex because he is due to donate semen, he positioned situations in which he would make excuses as difficult ones. At the same time, however, he also saw abstaining from sex as a pragmatic issue, something that

would happen naturally when people have been romantically involved for a number of years:

> When you have been together for some time then you probably also
> reach a point, when you have been together for four years, and you
> sleep together every day, then that is not the same as when you were
> newly in love. So, I think she is aware of it and then tests me by ask-
> ing: Well, is this because of that? But I mean before I started with this
> she never complained even when we were just watching TV together.
> This has not created any problems though, really. And she knows that
> this is only for a limited time period, you know, a year and half left.

Even though William gave the impression that being a sperm donor
is not a big problem in his relationship, it was also clear that he was
aware that he needed to honor his obligations to his girlfriend and
prove that he knows how to be responsible for the woman he loves.
For William, this meant that some of the monetary compensation
he receives for his semen samples should be used for intimate time
with his girlfriend:

> Tonight we are supposed to go out for dinner and I will be paying be-
> cause I promised her when I started (donating semen), I told her that
> I really appreciated that she accepted this, I mean, this was a big ges-
> ture. I have heard about others (sperm donors' partners) who can't
> accept it. And so I told her that I will make sure to take care of her be-
> cause this also affects her in some way. So, when we go out for dinner
> it is usually me that pays for the food, maybe 500 crowns or some-
> thing like that, which is only two times (at the sperm bank) in order
> to pay for that. So, that is how we have found a way to balance this.

Fully aware that being a sperm donor has an impact on his intimate life, William tries to negotiate the permissibility of donating
semen through positioning himself as the responsible life partner
who knows how to take care of the woman he loves. Being a sperm
donor is only permissible as long as this role is not compromised.
After finding that not telling his girlfriend about being a sperm donor compromises his position as the responsible boyfriend, William
actively involves her in his practical engagements as a donor. His
moral reasoning involves her to the degree that the two of them
made an agreement that donating semen is an acceptable way of
earning some extra money as long as it does not intrude on their
intimate life and as long as it enables them to have a better life together, with William having his own apartment, for example, and
the two of them enjoying quality time together. At the same time,

William's role as the responsible boyfriend is continuously actualized in intimate moments in which his sexual performance and his willingness to sexually satisfy his partner become the proof of his responsibility and commitment to her. Performatively remaking himself as the responsible boyfriend, William negotiates the moral permissibility of sperm donation in the sense that he weighs the pros and cons of donating semen in relation to having sex with his girlfriend. Thus, his biosocial subjectivation as a sperm donor involves an enticement of gender that enables him to experience himself as a man who can honor his obligations and assume responsibility for the woman he loves. He places himself in a gendered moral order by assuming a position that is recognizable to and acceptable for both himself and his girlfriend, legitimizing him being a sperm donor.

In the case of Emil, married and a father of two, it was not so much the ability to sexually satisfy his wife that played a part in assuming the role of the responsible husband, but rather his ability to act as a provider. Emil and I met at my office for our interview, and he told me that he had contacted me because he thought it was important to conduct research on sperm donors. As he saw it, my research could potentially lead to more men becoming donors, something that he deemed important: "I have two kids myself, and for me my family is very important. But there are also people out there who can't have children but who might really want some, and why not help them." Having family members who had tried to have a child for over seven years before they were finally successful, Emil knew from personal experience what it means to really want a child but to be unable to have one. By becoming a sperm donor, Emil thus in some way acted on his willingness to help those in need. But as well as assuming this kind of responsibility, Emil's decision to become a sperm donor was also connected to his role as a family provider and not least his role as a responsible husband. When I asked him why he had chosen to become a sperm donor, Emil said:

> Well, this might sound strange, but it was actually my mother-in-law who came up with the idea. When you are unemployed as I was and have all these expenses that have to be paid every month, well, I thought: why not. I mean, it was really hard; I could not even get a job as a cleaner, not even that. So, I thought: I am going to try this and see if there is some money to be made with this. And as it turns out, there is money in it. I was lucky that I at least could deliver that [laughing], you could say. And soon afterwards I actually also found a job. So, last year, I was able to take my wife on a tour to New York for a week, so there is some money in it.

As Emil's story reveals, he saw himself faltering as a responsible husband, being unable to provide for his wife and two children. Trying to find employment for some time and failing even to get jobs that did not require any kind of special qualification, Emil found himself in a situation in which he potentially would be unable to take care of his family. His remark, "I was lucky that I at least could deliver that," in regard to him being able to produce semen samples of good enough quality to become a sperm donor, reflects the potency of this experience, as it points to the frailty of his gender subjectivity that heavily relies on him being able to provide for his family. At the same time, assuming his role as a responsible husband required Emil to become a sperm donor, as it allowed him to honor his obligations as a husband, father, and even son-in-law. He took this responsibility upon himself and thus actualized his position as a responsible husband. While Emil never had to rely solely on the monetary compensation he receives for his semen samples, as he was able to secure employment shortly after he had applied to become a donor, it was his willingness to become a sperm donor that positioned him as a responsible husband (thus being able to take his wife on a trip to New York).

Victor, in his thirties, married, and father to a daughter from an earlier marriage, similarly legitimized his decision to become a sperm donor through the invocation of the role of the responsible husband. Yet whereas William's story had been about responsibility in the sense of taking care of his relationship with his girlfriend, and while Emil remade himself as a responsible husband by providing for his wife and family financially, Victor assumed the role of the responsible husband by actively engaging his wife in the decision to become a sperm donor. Victor and his wife had tried to have children for a couple of years, but were unsuccessful. His wife had been pregnant a few times but was never able to carry a pregnancy to term. This experience forced Victor and his wife to reconsider their initial wish to have children and thus to come to terms with the idea of growing old together without offspring. Accepting this future scenario had taken some time, Victor told me, but he and his wife had nevertheless accepted it. This acceptance and the experience of not being able to have children opened up the possibility for Victor to become a sperm donor:

> I had a child from my first marriage but my wife really wanted to have a child, and so we tried. When we found out that we could not have children a new situation emerged. My wife and I were watching a TV

program one evening about donor insemination and adoption and I mentioned that it could be a good idea to help those who can't have children. And then she surprisingly said: I think that would be a good idea. And then I said: Do you really think so? Because I have thought that I could do this (donate semen) before it all goes to waste. And that is how I began looking into sperm donation.

Here, Victor assumes the role of the responsible husband by involving his wife in the decision to become a sperm donor. Reasoning about whether donating semen is morally permissible or not, Victor and his wife open up the possibility of Victor donating semen through a joint decision. This decision is both enabled by and positions them in a gendered moral order by, in Victor's case, invoking the figure of the responsible husband. Compelled by the wish to help those who cannot have children, and based on their own experience of having to come to terms with being childless, the use of Victor's semen is legitimized as part of a larger common good—reproduction. At the same time, Victor and his wife remake themselves as gendered subjects by extending Victor's reproductive potential to other individuals, thus securing themselves a recognizable and acceptable position in the gendered moral order of reproductive heteronormativity. The enticement of gender enables the moral justification of sperm donation by aligning individual convictions with a larger moral order and thus providing a space in which both Victor and his wife can experience themselves as those gendered subjects that they would like to be—responsible reproductive citizens.

Sperm Donors' Regimes of Living

Understood as situated forms of moral reasoning, regimes of living provide the means for living life ethically, as Stephen Collier and Andrew Lakoff formulate it (Collier and Lakoff 2005). As I have argued throughout this chapter, sperm donors' moral reasoning relies on the enticement of gender in the sense that by assuming recognizable and acceptable gendered subject positions like the loving son, the caring father, or the responsible husband, sperm donors both legitimate and negotiate their partaking in sperm donation. When men make the decision to become sperm donors, they are faced with fundamental questions about the (im)morality of sperm donation and, as a consequence, they are required to come to terms with these challenges to their moral consciousness. Men will only ever become sperm donors if they are able to align the "normative, technical, and political elements" of sperm donation (Collier and Lakoff 2005: 31), that is, if they can find a way of balancing their own moral convictions, public attitudes, and their practical engagements as sperm donors. For sperm donors, this form of moral reasoning happens in and through the enticement of gender. It is the enticement of gender that helps sperm donors actualize certain gender subjectivities from which to make decisions as sperm donors. As the different stories of the men represented in this chapter show, being a sperm donor is a continuous process of biosocial subjectivation, which demands situated forms of moral reasoning through which men are enabled to come to terms with the (im)morality of sperm donation. Part of this process includes inhibitions due to the potential embarrassment that being a sperm donor might entail, as we saw in the stories of August and Oliver, as well as men's very real concerns about the well-being of their children and wives, as we saw in the cases of Malthe and Emil.

While the regimes of living that sperm donors construct clearly involve intellectual engagements, such as consciously weighing the (im)morality of certain decisions, as was the case with Mathias and William, who both postponed becoming donors due to their life partner's disapproval, or August, who talked with his mother about the pros and cons of sperm donation, regimes of living necessarily also require embodied forms of moral reasoning, as in the case of Chris, Malthe, or Emil, who all actualized their moral positioning through an embodiment of certain gender subjectivities—the loving son, the caring father, the responsible husband. For them, making decisions as sperm donors involved an emotional investment in a certain gendered moral order that offered experiences of positive gender normativity, that is, experiences in which men were able to emotionally recognize themselves in congruence with the expectations they have in regard to being a loving son, a caring father, and a responsible husband. Becoming a biosocial subject as a sperm donor thus happens with the help of regimes of living, forms of situated moral reasoning that entail positioning oneself inside a gendered moral order by assuming recognizable and acceptable gendered subject positions. These positions are assumed through the enticement of gender, as both an intellectual process of knowing what one's moral obligations are as sons, fathers, and husbands, and as an embodied emotional investment of gender self-recognition that provides for feeling the rightness of one's gendered moral self.

Chapter 3

AFFECTIVE INVESTMENTS
MASTURBATION AND THE PLEASURE OF CONTROL

Thommy should never have been a sperm donor. At least, that is how he put it when I met him at his house after work. In his thirties, he works for an investment firm and is in a long-term relationship with plans to marry in the near future. He also has a child with a woman from a previous relationship with whom he remains friendly. Thommy had first heard about the possibility of donating semen when he was a student, around twenty years of age. At the time, he did not consider it a real possibility, as he had been involved in an accident as a teenager that had damaged one of his testicles and left him with the prognosis that he might never be able to father children. Thus, when his then-girlfriend became pregnant many years later, Thommy was surprised. Neither he nor she had expected it to happen: "Before that, I didn't even consider the possibility because I figured if I were at all able to have children then my semen quality would be so bad that becoming a father would be pure luck." Over the next few years, Thommy saw different stories about donor insemination on TV and occasionally read about sperm donation in newspapers, so the awareness of it as a possibility stayed with him. As he was in a committed relationship, however, donating semen was still not an option for him even though he now knew that his semen quality was probably better than he had expected and although he liked the idea of helping people in that way. Being a registered organ donor and regularly donating blood, Thommy was convinced that giving one's bodily fluids to others in need of help is an honorable thing to do. To that end, he had a very pragmatic approach, not really differentiating between blood and sperm donation: "You give something that your body naturally produces. You give something that you will not be short of in the future since your body just produces more. And that is the same, no matter what you donate." It was only after he and his girlfriend decided to go their separate ways that Thommy first considered becoming a sperm donor. His reasoning was that, since he now was single, he would not have to coordinate between having sex with his partner and the requirement to abstain from ejaculation before providing semen samples at the sperm bank: "When we broke up, I thought: okay, now it doesn't matter anymore. Because now there was no problem anymore with waiting all those hours, you know, those hours that you need to wait [*at spare op*] before. This was the last nail in the coffin you might say, and it worked out just fine that way." Having been a sperm donor for more than two years when I met him, Thommy now had a weekly routine for donating semen, just like many other donors. When he started to donate, he only needed to wait forty-eight hours in between samples. At that time, he would donate twice or sometimes three times a week. However, his abstinence period had been increased to seventy-two hours, making it harder for Thommy to visit the sperm bank more than once a week:

> Usually I drive by there after work. I get off work at around four and then I can be there at about twenty to five, and then the whole thing takes ten minutes and I am on my way again. And this is not, you know, I have done this for such a long time now that you can't even compare it to, you know, when you masturbate normally. You really can't. This is some kind of service you are being paid for and that's what it is. There is nothing romantic about the situation: you go there with your donor card, you scan it and check in, and then you go into a room which is one meter and a half by one meter, and then there is a screen with a porno movie playing and that is that. So, there is nothing cute about it.

His weekly routine notwithstanding, and even though Thommy had acquired a pragmatic outlook on masturbating at the sperm bank, he also talked about the challenges involved in sticking to the control regime in place at the sperm bank. For him, the challenge lay in having to abstain from sexual activity for three days before delivering a sample:

> There are supposed to be seventy-two hours in between and that's why you need to plan all your other activities around that. You need to stick to those hours. For me this works best on a Friday. So, I am

there either Friday afternoon or maybe Saturday morning. At the beginning, I only needed to wait forty-eight hours and that was easier
to work with. But now Fridays usually work out for me. This is of
course no more a ritual than knowing out of routine that you are hitting a deadline: from now until Friday you need to have your fingers
on top of your blanket, you know. That is the only thing that sticks in
my head: no matter what the hell [*hvad fanden*] you're up to, it will
always be a no go.

This chapter explores biosocial subjectivation by attending to the
affective investments that sperm donors have to make in order to
be able to masturbate at sperm banks. The making of Danish sperm
donors as biosocial subjects requires that men learn to be affected in
certain ways so as to be able to masturbate at sperm banks and thus
produce semen samples on demand. As I will argue throughout the
chapter, learning to be affected in certain ways, sperm donors are
enticed by gender, that is, they seek ways of stimulation that allow
them to experience themselves in accordance with their own gender normativity by integrating the control regime in place at sperm
banks into their ways of being men. In other words, being able to
masturbate at the sperm bank is achieved by performatively remaking one's gender in the right way, where this right way depends on
men's ideals of a masculine self as well as on the biomedical evaluations of masculine performance as they take place at sperm banks.
Before men become sperm donors, their sexual experiences are
not likely to be framed by a control regime that demands that they
abstain from ejaculation for at least forty-eight hours in between
masturbation. Neither are they likely to be thinking of their masculine self-worth in terms of semen quality, nor will they relate to
their semen in terms of biomedical assessments of sperm cells. Once
they are sperm donors, however, the ejaculatory regimen in place at
Danish sperm banks and the biomedical evaluations of their semen
are part of how they live their (intimate) lives as men. Moreover,
the atmosphere at sperm banks and in donor rooms, and encounters with the materialities of sperm donation such as specimen cups,
pornographic magazines, and men's (own) bodily liquids, all make
up the affective and emotional landscapes that men have to navigate in order to be successful sperm donors. Thus, sperm donors
have to "sustain particular kinds of affective relations" (Ahmed 2012:
196) in order to be able to donate semen. They have to learn to be
affected in ways that produce "sexual capacities in [their] bodies"
(Alldred and Fox 2015: 907) so as to be able to ejaculate into a specimen cup. This chapter hence connects Danish sperm donors' talk

about masturbation at the sperm bank to my introductory discussion of affective investments in biosociality. The focus will be the making of Danish sperm donors as biosocial subjects through masturbation, that is, the incorporation of sperm donation's biomedical control regimes into men's gender performativity through masturbatory practices.

Thommy's experience of masturbating at the sperm bank is characterized by pragmatism and routine, something that he had in common with most of the other sperm donors that I was able to talk to. While, as we will see later, Thommy and other men also talked about the tantalizing effect of the boundary-breaking experience of masturbating in a semipublic space like a sperm bank, in order to be sperm donors and in order to commit themselves to the biopolitical objective of sperm donation, men need to learn to be able to masturbate on demand without necessarily being sexually excited about ejaculation as they would be when masturbating at home or when engaging intimately with sex partners. Rather, as Thommy's story makes clear, sticking to a strict time schedule and controlling one's sexual desires becomes paramount for the performativity of sperm donor masculinity. Knowing that he has to keep his "fingers on top of the blanket" for three consecutive days before donating semen at the sperm bank, in his more than two years as a sperm donor Thommy has learned to be affected in a particular way that allows him to be a donor. He puts his potential desire for sexually intimate contacts second, and his obligations as a sperm donor—abstaining from ejaculation for seventy-two hours in order to produce a semen sample that passes quality assessments—first. Part of learning to emotionally invest in a particular way of doing masculinity is connected to Thommy's desire to help others, his impetus to give his bodily fluids to those who are in need of them. Another part of Thommy and the other sperm donors learning to affectively invest in biosocial subjectivation through the enticement of gender are the control mechanisms in place at sperm banks and the materialities connected to the ejaculatory regimen to which sperm donors must adhere. From the personalized donor card held by every sperm donor, to the check-in procedures, to the specifications of and atmosphere in the donor rooms, Thommy names a range of things that become incorporated into the masturbatory practices of sperm donors that make them into biosocial subjects, and it is these ways of learning to be affected that Danish sperm donors acquire in order to be donors, and the enticement of gender this involves, that will be the focal point of this chapter.

The Biomedicalization of Masturbation

Even though sperm donation has been a huge social and commercial success, very little is known about sperm donors' experiences of masturbation and their masturbatory practices. Despite its central role for sperm donation, masturbation is not of importance for most researchers interested in biomedical regulation of reproduction (Garlick 2014). Rather, masturbation has been keenly avoided by social scientists conducting research on reproductive technologies (but see Almeling 2011; Inhorn 2012; Mohr 2010, 2016a). Simultaneously, male masturbation has a long history of being regarded as a personal vice, a corruptive practice that turns the masturbating male individual into a weakling by emasculating him (Laqueur 2003; Rosewarne 2014; Stengers and Neck 2001). This dynamic between necessity and taboo characterizes Danish sperm donors' experiences of masturbating at sperm banks, as we have seen in chapter 2.

But this dynamic also has a historical dimension. In Europe and America, anxieties about the corruptive nature of masturbation have existed at least since the infamous *Onania* was published, somewhere between 1708 and 1716 (Laqueur 2003). Onania, an anti-masturbation advice book, was connected to already existing beliefs about the sinfulness of masturbation. It had success because "it very aptly addressed some of the most pervasive moral, religious, social, and political concerns of the contemporary elites" (Stolberg 2000: 6). At that time, the negative effects of masturbation were thought to be physical (damage to genitals, loss of vitality, death) and psychological (nervous breakdowns and insanity), and were seen as directly harmful to men's gender identity (emasculation) and personality (corrupted soul, irresponsibility, lack of control). Moreover, the assumption was that the negative effects of masturbation would be passed on to future generations (the bad seed) and that it would be a threat to society in general, as it was believed that masturbation could potentially leave men unable to reproduce. Affective or emotional investments in a particular understanding of masculinity through masturbation were thus also at stake three hundred years ago.

As historical accounts of individual men's experiences of masturbation during the eighteenth and nineteenth centuries attest (Hall 1992; Stolberg 2000), men readily identified with the available interpretation of masturbation as a disease. They were concerned about masturbation as a personal tragedy, and had internalized "prevalent attitudes toward the solitary vice" (Hall 1992: 382) as a personal failure. At the same time, though, as the vigor of antimasturbation campaigns unfolded, scientists began to examine semen. Masturbation, even though it was shunned, was the most likely mode of procurement of semen for these examinations. When Antoni van Leeuwenhoek examined semen under the microscope as early as the 1670s, he "was repelled by the inquiry and quickly turned to other matters" (Ruestow 1983: 188). He found himself caught in the middle of debates about the permissibility of masturbation for scientific and medical purposes and felt the need to emphasize in his descriptions that the semen samples he had used had not been procured "by sinfully defiling himself but as a natural consequence of conjugal coitus" (Ruestow 1983: 189).

Yet alongside these dominant discourses, the eighteenth and nineteenth centuries also saw interpretations of masturbation as positive and fundamentally important to male development and masculinity; learning to be affected in certain ways through masturbation already back then encompassed a dynamic between ban and encouragement. Grounded in folkloric beliefs, as Lesley Hall argues, these interpretations constructed masturbation "as a site not of fear and guilt but of manly pride" (Hall 1992: 375). To masturbate was something good, something that men needed to do in order to become real men. Simultaneously, however, this manly nature also needed to be disciplined, to prevent sexual urges from taking control of the male individual. A real man was supposed to be "in charge of what his body did, not its victim" (Hall 1992: 375), and masturbation as a way of controlling the body was thus part of teaching men how to be affected in particular ways and thus do their gender in a way that was expected of them.

The availability of donor insemination as a medical treatment for infertility since at least the nineteenth century also signals that masturbation was encouraged as part of sperm donation even despite its controversial moral status. The onset of reproductive biomedicine was thus important for a change in moral attitudes toward masturbation. Whereas antimasturbation campaigns were about specific religious morals until the mid to late eighteenth century, in the nineteenth century masturbation became part of a scientific framework, making it instead a matter of medical reasoning and bodily needs (Singy 2003; Stolberg 2003), a dynamic that continued throughout the twentieth century. This shift enabled a reconsideration of the claim that all masturbation is vice, and, as a consequence, becoming a sperm donor was enabled by the biomedicalization of masturbation, which opened up spaces of positive experiences of gender normativity and thus allowed for masturbation as part of sperm donation. So-called "therapeutic masturbation" might have been one strategy used to justify masturbation as part of sperm donation in the nineteenth century (Singy 2003); it would have allowed young medical students or doctors to provide semen to cure infertility, a medical and therapeutic reasoning that would justify masturbation even though dominant moral codes condemned it.

While the moral and regulatory landscape of sperm donation has changed dramatically since then, Danish sperm donors nevertheless still need to make masturbation meaningful as part of sperm donation's biopolitical objective rather than being about sexual enjoyment. The regulatory regime of contemporary sperm donation does not accept sexual enjoyment as a legitimate reason for becoming a sperm donor (Mohr 2010), a stance that also characterizes sperm donors' own moral positioning. As chapter 2 showed, sperm donation is still connected with a taboo in regard to masturbation, and as Thommy's story makes visible, sperm donors' talk about masturbation happens first and foremost in terms of routine and pragmatism. As Thommy explained, there is nothing romantic about masturbating at the sperm bank. For him, it is a routine after work on Fridays, which takes ten minutes and cannot be compared to normal masturbation. Danish sperm donors learn to be affected in certain ways that enable them, on demand, to produce semen samples that pass quality assessments every time. Being sperm donors produces capacities in their bodies that allow them to be semen providers, and the remainder of this chapter will focus on how these capacities are produced. First, I will look at the dynamic between masturbatory taboos and boosted masculinity, and thereafter at the interplay between (self-)discipline, masturbatory routines, and flows of affect. Together, these dynamics make up the biomedical spaces of sperm donation in which men learn to be affected in particular ways and in which they become biosocial subjects through the enticement of gender.

Masturbatory Taboos and Boosted Masculinity

While social sciences have been silent about the masturbatory practices of sperm donors and the role they play in sperm donors' subjectivation processes, for sperm donors themselves masturbation is a central experiential arena for the actualization of sperm donor selfhood. However, due to the way in which sperm donation is regulated at Danish sperm banks and due to dominant moral codes, masturbation is also the part of sperm donation that is most likely to delegitimize being a sperm donor. For Thommy, this becomes clear every time he enters or leaves the sperm bank, as he told me:

> One of the most challenging moments is when you are on the street (in front of the sperm bank). There is a doctor's office, a sperm bank, and a recording studio in the same building, and either people think that there are a lot of male musicians here, or that this doctor has a lot of male patients, or, well, they think that there must be a sperm bank here. I don't know how many people actually know about (the sperm bank). But there are times when I am on the street and think: is he looking strangely at me? I mean, this is not a problem once you're inside the sperm bank. Everyone knows what is supposed to happen there. It can be a problem though when you leave, when you can feel those looks.

Thommy's experience reverberates in the narratives of most Danish sperm donors and is thus something that sperm donors need to consider as part of their moral reasoning, as we have seen in chapter 2. At the same time, this experience also points to the affective investments involved in being a sperm donor, as it actualizes the social taboo around masturbation as sensations and emotions when sperm donors "feel those looks." For Emil, in his thirties, married and a father of two, a similar affective investment was at stake. He talked about masturbation at the sperm bank as something "totally strange" and "awkward." Referring to the atmosphere inside the sperm bank, he said:

> It is a really nice little place, you know, very tidy and neat. It feels, in regards to the fact that you are supposed to go in there and do what you have to do, it feels, and this is totally strange [*vildt mærkeligt*], you get up there and there are two sweet girls behind the desk, and you are supposed to go into this toilet-sized room and do what you have to do, and they are just two meters away from you, you know. I know that the door is locked, and that it is soundproof and all those things, but it just feels kinda strange. So, that is strange. But also, you know, I am a very private person to begin with, and it was a little bit awkward to come up there and, well, yes, masturbate inside of this small shack [*biks*] there.

As Emil's elaboration shows, the social taboo around masturbation also actualizes affectively as part of the practical issues that sperm donors engage in every time they visit the sperm bank. Meeting staff and masturbating in a small room while knowing the staff are right outside becomes part of the experience of being a sperm donor. Oscar, in his thirties and a sperm donor for about two years, had similar experiences. Single and without children, Oscar had integrated being a sperm donor to the degree that his only sexual activity consisted of masturbating at the sperm bank, something he did three times a week. Nevertheless, he also said that he still gets embarrassed every time he has to hand over his semen sample to the staff at the sperm bank: "Well, actually it is very boundary-breaking [*grænseoverskridende*], you know, sometimes when you are there (at the sperm bank) and you come with your sperm in a small glass, and then you are supposed to hand it over, well, I feel a little bit stupid [*halvdum*]. . . . It is very, well, it is one's sexuality that all of a sudden is so, what is the word, that is so exposed all of a sudden, and that is very boundary-breaking."

Even when men have been donors for some time—Thommy, Emil, and Oscar had all been donating semen for two years—a feeling of awkwardness still actualizes the taboo of masturbation. Emil's way of wording things—"and this is totally strange"—points to the affective investments that this actualization demands of him as a sperm donor. Every time he masturbates at the sperm bank, "it just feels kinda strange." Oscar's narrative connects these feelings of awkwardness in addition to the materialities—semen in a specimen cup—and the moment of exchange of these materialities. His experiences show how sperm donors' affective investments are also bound to the material specificities of sperm donation. Handing over a specimen cup with his semen to sperm bank staff, he "feels a little bit stupid," as he terms it, a situation he will not be able to avoid and thus will have to find a way of dealing with. In other words, sperm donors need to find a way in which to develop bodily capacities to deliver semen samples, not because of sexual enjoyment—even though they might enjoy it—but because they are sperm donors and it is expected of them. In order to be successful sperm donors, men have to develop capacities that allow them to deliver semen samples on demand despite the taboos that they might experience.

Part of developing these capacities, this way of learning to be affected in a particular way, is connected to what I call the boost experience (Mohr 2014). The boost experience represents moments in which sperm donors are able to experience themselves as men in pleasurable ways that incorporate the control regime in place at Danish sperm banks as well as the biomedical registers that sperm banks use in order to measure their performance as sperm donors. It thus reflects how Danish sperm donors make the regulatory regime at sperm banks a meaningful part of their gender performativity by enacting sexual restraint and biomedical regulation in their ways of being sperm donors. The boost experience helps them to remake themselves as biosocial subjects by opening up a possibility for biomedical logics and regulation to become part of their positive self-experiences as men.

For some men, these experiences included what Emil and Oscar talked about as boundary-breaking. Yet while Emil and Oscar emphasized the negative sides of being subjected to such transgression, other men found the breaking of boundaries pleasurable. Felix, in his twenties, single, and a sperm donor for two years, described his interest in becoming a sperm donor in the following way: "I think my life was a bit boring somehow, a bit too rigid [*stringent*] in one way or another, and I thought, I should try, I mean, of course it is nice to get money and so on, but I also just thought that it would be fun to try something boundary-breaking, in one way or another. And this was the wisest thing I could think of instead of parachute jumping or something like that." Anton, in his thirties, married, a father of two, and a sperm donor for about a year, also described the first few times of delivering semen samples at the sperm bank as exciting. When I asked him why it was exciting, he said: "Well, it was boundary-breaking, you know, in regards to masturbation. That is something, you know, something that you normally do in private. But now you receive a small glass from a receptionist, and then you go into this little box, and the whole world knows what you are doing when you're in there." Thus, what figures as an embarrassing experience for some men can provide pleasure for others. Rather than being seen only as a restraint or a hindrance, a boundary-breaking experience might also figure as something that evokes lust and pleasure and thus represents a form of affective investment in sperm donor biosociality that relies on positive rather than negative actualization of gendered positionality.

A similar dimension was true for the sexual restraint that sperm donors experience due to the abstinence rule. Just as is the case with the masturbation taboo, being forced to abstain from sexual activity can also provide pleasure and thus boost men's self-experiences as sperm donors. For Haldor, a married father of two in his late thirties and with two years of experience as a sperm donor, this exercise of sexual restraint was a lustful experience. Talking about the necessity to abstain from ejaculation—in his case for seventy-two hours—before delivering a semen sample at the sperm bank, he said: "You know, you are more or less prepared for that in one way or another.

I mean, partly you have planned this (donating semen) three days in advance, that you are supposed to be there. In this way, strangely enough, it becomes some kind of boost, you know, yes, you know, just like the forbidden cake or something." Also invoking this image of the forbidden cake or fruit, Storm, in his twenties, single, and a sperm donor for nearly three years, talked about sexual restraint in a similar fashion: "Well, the way it works is that at the sperm bank (masturbation) happens every other day while at home it happens every day. That means you build up something, and then you are looking forward to it the hours before you go down there (to the sperm bank). So, it becomes more fun." The affective investments that sperm donors make when masturbating at sperm banks thus happen inside a dynamic between the experiences of taboo and restraint as negative transgression on the one hand and excitement and pleasure on the other. While abstaining from sexual activity can be troublesome for some, like Thommy who found it difficult to keep his hands "on top of the blanket" for three days, for others it is exactly this exercise of having to abstain from sexual activity that furthers lust and thus investments in being a sperm donor.

These more immediate affective investments into biosociality are connected to a continuous invocation of men's ways of doing masculinity in terms of biomedical measurements of their performance as sperm donors, such as the assessment of semen quality and the compensation they receive for delivering good-quality semen. Part of this continuous process of biosocial subjectivation happens in the interaction between sperm bank staff and sperm donors that ensues every time they visit the sperm bank. A short entry from my fieldnotes gives insights into what this might look like:

It is Thursday morning and I am sitting at the reception desk. A donor returns from the donor rooms to the desk with his specimen cup on the papier-mâché tray that donors receive here together with specimen cups while another donor who returned before him receives his compensation in cash. Lise, one of the lab technicians, is counting the money. Maria, the secretary, is standing by while Lise is counting. The donor and Lise and then Maria sign the receipt stating that the donor has received his compensation. Now, the donor who had just arrived with his specimen cup scans his finger and then enters his pin code on the keypad. Lise says: "It didn't work." The donor smiles and wants to leave. "No," says Lise, "you have to scan your finger again." The donor laughs and says that he had understood that his sample was not good enough. Lise smiles and responds that even though they would be working fast, they were not that fast. When the donor scans his finger the second time, everything works. "That was a nice sample last time," Lise says. The donor smiles. "You will be getting money soon," she adds. The donor inquires about the quality of his last sample. Lise says that it was a MOT 20, which indicates that his sample had 20 million sperm cells per milliliter after thawing. "No, no, in money. That is the only way I know how good it is," says the donor, and laughs. Lise checks a list and replies that it would be 500 Danish Crowns.

As a continuous invocation of the biosocial subject, sperm donors are positioned according to their performance as semen providers at sperm banks. As the fieldnote makes clear, interaction between staff and sperm donors centers on the evaluation of men's biomedical value, that is, sperm donors are talked to and referred to in interactions with staff through their semen samples. This evaluation actualizes through numbers, both in terms of sperm counts as well as in the amount of money that sperm donors receive for their samples. As the reaction of the sperm donor in the fieldnote shows, this has performative effects. For him, the value of his semen is connected to the amount of money he receives for his samples. It becomes a way of knowing his semen and himself and thus a measure of his quality as a sperm donor or, as he says, "No, no, in money. That is the only way I know how good it is." As was also the case for William in chapter 2, thinking about one's semen in terms of monetary compensation is part of a sperm donor's biosocial subjectivation. Sperm donors develop a different relationship to their semen due to being sperm donors. While this effect of being a biosocial subject as a sperm donor could be called commodification (Almeling 2011), it also points to the meaning making and to the particular affective investments that men make when they become sperm donors. Thinking about one's semen and one's worth as a sperm donor in terms of the monetary value that is put on the amount of sperm cells one is able to provide requires men to recognize and feel themselves in a different register than they did before they started to donate semen. It requires men to embody the evaluative logic in place at sperm banks.

The positive experience of being good enough that is actualized in encounters between sperm donors and staff at sperm banks becomes for the donors a way of thinking about themselves as men. Over time, the continuous invocation of having good semen quality impacts how sperm donors think about themselves as men, and not least how they do their masculinity. Becoming a biosocial subject is boosted by the continuous experience of being good enough that is provided by masturbating and producing semen samples on demand. For William, in his twenties and in a long-term relationship, having good semen quality was very satisfying. For him, good semen quality was a sign of being healthy and of having good genes. When I asked him what being proud of good semen quality meant for him, he said: "Well, just that feeling, you know, that you are healthy and well, just as when you are at the doctor's and he says: you are a healthy young man. Then you feel like: ahhh, this is beautiful. Wouldn't you agree, to know that you don't have any illnesses? The worst thing is to be sick. And it was just wonderful to know that one has good genes." For Mathias, also in his twenties and in a long-term relationship, this confirmation of being healthy and having good genes clearly supported his male ego. When considering the quality of his semen, he proudly announced that he would be very popular as a sperm donor: "I have genes that they are really interested in, with dark hair and brown eyes, so in theory I can stop by there as many times as I want to. Normally you're only supposed to come once a week, but I can stop by there two or even three times a week if I want to." Knowing that one has "genes that they are really interested in" thus translates into feeling better about oneself, and, in the case of Mathias, even to a feeling of male pride. Oliver, in his twenties, single, and a sperm donor for less than a year, talked about the impact that knowing he has good semen quality has on him in the following way:

> When I found out about it (having good semen quality) I also found out that I was very healthy [*sund og rask*]. Until I became a sperm donor, I had this image of myself as weak because I have never been good at sports, I have never used my body for much physically, and I never felt especially attractive or anything like that. I was sick quite often as a child and I had this image of myself as very vulnerable in some sense. But after all of this (becoming a sperm donor) I have a totally different picture of myself and my body. Now I have a picture of myself as someone strong and someone you can rely on, that I am, even though it sounds weird, part of an elite. I am healthier than the average person, I have high semen quality, and I feel more attractive in some way. I actually feel that I can be more picky about potential girlfriends, you know, because I am a more attractive partner because I have high semen quality, and I know that I will have healthy children.

This continuous experience of being healthy and having good genes is also supported by the regular blood tests and physical exams that sperm donors have to go through. While physical exams also always contain transgressive moments of male shame, which potentially can lead men to reevaluate their decision to become sperm donors, as we will see in chapter 5, most donors talked about these exams as a positive experience that additionally boosted their feelings of male self-worth. Being checked regularly furthermore proved to them that they were part of a professional and responsible endeavor that was about doing good in the world. When asked, for example, whether excluding gay men and drug users as donors was reasonable, as regulations in Denmark require, most men were convinced that sperm banks had a responsibility to minimize health risks. For example, Jeppe, single, in his late teens, and a sperm donor for just about a year, said:

> I think, you could say, the things that you risk with, for example, sex with other men or when you use needles (for drugs), that is, you could say, a fatal thing that could happen to an eventual donor child if it is born with HIV or something like that. So, I think that it is actually okay to have that kind of requirement (to exclude gay men and drug users as sperm donors). You could say there is also an economic reason in that you don't need to check, you don't have to be paranoid; and it also gives assurance to those who receive the donation that there are rules for this and that certain measures are taken.

Continuous control of lifestyle and sex life are thus seen by sperm donors as a necessary means to guarantee the legitimacy of sperm donation, and by accepting these kinds of interventions, donors come to understand themselves as individuals who have all the mandatory qualities and characteristics. They understand themselves as responsible and healthy men who can make a difference.

Making a difference thereby rested on a feeling of pride about having good-quality semen and good genes, as was made clear earlier. This continuous experience is likely to have performative effects inasmuch as it influences sperm donors' ways of thinking about themselves and ways of doing their masculinity. One donor in whom this was rather obvious was Storm. He was convinced that he was one of the best three donors at his sperm bank. He even knew what the average sperm count of his semen samples was, something that not all donors were interested in: "I think the lowest I have had was 37 million (sperm cells per milliliter) and the highest was 136 million. But the majority of my samples are between 85 and 115 million." Knowing what he was worth as a sperm donor, Storm was very open about donating semen. In comparison to other men, he did not feel ashamed about being a sperm donor, but instead actually used it as a pickup line when flirting with women, as he told me: "You know, it is not like: hi my name is Storm and I am a sperm donor. No, that's not how it works. It flows into the conversation naturally. I am very good at steering the conversation in that direction. I think it is wonderful to have that quality stamp." Telling me that he would have to be careful with those women who might try to come after his semen, he explained that he would always use a condom when having sex with them, and that he would dispose of the condom himself in order to ensure that they did not use his semen secretly without his knowledge: "Imagine a woman in her thirties who really wants to have children and that has the idea that she doesn't want children with a husband but from a sperm donor instead. When you meet that woman her hormones go crazy [*slår kolbøtter*]." Feeling astonished and also partly provoked by his narrative, I asked Storm what his semen quality meant to him: "It is in some way the physical side of me and what I am in flesh and blood. I have begun to be more proud about this than I was before, sometimes even to the point of being arrogant. I mean, it is what it is. I have changed since I found out that I have such good sperm quality. And usually most of the samples are of the same quality." And when I wanted to know how this feeling of pride expresses itself, he added:

> More self-confidence. When I am talking with someone who says something annoying or irritating, then you can look at them once and say (to yourself): He has probably just 10 million sperm cells or just 5 million. And then you can say (to yourself): I have without doubt sperm quality ten times better than yours. I can be the father of your children because you are not able to impregnate your wife. And with that you feel uplifted and can be a little bit more relaxed about the whole thing.

The affective investments that sperm donors make in biosociality through masturbation at sperm banks are thus positioned within a dynamic between taboo and transgression on the one side and pleasure and lust on the other. While some men might find it difficult to masturbate at the sperm bank because it actualizes the social taboo around masturbation, for other men it is precisely this actualization of taboo that contributes to them continuing to donate semen. The same can be said about the sexual restraints that men have to live with as sperm donors. Though some donors find it difficult to wait forty-eight or even seventy-two hours before being able to ejaculate, others are enticed by the idea of having to abstain.

Whatever their personal relationship to the social taboo around masturbation, as well as to the necessity of sexual abstinence, they all have to learn to be affected in such a way that they are able to produce semen samples on demand. As the experiences of the men cited in this section of this chapter show, this process of learning to be affected in a particular way involves incorporating biomedical evaluations of semen quality and sperm donor performance into men's gender performativity. What I call the boost experience, the continuous experience of being an excellent sperm donor, enables this incorporation and thus allows men to become biosocial subjects who adhere to the biopolitical regimen at place at sperm banks. The boost experience represents successful affective investments in biomedically evaluated masculinity by enticing men to performatively remake themselves as the men they want to be—men who produce good-quality semen. Being a sperm donor enables them to feel that they are doing their gender in the right way, as they are continuously reminded of being those men who have what it takes. Sperm counts, monetary compensation, assumptions about being healthy and having good genes—all these dimensions of being a sperm donor become part of how sperm donors think, embody, and not least do their masculinity.

(Self-)Discipline, Masturbatory Routines, and Flows of Affect

As we have seen in the previous section, masturbating at the sperm bank becomes a routine practice at some point. This routine functions on a number of different levels, from a more general acceptance of being a sperm donor and the moral reasoning this involves, as we saw in the previous chapter, to a more individualized routine for each sperm donor, such as stopping by each week on the same days and at the same time, to a micromanagement of donors' routines at the sperm bank through interactions with staff as well as donors' particular ways of masturbating in the donor rooms. The masturbatory routines of donors are thereby characterized by a dynamic between being disciplined by sperm bank staff on the one hand and each donor disciplining himself in accordance to what is expected of him as a man who can provide semen on demand on the other.

This dynamic of (self-)discipline depends on different layers of formal and informal types of regulation (Graham, Mohr, and Bourne 2016). Sperm donors are of course formally regulated by the contracts they sign with sperm banks. These contracts obligate sperm donors to deliver a certain number of semen samples so that sperm banks are guaranteed a capital return on their investments. Signing contracts with sperm banks, sperm donors also accept possible reimbursement claims from sperm banks in the event that they fail to live up to their contractual obligations, for example by not delivering enough samples or by donating semen at another sperm bank simultaneously. While these formal types of regulation work through the punitive power of contract law, the more informal types of regulation in place at Danish sperm banks work through the invocation of the (self-)disciplined individual, with masturbation as the central arena in and through which (self-)discipline is made to work. At some sperm banks, for example, donors are given a sheet of instructions for what to do while in the donor room. These instructions contain advice, such as locking the doors so that outside signal lamps are activated, washing the penis with only clear water before masturbating, collecting semen directly in specimen cups (especially the first few drops, as they contain the most sperm cells), turning off pornographic movies when leaving the room, and making sure that samples are registered properly by sperm bank staff. These kinds of instructions ensure the proper collection of semen in specimen cups and thus remake masturbation at the sperm bank into a performance of (self-)discipline rather than a sexual act. Being a good sperm donor requires men to adhere to these rules, and adhering to these rules positions them as good sperm donors. This becomes most obvious in situations in which men do not follow the established rules, as the following fieldnote shows:

Christian, the leading technician, and I are talking about what qualifies men as good sperm donors. He tells me that whether a man is a good sperm donor or not would depend on many different things: his semen quality, his genetic profile, his medical evaluation, all that would come together when determining whether or not someone would make a good sperm donor. "And of course it is also important that a guy behaves properly," Christian adds. Explaining what he means, Christian says that he would make sure that men would not fall outside of what he would consider normal behavior: "They should not be too extreme." Asking Christian whether that would include someone lying about his time of abstinence, for example, he replies that lying about the time of abstinence would definitely be unacceptable, and he would make sure that sperm donors are aware of his standpoint in regard to this: "I mean, how difficult can it be. Get yourself together and tell me when the last time was."

He then tells me the story of a donor whom he had caught trying to cheat. According to Christian, this donor had collected his semen in a condom at home and taken the semen with him to the sperm bank, where he then transferred it to a specimen cup. When receiving the specimen cup from that donor, Christian had wondered about the sample's smell and consistency: "It just smelled completely different from what samples normally smell like." The quality assessments then revealed that the sample was of really poor quality and well below what this donor's samples were usually like. When the donor came in the next time, a few days later, Christian confronted him and asked whether something unusual had happened with the last sample. At that point, the donor confessed to collecting the sample with the help of a condom at home: "He told me that his girlfriend also needed to be taken care of." Shaking his head, Christian tells me that he made it clear to the donor that that kind of behavior was totally out of line and should the donor try it again, he would immediately be dismissed as a donor.

While from the donor's point of view this could be said to be an attempt to negotiate his obligations as a boyfriend and lover while also donating semen, something that is not necessarily always easy, as we have seen in the previous chapter, for Christian this behavior signals an attempt to cheat the regulations in place at the sperm bank and is thus unmistakably what he considers unproper sperm donor behavior. Good sperm donors do not cheat; they masturbate at the sperm bank and they also abstain from sexual activity, no questions asked. What is more, they need to be able to ejaculate properly, that is, they need to collect their semen in a specific specimen cup provided by the sperm bank, and they need to collect their semen at the sperm bank and not at home or anywhere else. While it is common practice that men undergoing infertility treatment masturbate at home and bring their semen samples to the clinic, sperm donors are required to have bodily capacities that enable them to ejaculate on demand at the sperm bank. Enforcing (self-)discipline like in the example above, formal and informal regulation in place at sperm banks thus aim to ensure that men develop these capacities and, as a result, become good sperm donors.

Being forced to masturbate at the sperm bank and to collect semen in specific specimen cups, men learn to discipline themselves in and through the ways in which they masturbate. They develop routines that ensure ejaculation as well as the proper collection of semen. Elias, in his thirties, single, and a sperm donor for about two years, definitely had to get used to masturbating at the sperm bank. As became clear in chapter 1, he had difficulties reaching orgasms at the sperm bank. As with most other donors, he had developed a certain technique for collecting his semen, which included him being on his knees while having the specimen cup in his left hand and then concentrating on getting all the semen into the cup. When I asked him what he thought about the specimen cups, he said: "Well, it totally fucks up the orgasm. You need to concentrate on the cup, only on the cup, only on the cup and all of that. And that makes it, well, you know."—"So, it's no fun or what?"—"No, not really. It could be that it is for some, but not for me. That is simply too distracting." Anton had less difficulty masturbating at the sperm bank and did not need to concentrate as much on ejaculation. Nevertheless, he had also developed a routine that enabled him to provide semen samples and collect them properly. After some of his samples had turned out to be of low quality, staff had asked him to try and produce what are called split samples. Producing split samples demands men to only collect the first parts of an ejaculate, since these contain the most sperm cells. As a result, men are more likely to have higher sperm counts because their samples will contain less seminal fluid and thus have a higher concentration of cells per milliliter. This, at least, is the reasoning behind asking donors to provide split samples. While skeptical about it at first, Anton had been able to train himself to split his samples and was now able to collect only what are considered the best parts of his semen. When I asked him how he does it, he said: "Well, it is all about hitting the cup right the first time and then you have the number of squirts that you know your dick produces. The first two, three squirts should be in the cup, and then you need to squeeze it tight and the rest ends up in a piece of paper." According to Thommy, hitting the cup right the first time requires training, and takes some time to get used to. While he said that he has never missed the specimen cup, he also admitted that spilling semen would be relatively easy when one is not used to ejaculating into a specimen cup. When he and I were talking about hitting the specimen cup, he said:

> I have hit the cup every time so far. But if you don't place the cup right or if you can't hold back so that you can stop it until you have the cup right, well, yes, then of course it is easy to spill something. But after a while this becomes less and less of a problem because you learn to control [*at styre*] it better the more often you do it. This cup, I remember when I had to do it for the first time. I was like: are you

serious? But if you have done this 150 times then you get the hang of it. Usually, I can feel it a bit before and then I simply take the cup into my hand and finish it off.

By training themselves to hit specimen cups just right, and even controlling the ejection of semen so that samples with higher sperm counts can be delivered, sperm donors connect their masturbatory practices to the goal of producing good semen samples. They control their affective states of excitement and pleasure in order to produce good-quality semen. Noah, in his twenties, single, and a donor for about a year, described this control of affective states as follows, when he talked about the difference between masturbating at home and doing it at the sperm bank:

> Well [laughing], the whole thing about that you need to hit the cup, that doesn't really, I really think that you can enjoy it more when you don't need to hit the cup. It is a little bit of a deal breaker. Your thoughts have to follow two lanes instead of only being focused on lust since you also need to coordinate getting all of it into the cup and that kind of thing. So, in this regard it is very different from when I do it at home. . . . But I also have to say, I have the feeling that when I can hold on a little bit longer (keep on masturbating) then I also donate more. So, I try, I am just as relaxed (as at home), but I try to perform better in that way, you know, I try to hold on a little bit longer, so that I can also deliver a proper [*ordentlig*] donation. I mean, at home I don't really care about how much it is.

In Noah's narrative, a masturbatory routine is very much about producing what he calls a "proper donation," a semen sample that has good quality. It is in and through his masturbatory routine—holding on a little bit longer—that he tries to live up to the expectations that he faces as a sperm donor. Masturbating the right way thus not only ensures the proper collection of semen samples, but for men like Noah it is also connected to the quality of the semen they deliver. In other words, masturbation becomes a way of doing sperm donor masculinity by incorporating the evaluative logics of reproductive biomedicine in the ways that gender is performed in and through masturbation. Sperm donors become men who have good semen samples through their masturbatory routines.

These experiences testify to what degree sperm donors are able to discipline themselves. As donors, they not only need to abstain from ejaculation for at least forty-eight hours before providing a semen sample at the sperm bank. They also need to control their orgasmic function to the point of being able to interrupt ejaculation so as to collect semen samples properly, and they train themselves to masturbate in the right way in order to produce good-quality se- men. This kind of (self-)discipline contains regulatory elements in the sense that men try to live up to their contractual obligations as sperm donors. At the same time, this (self-)discipline also involves an experience of doing it right and being able to hit the cup, and producing good-quality semen. While sperm donors' orgasms might also be about sexual fulfillment for some men, they are similarly most likely to be about living up to the expectations that men are met with when they become sperm donors. Being able to produce a semen sample on demand means being a good donor, and being a good sperm donor in this sense requires men to incorporate (self-) discipline as part of their masturbatory routines. In this way, every time sperm donors masturbate and ejaculate, they remake them- selves as biosocial subjects, because it is through successful mastur- bation that they live up to what is expected of them as men. As the experiences of Elias, Anton, Thommy, and Noah attest, the develop- ment of masturbatory routines ensures this success. Sperm donors train themselves and thus learn to be affected in particular ways: ejaculating with spoiled orgasms, knowing the number of ejections during orgasms, holding off ejaculation until a specimen cup is in place, and, not least, feeling ejaculation coming so that you know when to "finish it off" in order to produce the perfect semen sample.

Learning to be affected in these ways, and thus developing a mas- turbatory routine, requires disciplining one's body. In that sense, sperm donors are masters of micromanaging their affective states. Yet in order for this micromanagement to be affective so that men are able to produce good-quality semen on demand, affect needs to flow in a specific way. This demands a number of elements to be in place that are not necessarily controlled by sperm donors them- selves. As we have already seen, knowing that sperm bank staff are right outside while one is masturbating can have an influence on whether men are able to produce a semen sample. Another import- ant part of this affective landscape is the atmosphere in the donor rooms, and sensory experiences like smells or having to use mag- azines and computers, but also possibly encountering other men's semen. These experiences have an impact on whether or not men are able to masturbate and thus perform sperm donor masculinity and, as a consequence, sperm donors work toward making sure that flows of affect are disturbed as little as possible.

For Thommy, for example, two things were especially important. First, he would avoid using the donor room that has a window facing the street. When we were talking about the atmosphere in the donor rooms, he jokingly said: "It is always exciting to be in room number three. That one has window blinds and you can see right down onto the street. And sometimes you're wondering whether people on the street can see you, or those on the floor above in the building on the other side." Second, he would avoid touching the magazines, something that he did not like at all: "Sometimes the computers on which you watch the movies don't work right. And then you have to resort to [*ty til*] those old magazines which can be, well, a bit used." When I asked specifically about these magazines, Thommy added: "The internet has really revolutionized this business, because I can just imagine what it must have been like with just those dirty/icky [*snuskede*] magazines. If there were just them, I don't think I could get out of there fast enough either. There is no doubt that I try to avoid having to touch those magazines because they can get really nasty." As a consequence, Thommy usually uses the same donor room when he is at the sperm bank—a room without a window and with a properly functioning computer—a routine that ensures that flows of affect lead to successful performance as a sperm donor.

Another routine that ensures these kinds of flows of affect is the cleansing and disinfecting of rooms, as well as washing oneself and thereby erasing any possible traces of semen that was not collected in the specimen cups. These routines aim to contain semen's potential to matter as more than just a reproductive substance, when encountered in donor rooms for example (Mohr 2016a), encounters that were positioned as disgusting by most donors. Lucas, in his twenties, single, and a sperm donor for about a year, had experienced encountering semen in a donor room: "I have been subjected/exposed to splotches (of semen) on the floor and that I think is, well, of course it is up to the individual person how they, but, again, you wouldn't be able to prove who that was anyways. I mean, you would assume that people clean up after themselves, but that was disgusting." Victor, in his thirties, married, and a father of one daughter, also thought that encountering semen in donor rooms was disgusting, and, as a consequence, he had a routine of cleaning the donor room before and after masturbating. When I asked him whether he liked semen or not, he said: "Well, as I said, now I have gotten used to it, and I don't have any problems with sperm as such as long as it is my own we are talking about. Other people's sperm, that they are welcome to keep to themselves." When I asked him whether he would clean the donor room every time, Victor said: "Yes, both before and after, because I don't know who the other guy was. And I don't know what it looks like after he is done, that I don't know, especially if you should be unlucky with one thing or another." Anton had a similar routine. He also cleaned the donor room both before and after masturbating. In addition, like many other donors, he also washed himself after masturbation. He explained this habit as a way of avoiding the smell of sex for the rest of the day, as he termed it. When I asked him why he washes his penis after he has collected his semen, he said: "I think that it smells. The next time you take a piss you will smell of sex. So, I like to wash myself afterwards." Among all donors there was an agreement that donor rooms should be cleaned, and every man I talked to positioned himself as sticking to this shared routine. Alfred, in his twenties, single, and a sperm donor for roughly a year, was probably most adamant about cleanliness, and tried to avoid touching anything at all inside the donor room. Implying the image of conveyor belt efficiency, in his ideal masturbatory routine at the sperm bank, cleanliness would be ensured by how the different elements inside the donor rooms are arranged and by each donor sticking to the established routine. He and I were talking about how the donor rooms could be improved, when he said:

> It seems as if they just put a roll of kitchen paper, a computer mouse, and a TV in there. The sink doesn't work properly all the time either. They could really improve things, like where you get the sanitizer, that should be a dispenser that hangs on the wall. They could have better soap and maybe hand lotion. And it shouldn't be necessary that you need to press on (the dispensers) to get something out of them. You should just be able to stick your hand under it and then it just dispenses by itself. The whole thing should be more like a course which you complete. You start here, hang your bag, hang your jacket, and then you would go over there and place your cup there, open the lid, and then you watch TV, and then you just move on to another part of the room where you wash and dry your hands, so that you would do a natural circuit of the room.

Connected to the cleanliness routine was the sensory experience of smell in donor rooms. Strong odors in donor rooms were positioned as disgusting by most donors, with some men also saying that the distinct smell of the donor rooms would stick to them even after they left the sperm bank. While spilled semen can be cleaned away, and while washing oneself can ensure that men do not smell of sex once they have delivered their sample, the smell in donor rooms is a more persistent sensory experience over which sperm donors have no control and that they thus have to find different ways of dealing with. Thommy was rather pragmatic about the smell in the donor rooms: "It can easily start to smell in there. When you have forty men in and out of the same room every day and when the only thing that they are doing in there is to whip the willy [*at finde pjer-roten frem*], then it easily starts to smell. And it sure does and that's just how it is." Other men had more difficulty with the smell in donor rooms. Storm, for example, wanted donor rooms to be better ventilated. Talking about the interior of the donor rooms, he said: "It really smells in those rooms. And that's because ventilation is pretty bad in there. And some people just take too long. I mean, what is it with guys who don't know how to masturbate? Why does it take them fifteen, twenty minutes? That's too long. No wonder it smells." Felix had a similar attitude in regard to the smell in donor rooms. While the boundary-breaking appeal of having to masturbate in a semipublic space like a sperm bank also figured as an enticing element of being a sperm donor in his narrative, the smell in the donor rooms definitely did not. He had recognized the particular smell of donor rooms the very first time he masturbated at the sperm bank: "It was so strange to come into this room which smelled like, yeah, what do you call that, musk." This experience stayed with him and, as he told me, every time he enters one of the donor rooms, he still notices the smell. Explaining to me what he associates with semen, Felix said: "Well, it has this special, not that I have played with it, but it has this special, I mean, I am not that interested in it, but it has this distinct smell. When you go into one of those rooms there, that's where you can smell it because those rooms are only used for that." After almost two years of being a sperm donor and delivering a semen sample twice a week on average, Felix had found a way to deal with the smell in the donor rooms. As he termed it, masturbating at the sperm bank was now business as usual for him. Nevertheless, he also still lived with the transgressive experience of the smell, sometimes even feeling that it stayed with him after he had left the sperm bank. Talking about the atmosphere at the sperm bank, he said: "As I said earlier, there is this characteristic smell inside these rooms there, and sometimes you get the impression that you smell of it when you sit on the bus on your way home, and that can be a really weird experience. But that is of course also psychological, I mean, of course you don't smell like it." Rationalizing his own sensory experiences at the sperm bank and the affective investments in being a sperm donor that they require of him as purely psychological, Felix had taught himself to set his inhibitions aside. If he had not been able to do so, he would not be able to be a sperm donor: "What are you thinking of when you think of sperm donation?"—"I can't help but think about those smelly rooms. So, I guess I am thinking about that smell when I think of sperm donation. But there is nothing special about it any longer. That boundary has been crossed a long time ago, you might say. So, now it's just a funny thing I joke about with friends."

Masturbatory routines enable sperm donors to produce good semen samples on demand. Routines ensure that affects flow in a specific way and thus men can overcome possible inhibitions that might hinder them from masturbating and ejaculating. These routines require (self-)discipline and specific affective investments so that ejaculation and the proper collection of semen samples is accomplished every time sperm donors visit sperm banks. Disciplining happens partly through formal statutes like contracts and regulations, but, as this section has shown, also through more informal engagements between sperm bank staff and sperm donors. Furthermore, donors need to learn to be affected in particular ways, that is, they need to develop specific affective capacities that enable them to deliver good-quality semen samples every time. By incorporating (self-)discipline as part of how they masturbate, sperm donors make sure that they live up to these expectations and thus help to produce the experience of doing gender the right way. Central to this experience is masturbation and the masturbatory practices in which sperm donors engage. It is in and through masturbation that men are able to experience themselves as men who live up to the expectations that sperm donors are faced with. Hitting specimen cups right the first time, timing one's ejaculation perfectly, and being satisfied by high sperm counts rather than good orgasms are all performative moments of sperm donor biosociality through the enticement of gender. Sperm donors are enticed to remake themselves as particular gendered subjects, namely, men who deliver good-quality semen, and donors' masturbatory routines ensure this gender performativity through flows of affect.

Sperm Donors' Affective Investments

Becoming a sperm donor requires specific affective investments. As Sarah Ahmed argues, norms are sustained in their social potentiality through specific emotional and affective relations that we develop toward them, that is, they are sustained through "what we do with our bodies" (Ahmed 2012: 196). It is in this sense that men's bio-social subjectivation as sperm donors through masturbation might be understood. They remake themselves as men and sperm donors through their ways of masturbating at the sperm bank. Masturbating in a specific way, sperm donors become biosocial subjects due to what they do with their bodies: they develop affective relations to being a sperm donor through masturbation. As I have argued throughout this chapter, these affective investments are enabled by the enticement of gender in the sense that being able to produce good-quality semen samples on demand involves a positive experience of gender normativity for men, that is, they experience themselves as men who produce good-quality semen. This experience relies on sperm donors' ability to develop capacities that allow them to masturbate and ejaculate at sperm banks. As Nick Fox and Pam Alldred argue, such sexual capacities are developed through specific territorializations of flows of affect, codifications of gender subjectivity that entice men to do gender and live sexuality in a specific way (Alldred and Fox 2015; Fox and Alldred 2013). As this chapter shows, territorializations of flows of affect happen through masturbatory routines in which sperm donors engage. These routines ensure that sperm donors are stimulated affectively in a way that ensures ejaculation and the proper collection of semen samples. Whereas sperm donors might experience these routines as free flows of affect, meaning men's stimulation is not disturbed by internal or external interferences, these flows of affect are specifically territorialized in the sense that they remake sperm donors as biosocial and specifically gendered subjects, namely, men who understand themselves and their ways of being men in terms of biomedical registers and biopolitical valuations.

The experiences of men as presented in this chapter provide insights into how the enticement of gender territorializes flows of affect in a particular way so as to ensure men's biosocial subjectivation as sperm donors. The dynamic between masturbation as a taboo on the one hand and ejaculatory abstinence as a boost experience on the other, for example, enables flows of affect that entice sperm donors to remake themselves as (self-)disciplined men through masturbation. While for some men the experience of taboo is a reassurance of their commitment as sperm donors—since they are reminded that they are in it for the right reasons and not because of sexual enjoyment—the pleasures of being able to masturbate after three days of abstinence actualize other men's gender subjectivities as men who can perform successfully just when it is needed. Continuous invocations of men's biomedical value in terms of sperm counts and monetary compensation connect to these territorializations of affect, as they provide men with the experience of doing gender in the right way, that is, information on semen quality and compensation for good-quality semen continuously reassure sperm donors that they are men who have qualities that are in demand. Furthermore, masturbatory routines ensure that sperm donors can provide quality semen every time they visit the sperm bank. As such, routines territorialize flows of affect in such a way as to enable men to ejaculate and collect semen in particular ways that ensure its biomedical value. Through all of this, men are enticed by gender. As sperm donors who know how to hit specimen cups the first time, and who have excellent sperm counts, men experience themselves in accordance with what they themselves and what sperm banks expect of them—they are men who produce good-quality semen. The masturbatory practices that men engage in as sperm donors thus make them into biosocial subjects because it is through masturbation that sperm donors incorporate biomedical registers and biopolitical valuations into their ways of being men.

Chapter 4

BIOSOCIAL RELATEDNESS

BEING CONNECTED AND
THE PLEASURE OF RESPONSIBILITY

When Magnus met a lesbian couple looking for a sperm donor a few years ago, he decided that being a sperm donor at a sperm bank was not enough. Having donated semen at a sperm bank for some years by that point, he was convinced that direct contact with recipients of donor semen, and knowing what your semen was being used for, was more responsible than simply relinquishing semen to a sperm bank without ever knowing what happens to it. Magnus had contacted me after having seen an advert about my research on the website that he used in order to make contact with women looking for donor semen outside of the international biomedical network of fertility service providers, of which Danish sperm banks are part. In his forties and working in manual labor, Magnus lives with his long-term partner and her child, whom he regards as his own. Magnus had not always had the feeling of responsibility toward donor semen recipients and donor-conceived individuals that he exhibited when talking about them during our interview. As he explained to me, he had originally applied to become a sperm donor because he wanted to earn some extra cash: "I don't remember whether I saw an ad or whether I read something about it (becoming a sperm donor) in a newspaper, but I liked the idea of earning something extra. So it was definitely money that was my motivation in the beginning, there is no doubt about that." However, after reading more about becoming a sperm donor on the sperm bank's website, Magnus felt that something else was at stake for him as well: "It was really interesting to see whether I could do it or not (become a sperm donor). I didn't have any idea about the economic part of it since I didn't know how much one would earn. But it became more and more interesting when I realized what else it meant for me: either I would find out that I would not be able to have children or I would make it through the needle's eye and would actually be able to reproduce [*forplante mig*]." This preoccupation with whether he had what it takes to become a sperm donor receded into the background once Magnus had been accepted as a donor and when donating semen became part of his usual routine. For many years, Magnus donated semen twice a week on average. When he started as a sperm donor, the possibility of donating semen without anonymity, as is an option in Denmark now, did not exist, and as a consequence Magnus had to unwillingly accept the fact that individuals conceived with the help of his semen would have no official way of contacting him. At some point, however, Magnus was no longer able to morally justify this arrangement and began registering on different websites that facilitate direct contact between men willing to provide semen and women looking for options outside the biomedical network of fertility service providers. Critical of the business side of sperm banking, he liked the idea of personally meeting the women who would use his semen: "When you look at the sperm banks' donor catalogues, you will read that they (the donors) are tall and blond and handsome and have an IQ of over 200. But that is not true, that is not what the world actually looks like. But of course, that is a product brochure [*handelskatalog*], that's what they live off, selling semen. But I like to actually meet those people for whom I provide semen, and it seems as if recipients also think that that is a good idea." In addition, Magnus registered with internet sites that connect donor-conceived individuals with sperm donors. He made this decision because he disapproves of leaving donor-conceived individuals with no possibility of contacting the men who provided semen for their conception, a decision that actually violates the contract he signed as a sperm donor, but also one that he deems necessary if one is to take responsibility as a donor:

> Back in time, all of them (sperm donors) were medical students who got some quick cash [*håndører*] for doing it. There was no official register. And I see that very critically: there were no registers back then. You might remember the story in the media about this girl who came forward because she wanted to meet her father (sperm donor) who in all likelihood was a medical student. I mean, that is just hopeless. She actually carries this big burden with her [*hun har et kæmpe hul i maven*]

because she doesn't have the option to check a register and say: hey, you are my father and that is good to know. And that I think is wrong.

Yet while Magnus feels passionate about the right of donor-conceived individuals to know the man who provided the semen for their conception, and while he uses the word father to refer to himself in relation to donor-conceived individuals, he nevertheless is also very clear that connections to donor-conceived individuals are not kinship relations. As a sperm donor, he sees a different kind of responsibility bestowed upon him than the responsibilities of a father in the traditional sense: "I am not building a family with them. I am the guarantee, so to say, that the kids won't worry to death about having a father whom they don't know. Yet, I am not going to be the father in their lives."

This chapter explores biosocial subjectivation as a matter of relatedness. What will be in focus here are the ways in which Danish sperm donors negotiate the kinds of responsibilities that come with partaking in sperm donation and therefore relating or being connected to other people through the use of reproductive technologies. Engaging with questions of relatedness in this sense demands specific forms of moral reasoning as well as particular affective investments from sperm donors, since questions of relatedness are moral decisions at the same time as they are about affective and emotional (de)attachments. As I will argue throughout this chapter, biosocial relatedness is about taking responsibility for the performative effects of reproductive technologies for one's relational life by caring for those one relates or is connected to. Biosocial relatedness means that sperm donors have to negotiate the tension that arises between potential claims to traditional notions of kinship that sperm donation involves on the one hand, and forms of relatedness that go beyond kinship produced through sperm donation on the other. Being connected through the use of reproductive technologies means that certain elements of what could be called kinship become part of being connected, such as biogenetic connections between sperm donors and donor-conceived individuals. However, biosocial relatedness cannot be reduced to these elements since being connected through the use of reproductive technologies also bears moral dimensions that are neither purely about kinship matters nor plainly a manifestation of geneticization. Sperm donors negotiate this tension through the enticement of gender as responsibility, that is, when faced with the moral and emotional challenges of biosocial relatedness, Danish sperm donors claim positions as responsible men and

thus become biosocial subjects through the performativity of gendered responsibility. Before becoming sperm donors, men are not
necessarily forced to think about what difference reproductive biomedicine makes in how they relate and are connected to people, but
once they become sperm donors this question becomes paramount
in all aspects of men's relational life. As became clear in the previous chapters, sperm donors' specific affective investments as well
as their ways of moral reasoning involve and touch upon their intimate social relations. Put differently, sperm donors have no choice
but to ponder questions of relatedness as they are reformulated in
a biomedical day and age. By taking care of those one relates or is
connected to through the use of reproductive technologies, sperm
donors accept this responsibility. How this translates into specific
forms of relating in the lives of Danish sperm donors will be the focus of this chapter.

Magnus's decision to start donating semen privately to women
whom he meets through internet contact sites can be understood as
taking responsibility for biosocial relatedness, as he is convinced that
doing so is more responsible than donating semen to a sperm bank,
which does not allow for personal contact between the different parties involved. Taking care of those whom he is connected to through
the use of reproductive technologies, Magnus remakes himself in
that way as a man who knows what kinds of responsibilities he has
as a sperm donor. He makes the performative effects of reproductive
technologies for his own relational life and that of donor semen recipients and their future children his personal responsibility rather
than expecting sperm banks to take care of it. While signing a contract with a sperm bank would protect him from fatherhood claims
and child support payments, Magnus chooses to relinquish this protection in favor of sorting out biosocial relatedness himself. As he
terms it, "it is wrong" when donor-conceived individuals are bereft
of the opportunity to contact the men who provided the semen for
their conception, and thus he acknowledges the social significance
of biogenetic connections in a society in which the dominant understanding of kinship equates these connections with kinship relatedness. At the same time, however, Magnus does not understand
himself—or for that matter sperm donors in general—to be the father of those individuals who are conceived via donor insemination
with the help of his semen. While he uses the term "father" to talk
about himself in relation to donor-conceived individuals, he is also
very clear in distinguishing between father as progenitor on the one
hand and father as social figure in relation to institutions such as

family and kinship on the other. Rather than taking on the responsibilities of a father in this latter sense, he sees himself as having to act responsibly as a sperm donor, which in his case requires knowing the recipients of donor semen and donor-conceived individuals personally without being a father in the traditional sense. In addition, Magnus criticizes the business approach that characterizes sperm donation in Denmark by positioning his decision to meet personally with women who are looking for donor semen as the more responsible option in organizing sperm donation. From his perspective, it could be argued, being in direct contact with donor semen recipients thus allows for more responsible engagements, as it provides for the opportunity to negotiate the at times difficult moral as well as affective and emotional challenges of biosocial relatedness directly between those who are affected by them. While taking this step was certainly an exception among the sperm donors whom I met, Magnus's insistence on the specific kind of responsibility sperm donors have in relation to questions of relatedness was shared by all donors. Though they all had their own ways of navigating the terrain of biosocial relatedness through specific gender performativities as responsibility—that is, different sperm donors remade themselves as responsible men in different ways—all donors nevertheless shared Magnus's sense of responsibility as the result of being sperm donors. No matter what their personal circumstances looked like, all sperm donors aimed to be responsible men who know how to navigate the terrain of biosocial relatedness. How this enticement of gender as responsibility works by caring for those one relates or is connected to through the use of reproductive technologies will be explored in what follows.

Biosocial Relatedness, Transilience, and Wayward Relations

The advent of what has been termed the new reproductive technologies has not only brought about new ways of conception, such as in vitro fertilization (IVF) and intracytoplasmic sperm injection (ICSI), but has also reinvigorated anthropological and sociological debates about the meanings of kinship. Important in these current debates is a fundamental distinction between kinship and relatedness as two interrelated but nonetheless different analytical terms for how to understand what being related might mean in a biomedical day and age. Whereas kinship for a long time was made out to be the fundament of human sociality in any society (Holy 1996), in contemporary scholarship kinship is recognized as one particular way of making connections between specific individuals and groups of people meaningful as a specific form of being related (Strathern 1995). This important analytical distinction between relatedness as a term that captures a variety of ways of being related on the one hand and kinship as a particular Euro-American way of being related on the other opened up the possibility to attend to how people actually go about and live kinship and relatedness rather than simply assuming that kinship systems and structures would be important for any society (Carsten 1995, 2000, 2004).

Reproductive technologies were important for this intellectual development insofar as they complicated the picture of what was deemed natural (kinship) and what was deemed cultural (relatedness). Whereas before the onset of contemporary reproductive biomedicine some might have argued that kinship is a social fact modeled after nature, anthropological and sociological analyses of the uses and experiences of reproductive technologies have made obvious that this divide was never anything but artificial. The use of reproductive technologies makes clear that kinship is in and of itself a technology "that organize[s], facilitate[s], and activate[s] human reproductivity" as Sarah Franklin terms it (Franklin 2013: 29), that is, rather than being a representation of natural facts, kinship makes reality in the sense that it (re)creates specific ways of being connected and being related, including reproductive technologies. Central to this kind of thinking is Janet Carsten's conceptualization of the term *relatedness* (Carsten 1995, 2000, 2004). She argues that it is important to resist distinctions between biology and culture and instead to attend to how such distinctions are done and undone in and through local practices that make for experiences of being related. With particular attention to reproductive technologies, Carsten observes that they configure kinship both in traditional as well as in nontraditional ways and that people very explicitly "define who is kin and who is not and what kinds of kinship count and what kinds do not," thereby opening up the possibility of destabilizing the "taken-for-granted quality of the relations themselves" (Carsten 2004: 180).

In this sense, Danish sperm donors also very explicitly decide who is kin and who is not (Mohr 2015). As will become clear in this chapter, it is not so much confusion about who counts as kin and who does not that troubles sperm donors. Rather, they contemplate what kinds of responsibilities they might have to people they relate or are connected to through sperm donation. On the one hand,

Danish sperm banks' insistence on the importance of kinship by invoking sperm donors' kin relations in terms of their biogenetic profile, something that could be called the *biomedicalization of kinship*
(Finkler 2000, 2001; Mamo 2005, 2007), forces sperm donors to
consider the kinds of responsibilities that come with biogenetic connections in a context that values these connections first and foremost for the biomedical value assigned to them. On the other hand,
the denial of what usually would count as kinship by contractually
and legally forcing sperm donors to disregard genetic connections to
donor-conceived individuals as kinship begs sperm donors to consider what kinds of responsibilities they have toward those to whom
they are not allowed to be related as kin.

It is this biosocial *kinship trouble* (Mohr 2015) that Danish sperm
donors have to navigate, and the legal, institutional, and practical
specifications of how sperm donation is organized are thus important when trying to understand how sperm donors navigate the terrain of biosocial relatedness. As Rene Almeling shows, this context
is important because it influences how sperm donors will make
connections to donor-conceived individuals meaningful (Almeling
2011). She argues that in the context of her study of American egg
and sperm donors in which sperm banks encouraged nonanonymous donations and in which paternity is predominantly equated
with a biogenetic model of father-child relatedness, sperm donors
could not help but "think of themselves as integral in the lives of
offspring" (Almeling 2011: 163), and thus talked about themselves
in terms of being fathers to donor-conceived individuals. As Magnus's story makes clear, and as this chapter will unfold in more
detail, Danish sperm donors—independently of whether they are
donating semen anonymously or nonanonymously—do not regard
themselves as fathers of donor-conceived individuals, an empirical
observation that has also been made in other comparable societal
contexts (Baumeister-Frenzel et al. 2010; Hammarberg et al. 2014;
Kirkman 2004; Kirkman et al. 2014; Riggs 2008, 2009; Riggs and
Scholz 2011; Speirs 2007, 2012). Thus, the specific context of organizing sperm donation in Denmark—emphasizing biogenetic connections due to the biomedical value assigned to them on the one
hand and negating kinship relations between sperm donors and
donor-conceived individuals through laws and contracts on the
other—has a particular effect on how sperm donors in Denmark
make connections established through sperm donation meaningful.

When considering the legal, institutional, and practical specifications of how sperm donation in Denmark is organized, it could thus

be said that, rather than simply mimicking traditional kinship relations, biosocial relatedness is about the kinds of responsibilities individuals have when they relate or are connected to one another through the use of reproductive technologies. In this sense, biosocial relatedness involves kinship elements as well as modes of relatedness that go beyond kinship. Sperm donors ponder, for example, what kinds of responsibilities they have to donor-conceived individuals, people to whom they are biogenetically connected, without considering them family or kin. At the same time, sperm donors also ponder what responsibilities they have toward loved ones and family, people whom they consider kin without necessarily being biogenetically connected to them. As biosocial relatedness, what makes these ways of relating and being connected a particular mode of relatedness are the specific kinds of responsibilities that come with participating in the creation of new life through the use of reproductive technologies. Being sperm donors changes the ways in which men engage with the world, and thus also how they live their social lives.

In addition, it is not certain how biogenetic connections between sperm donors and donor-conceived individuals will be made meaningful in the future. It is not clear whether they will remain meaningless as kinship or whether they will morph into kinship or kinship-like relations. Rather than just being about kinship, connections forged through the use of reproductive technologies have a potential to come to matter in a variety of ways, something that Monica Konrad calls *transilience*. Based on her study of ova donors in Britain, Konrad argues that transilient relations can be understood as relations that hold the potential of being understood and lived as ways of being related by eliciting the other in the relational equation through an activation of "what would otherwise remain hidden as concealed relations" (Konrad 2005: 49). In other words, biosocial relatedness might be said to be characterized by a specific relatedness potential—transilience—that connections established through the use of reproductive technologies hold without knowing beforehand whether that potential will be actualized or not. Whereas traditional kinship from the outset declares certain connections to be about being related, in a biomedical day and age the actualization of a relatedness potential is not a preset given. Rather, as is the case for Danish sperm donors, one cannot be sure whether biogenetic connections between certain individuals will actually lead to kinship relations or whether they will translate into other ways of being related.

These other ways of living relatedness neither substitute kinship relations nor are they supplanted by kinship. Rather, they are what Maren Heibges (formerly Klotz) calls *wayward relations*, that is, relations that "reaffirm notions of kinship as genetically grounded" while also going "beyond simple notions of geneticization" (Klotz 2014: 265, 2016). Wayward relations draw on the authority of genetic knowledge without reducing relations to biogenetic kinship. Based on her ethnography of the kinship knowledge management practices among families in Germany and Britain who used reproductive donation and among donor-conceived individuals, as well as at German and British fertility clinics and sperm banks, Klotz argues that these relations are best understood as ways of reclaiming authority in a context characterized by knowledge monopolies. While fertility clinics and sperm banks know who is connected to whom when their services are used, recipients of donor semen, donor-conceived individuals, and sperm donors often do not know whom they are connected to through sperm donation and donor insemination. Employing strategies such as registering with online databases that connect donor-conceived individuals with sperm donors and other donor-conceived individuals, sperm donors and donor-conceived individuals exert agency in terms of biosocial relatedness and reclaim their authority to enable and disable certain connections in a context in which their ability to know whom they are connected to is limited. In this sense, wayward relations exist alongside and parallel to traditional kinship relations. They give biosocial relatedness its form insofar as they are constituted in and through particular practices of relatedness that come about by caring for those people whom one relates or is connected to through the use of reproductive technologies.

Magnus's decision to register with internet sites that connect donors and donor-conceived individuals, and to also arrange sperm donation outside of officially regulated pathways, might be understood as biosocial relatedness in this sense. Magnus acknowledges connections that are established through the use of donor insemination and thus remakes himself as a man who takes responsibility for being connected in this particular way. While his way of taking responsibility was an exception among the sperm donors I met insofar as the vast majority of them neither donated semen privately nor were registered on internet sites that establish contact with donor-conceived individuals, taking responsibility for the fact that one relates and is connected to specific individuals in a particular way—sperm donation—was something that all donors did in many different ways. In what remains of this chapter, I will go into detail about how sperm donors act on the sense of responsibility that biosocial relatedness bestows upon them. What I will first focus on are sperm donors' ways of caring for donor-conceived individuals and recipients of donor semen by protecting their health and well-being. This involved first and foremost making themselves available for rigorous health screenings at sperm banks and incorporating the objective of protecting the health of the yet unconceived child into their self-images as responsible reproductive men. Thereafter, I will look at the ways in which sperm donors care about their families and those they love by protecting them from possible outside interference from donor-conceived individuals and their families and by warding off possible moral judgments by third parties about their decision to become sperm donors.

Caring for Donor-Conceived Individuals and Donor Semen Recipients

For sperm donors, caring for donor-conceived individuals and donor semen recipients means making oneself available for a number of biomedical tests and assessments that are put in place to ensure the health of the yet unconceived child and the safety of donor semen recipients. Becoming a sperm donor thus requires men to provide information about their health and biomedical status. Because sperm banks first and foremost locate this information in the biogenetic connections that donors have to parents and other family members, as well as to the children who will be conceived using their semen, sperm donors are forced to actualize biogenetic connections in terms of their biomedical value. At the same time, laws regulating paternity rights clearly state that sperm donors have no parental rights in regard to the children conceived with the help of their semen, while contracts that donors sign with sperm banks position donor-conceived children outside of donors' kinship relations. Furthermore, sperm donors almost never receive information on whether their semen is used, who the recipients are, and how many children are conceived and born with the help of their semen. Accordingly, the majority of sperm donors consider biogenetic connections to donor-conceived individuals and relations to donor semen recipients in terms of their biomedical value rather than as part of kinship. This reasoning provides the context in which men take on responsibilities as sperm donors by caring about donor-conceived individuals and the recipients of donor semen.

As shown in chapter 1, sperm donors enter a confessionary regime that is part of the continuous process of biosocial subjectivation and that is put in place as a way of accounting for the (biogenetic) health of donors. The biomedical value of information as it is captured in medical questionnaires and through conversations between sperm bank staff and sperm donors is thereby determined through the biogenetic character of the connections this information is attached to. On forms and questionnaires in regard to sperm donors' own and their family's medical history, for example, men are instructed to provide information on "biological (blood) relatives only." In addition, these forms reify race and gender as important categories when determining the value of health information through the use of traditional kinship diagrams. Furthermore, the significance of biogenetic connections is also marked linguistically in conversations between sperm bank staff and sperm donors when staff reify the importance of information about biologically related family members as essential to the health of the future child. For example, in a conversation between a staff member and a sperm donor about the necessity of medical checkups when no longer actively donating semen the staff member defended these checkups by saying: "You don't want to be responsible for killing the child."

Caring for donor-conceived individuals and donor semen recipients happens thus through the incorporation of this moral appeal in sperm donors' self-images as men. As chapter 2 showed, legitimizing being a sperm donor and thus living life ethically is achieved by taking recognizable positions in a gendered moral order, such as the loving son, the caring father, or the responsible husband. Similarly, men claim responsibility for biosocial relatedness by acknowledging the stipulated biomedical value of biogenetic connections to family members and donor-conceived individuals. One way of doing this is by providing coherent information about one's biogenetic connections during donor candidate interviews, which men have to go through in order to become sperm donors. In these interviews, sperm donors work toward becoming recognizable as responsible men who subscribe to the moral code of contemporary reproductive biomedicine, which holds that the health of the yet unconceived child needs to be protected by any measure. To this end, they do their best to provide as much coherent information as possible. In addition, sperm donors try to distance themselves from biogenetic connections that could potentially be interpreted as compromising the health of the yet unconceived child.

The intertwinement of these dynamics is captured in the following fieldnote in which Elisabeth, the donor coordinator, interviews Matti, a donor candidate in his twenties who recently applied to become a sperm donor and whose first semen sample passed quality assessments. As is the case before any of these interviews, donor candidates fill out a lengthy questionnaire about their medical history, which is then checked for accuracy by the donor coordinator during the actual interview. As will become clear, Matti is able to position himself as responsible by providing coherent information about his biogenetic connections on the one hand, while on the other also denying the importance of biogenetic connections that could be understood as problematic, a strategy that I have witnessed repeatedly during these interviews:

Elisabeth begins the interview by remarking that the information that Matti has provided on the questionnaire looks good but she also adds that it would not be she who decides whether or not Matti will be accepted as a donor. Rather, that decision will lie in the hands of the sperm bank's geneticist. After checking Matti's eye color and his recent travel history, and after making sure that Matti really wants to sign up as a non-anonymous donor, Elisabeth explains the abstinence rule, reimbursement details, and reminds Matti that he will have to provide additional information such as baby photos and a psychological test once he is approved as a donor. She then prints Matti's contract and while we all wait for that to be done, Elisabeth explains that Matti is expected to be sperm donor for at least a year and that he will be responsible for informing the tax authorities about the reimbursement that he receives for his semen samples. Matti does not ask many questions through any of this, and nods only here and there to signal that he understands.

Once the test for colorblindness is complete, Elisabeth turns to the medical questionnaire. As usual, Elisabeth begins by asking whether Matti is well and healthy. "Yes, I am," answers Matti promptly. "You don't have any allergies either?" Elisabeth continues. "No. I don't even take vitamin pills," says Matti. Turning to Matti's parents next, Elisabeth inquires about their health, and in the case of Matti's father, the cause of death. "My father died of a stroke," Matti explains. "We had it checked whether that was something inheritable but that was not the case. That was due to his lifestyle." According to Matti, his father had smoked and drunk too much. Elisabeth wants to know whether Matti's father had been an alcoholic. "Yes, he was. But I grew up at my mother's," Matti answers. Matti's mother has no health problems. Matti's maternal grandmother, on the other hand, had died of cancer and had one of her breasts as well as her uterus removed due to the disease. Elisabeth wants to know when the operations took place, and after some moments of reflection Matti says, that it must have been in the mid-nineties. His maternal grandfather had diabetes and died seven years after he had had a stroke. "But that was also due to lifestyle," Matti adds right away. His grandfather had too much fat in his blood, which accumulated in the wrong places, Matti continues. His paternal grandparents did not fail anything and Matti provides this information convincingly, even though contact with his father's parents had been sparse. When all questions in regard to the family medical history are answered, Elisabeth sums up the information Matti has provided by repeating his answers. "This looks alright," she then adds, "but I will send this to our geneticist and once she approves it, I will call you in for a blood test and a medical exam."

Taking place inside a biomedical framework that ascribes particular value to information as understood as being attached to biogenetic connections, these conversations point to the ways in which men who want to be sperm donors learn how to integrate the biomedical logic of valuing knowledge about one's biogenetic connections into their ways of understanding and presenting themselves. While it is unclear whether or not Matti and other sperm donors consciously decide to downplay the importance of certain connections, namely, those that can potentially be understood as problematic, the attempt to appear as someone who values the information attached to biogenetic connections is captured here nonetheless. Matti answers all relevant questions satisfactorily and thus lives up to what is expected of him as a sperm donor. At the same time, he also distances himself from connections that might be understood as problematic, thereby linguistically marking the fact that he knows the importance of this knowledge and how knowing about one's biogenetic heritage as a sperm donor is directly connected to the health and well-being of the yet unconceived child. Matti's ability to answer coherently, and his way of wording things, give a convincing impression of him as someone who tells the truth, someone who can be trusted, and not least someone who honors the significance of biogenetic connections as holding important biomedical information. Whether or not the information he provides is in fact accurate, as I will attend to later, is not as important as his performative becoming as a responsible sperm donor in these instances. Answering coherently and convincingly signals that donors take the endeavor of sperm donation seriously. It makes them recognizable as individuals who act according to the responsibility that has been bestowed upon them through biosocial relatedness.

I noticed the same dynamic when talking to sperm donors about being tested and screened for a number of conditions when signing up as donors. As is legally required, Danish sperm banks test for a number of sexually transmittable diseases (HIV, hepatitis, chlamydia, syphilis, gonorrhea), including human T-lymphotropic virus (HTVL), even though there is no legal requirement for it. In addition, sperm banks demand full karyotypes from all of their donors and some also test specifically for cytomegalovirus (CMV) as well as sickle cell anemia and cystic fibrosis. All donors appreciated that sperm banks screen applicants in regard to their medical history, and all donors directly related the benefits of this screening to the health of the children being conceived with the help of donor semen as well as to the health of the women who will be inseminated with their semen.

Jeppe, a sperm donor for about a year, single, and in his late teens, talked in the following way about the importance of being screened as a sperm donor: "I think that is important. I mean, other people's safety genetically speaking is at stake here and that is very important to consider. You could almost call this product safety in the sense that people who are undergoing fertility treatment can be sure that the treatment is good enough, that they don't take any chances, that I think is important." Elaborating on this point, he then added:

> This has to do with the fact that you don't know the person whose donation you will receive. There is no way you will know who they are. And under those circumstances I think it is nice that when people have the chance to make sure that their children will be healthy, that they make use of it. I mean, you can get genetic tests online and people have become more aware of what is important. And I think there are people who like the idea of having reassurance that there is nothing wrong with their child.

The health of the yet unconceived child justifies the rigorous screening of sperm donors and the continuous interventions in sperm donors' intimate life through tests, questionnaires, and assessments. As Jeppe argues, it is only reasonable to aim for a healthy child when one has the chance to. At the same time, this viewpoint also translates into sperm donors' sense of responsibility, as they expressed being personally responsible for the genetic health of the yet unconceived child. This was the case for Mathias, a sperm donor for about a year who was in his twenties and in a long-term relationship with no children. When talking about whether there were circumstances that would make him stop donating semen, he said, without hesitation: "If I knew that I had a gene in my body with the slightest possibility, just a tiny chance of causing disability or something like that in the children who are born with my donations, then I wouldn't be able to do it anymore. . . . I know my family is healthy but if there was just the tiniest possibility, I would be too worried to continue." The logic of protecting the yet unconceived child was so prominent among sperm donors that even asking questions about the necessity of health screenings during interviews with them was looked upon by some as nonsensical. Protecting the health of future children born with the help of donor semen by providing information about their biomedical status seemed to be self-evident. What is more, not taking responsibility in this sense would be unacceptable since the requirement for becoming a sperm donor is to make oneself accessible to biomedical scrutiny. If Matti had been unable to provide coherent information about his biogenetic connections during the interview with Elisabeth, he would have had a hard time getting accepted as a donor. Thus, the way in which sperm donation is organized—attaching biomedical value to biogenetic connections—makes a difference for what kinds of responsibilities sperm donors see bestowed upon them in the context of biosocial relatedness.

Caring for the yet unconceived child also went beyond matters of health as attached to biogenetic connections between sperm donors and donor-conceived individuals. Sperm donors also contemplated the importance of the right parents for the well-being of the yet unconceived child, and thus, when directly asked about it, made comments about whom they would consider to be good recipients and whom they would prefer not to give semen to. Making these comments, donors always relativized their opinions by stating that they did not have the right to determine who should use donor semen and who should not. However, by talking about what kinds of people donor semen recipients should be, sperm donors found another way of expressing the kinds of responsibilities that come with being a sperm donor and thus being connected and relating to people through the use of reproductive technologies. Noah, single and in his twenties, and a sperm donor for about a year, talked about the personal message for recipients and donor-conceived individuals that sperm banks demand from sperm donors in the following way: "Well, I can hardly write much more than good luck with everything and I hope all goes well. To be honest, I don't feel that it is my place to say anything about how their children should be raised, for example raising them according to the Christian faith or anything like that. I can only wish them good luck with everything. I think it is strange to write a message to people toward whom I don't feel any kind of obligation [*forpligtelse*]. I can't tell them what to do." At the same time, however, Noah, like many of the other donors, also had specific expectations of recipients when directly asked about them. He expected recipients to treat their children in a "loving and caring" way, as he put it. Furthermore, and similarly to many of the other donors, he would also prefer it if particular people were excluded from using donor semen or reproductive biomedicine in general. Noah's list of people included pedophiles, people who would abuse their children, and people who would generally have problems being around children. Other donors included in this category people who in their eyes did not have the psychological or financial resources to take care of children, and two donors, even while accepting that their semen was also used by lesbian women, stated that they would prefer it if lesbian women did not have access to donor semen as their future children would grow up without a father. While donors at Danish sperm banks have no influence on who gets to purchase their semen, expressing concerns about what they deemed parental fitness was also a way of positioning themselves as men who are sperm donors for the right reasons, namely, men who are concerned about the health and well-being of the yet unconceived child.

For some donors, this reasoning also extended to their choice of whether to donate semen anonymously or nonanonymously. While Denmark has a history of supporting anonymous sperm donation, and while under current legislation men can still choose to donate semen anonymously, most of the donors I talked to who had decided to donate semen nonanonymously (fourteen of the twenty-six men who donated either at a sperm bank or through private arrangements) had also considered the well-being of donor-conceived individuals when making their decision. Many of the men had a similar reasoning to Tristan, in his twenties, a father of one but not in a relationship, who, when asked why he donates semen nonanonymously, simply said: "I think it is okay when the children have an opportunity to get to know who their biological father is. And I also think that the chances of meeting one's in quotation marks 'children' are next to nothing. So, I think it is great when the young ones know who their father is, that is actually nice." Others, like Felix, in his twenties, single, with no children, were more outspoken about why they chose to donate semen nonanonymously. Having never even considered the possibility of donating semen anonymously, Felix argued:

> I don't think this (sperm donation) should be anonymous. I had made up my mind: if I was to do it, I would only do it openly. I hope that there will be somebody in eighteen or twenty years' time who wants to contact and meet me. I am not under any obligation, I only have to meet them. It is not like I have to buy birthday presents for eighteen years or anything like that, I only have to meet them and that is the least one can do I think. If people think that it is my twenty-three chromosomes that define them, if they think that is important and not the eighteen years they have spent with two parents. I mean, I believe more in nurture than in nature you know, and I would never have made it through all those tests if there was anything wrong with me anyway. But I do understand if people want to know where their nose is from or their eyes or anything like that, that I understand.

While donors like Tristan and Felix did not consider themselves to be fathers of those children whom they helped to be conceived, they nevertheless saw it as part of their responsibility as sperm donors to provide donor-conceived individuals with the opportunity to contact the men who provided the semen for their conception. Positioning themselves in this way, sperm donors express caring for the well-being of donor-conceived individuals and thus acknowledge the responsibility that comes with biosocial relatedness.

In addition to sperm donors internalizing the need to protect the health and well-being of the yet unconceived child as part of their sense of responsibility, they simultaneously also feel that they have a particular responsibility toward recipients of donor semen. This particular responsibility takes a similar form as when considering the value of biogenetic connections to donor-conceived individuals, namely, that sperm donors' particular role—providing a reproductive fluid—includes the responsibility to be healthy and to provide adequate information about one's health status. Emil, married, a father of two, and in his thirties, for example, talked about providing information for his donor profile in the following way: "For me it was important that I describe myself as accurately as possible. Because people shouldn't be buying the cat in the sack [*katten i sækken*], you know, after eighteen years they end up with a child that they didn't anticipate having and then they can't exchange it. It is important to be precise here. I was very careful not to make myself look better than I really am. This should be honest, honest and fair [*ærligt og redeligt*]." Lucas, a sperm donor for about a year, in his twenties, and single with no children, saw it the same way. The task of providing accurate personal information was important to him. This importance emerged out of a self-image in which providing accurate information was the only responsible thing to do as a sperm donor. Talking about the time he spends filling out forms as part of the screening procedures at the sperm bank, he said: "Well, this is also because I really want to do this properly. I take my time and go through the different things properly, since these things are supposed to be read by future parents, and that's why things should be in order, of course they should be. . . . That I get paid to do this is not important for me. But it matters to me that things are, that I do things properly."

The same kind of logic is also at stake for sperm donors like Magnus, who donate semen through private arrangements. After many years of donating at a sperm bank, Magnus now provides information about his biogenetic connections to parents and family members himself when meeting women for insemination. He feels responsible for guaranteeing that he is healthy and that he will not transmit diseases to either the women themselves or their future children. Being met with questions in regard to his health and possible inheritable genetic conditions, Magnus claims the position of the honest man who can be trusted, a person with integrity:

> When they ask me anything, I tell them exactly as it is. For example, when they ask about my parents, whether they were well and healthy [*sunde og raske*], I tell them: no, my father is actually an alcoholic and has suffered from that for many years. So, what about you, they then ask, do you like beer as well? Yes, I do. You know, I am hopelessly honest. I don't want to hide anything. They should feel that the answers I provide are exactly what they wanted to know. It is not a secret how I am. There is no reason to make myself look any better than I really am.

Positioning himself as "hopelessly honest," Magnus performatively (re)creates himself as a responsible man who is committed to a reproductive endeavor in which neither the women who want to use his semen nor the children these women want to give birth to are at risk health-wise. Being honest becomes a way of caring about donor semen recipients and the children they want to give birth to.

At the same time that they care for donor-conceived individuals and recipients of donor semen by accepting the responsibility that biosocial relatedness has bestowed upon them, and they thus make themselves available for continuous biomedical scrutiny, sperm donors also know very well how to handle this responsibility pragmatically. While all of them tried to live up to the expectation of

providing as much information as possible about biogenetic connections to parents, siblings, and other family members, and while
they all made an effort to inquire about their different family members' medical histories, they also made authoritative decisions about
when it was acceptable not to provide accurate information or not
to inquire about certain health conditions among biologically related
family members. In other words, sperm donors also find themselves
in situations in which the accuracy of the information is less important than the need to provide coherent health information. Haldor,
for example, married, a father of two, in his thirties, and a sperm
donor for about two years, told me that not all information he provided on medical questionnaires was based on factual knowledge.
When he and I were talking about the difficulty of filling out long
medical history questionnaires, he said: "Well, it could very well be
that I have not always answered correctly. I mean, I think I did, but
if I don't know whether they (family members) have anything then
I can't write about it either." Lucas had a similar approach to filling
out medical questionnaires. In his reasoning, it would be his responsibility to inquire about possible medical conditions in his family,
whereas it would be the responsibility of sperm banks to check up
on it, as it is they who sell semen to donor semen recipients. We
were talking about genetic screening as part of sperm donation when
he said:

> You can't check for everything. I think it is fine that they (sperm
> banks) check for the basics. But I also think, when you sit there and
> look at this piece of paper and fill out one thing after another, I don't
> know how many of the diseases they ask about I have checked no
> because I didn't know what they meant. I mean, I have never heard
> of them and I have never heard that someone in my family has had
> them. I can't gather all information anyway, information on my
> grandparents or something like that. I know that they haven't been
> terminally ill and that they had a good and long life. That is what I
> know. So, you assume that they (sperm banks) will check up on this
> with all the blood tests they do all the time. I mean, I am not a labo-
> ratory technician and it is not my task to understand all of this. I can
> only answer yes or no. I also can't answer whether one of my previ-
> ous sex partners has had chlamydia or anything like that. I know that
> I have never had it and that's why that question is completely irrele-
> vant for me. You can't answer everything.

Magnus also knew very well when providing information about
his health and his biogenetic profile went too far. To that end, he
had made the decision that he would not undergo genetic testing,

since in his eyes it would mean promising something that he cannot and does not want to live up to, namely, the promise of producing the perfect child: "I don't make superhumans because I am not a superhuman myself and that's why I can't promise everything. I know that nothing is wrong with me [*at jeg ikke fejler noget*] and they will have to trust me on that. If they feel that they can't, then it is better that it (arranging sperm donation and donor insemination) doesn't work out."

Relating and being connected to people through the use of reproductive technologies demands specific kinds of responsibilities. Sperm donors acknowledge these responsibilities by caring for those whom they relate or are connected to by being a sperm donor. In regard to donor-conceived individuals and donor semen recipients, this takes the form of making themselves available for continuous biomedical scrutiny. All sperm donors that I talked to understood themselves as men who try their best to live up to the expectations they are met with in terms of recurring questionnaires and medical exams and a number of different periodic tests. All of them acknowledged the importance of this biomedical control regime, as the health of the yet unconceived child needs to be protected, as Magnus's, Jeppe's, Emil's, Lucas's, and Mathias's ways of reasoning show. What is more, they see the health of the yet unconceived child partly as their own personal responsibility. At the same time, they also approach this responsibility pragmatically in the sense that they set boundaries for what health information they want to and are able to gather about themselves.

Sperm donors cannot ignore the responsibility that comes with providing semen for the conception of children through donor insemination, and it is in this sense that relations between sperm donors and donor-conceived individuals and sperm donors and donor semen recipients can be understood as biosocial relatedness. Danish sperm donors develop a feeling of responsibility for donor-conceived individuals as well as donor semen recipients due to the moral obligations installed in people connected through the use of reproductive technologies. These moral obligations are partly bound to the presence of biogenetic connections—sperm donors and donor-conceived individuals share parts of their biogenetic profile; donor semen recipients and sperm donors partake in forming the biogenetic profile of future children—and partly bound to the way in which these biogenetic connections came about—by sperm donation and donor insemination. While it cannot be determined from the outset how these connections and these ways of relating to one another will come to matter in the future, the moral obligation bestowed upon sperm donors by participating in the conception of a child through the use of donor insemination is clear from the very beginning: sperm donors have the responsibility to be healthy and to provide accurate information about their health, and it is on this sense of responsibility that sperm donors act. How biosocial relatedness translates into specific ways of caring for family members and loved ones will be the topic of the next section.

Caring for Family Members and Loved Ones

Regardless of whether or not men have considered the repercussions of becoming sperm donors for their social relations before signing up, once they are sperm donors the pivotal importance of this decision for how they relate to people makes itself noticeable in all aspects of men's relational life. The particular dynamics of biosocial relatedness require sperm donors to consider what responsibilities come with being a sperm donor and the different ways of relating and being connected that follow on from it. As the previous section has shown, biosocial relatedness demands a specific kind of responsibility from sperm donors in regard to donor-conceived individuals and recipients of donor semen. Yet whereas this responsibility is meant to help guarantee the health of the yet unconceived child and the well-being of donor semen recipients, caring for family members and loved ones as a way of honoring the particular kind of responsibility that biosocial relatedness bestows upon sperm donors rather takes the form of protecting sperm donors' family life from outside interference from donor-conceived individuals and their families as well as from possible moral judgments about sperm donation from third parties.

As chapter 2 already alluded to, many sperm donors avoid telling colleagues and friends that they donate semen, because they see themselves faced with possible embarrassment due to still existing taboos around it. Alfred, for example, in his twenties, single with no children, and a sperm donor for about a year, chose to donate semen as an anonymous donor because he felt that colleagues and friends would not be able to accept his choice to become a sperm donor. Explaining to me why he chose to donate semen anonymously, he said:

> That is definitely because of the offense [*forargelse*] people take when I tell them about it (being a sperm donor). There is this paradigm which, it is still a big taboo and there seems to be no understanding

for it. When you meet people who are very academic, they think that this (donating semen) is something disgusting [*ulækkert*]. Other people who are more practically trained and have more of an understanding of the body, those people are more sympathetic. But the reason I am anonymous is simply the offense that people take at this issue.

Whereas the decision to keep being a sperm donor to oneself is of course also a measure to save face, sperm donors acknowledged that by becoming donors they would also interfere with the lives of parents and siblings, and not least life partners and children, and thus also took precautions to minimize the impact their decision would have on them. Jeppe, for example, directly involved his family in his decision to become a sperm donor, as he felt it concerned them as well: ". . . I also thought about, that this is not only about me, this is also about my family, these are also their genes. So another priority for me was, what they think about all of this. I asked them their opinion, and they told me that this is not something they are crazy about, but if I thought it wouldn't be a problem, then I should go ahead and do it." Anton, in his thirties, a father of two, married, and donating semen for about a year, had become a sperm donor after his wife had suggested it to him in a time of financial hardship. Yet while the compensation Anton receives for his semen samples helps him to fulfill his role as a responsible father and husband, he and his wife also agreed that being a sperm donor should not come at any price, meaning it should not have any impact on their family life. When I asked him what he thinks would be important to consider when being a sperm donor, he answered: "Well, as long as it works out here at home and it doesn't influence my family and my life here at home with my family in a negative way, then I don't have a problem with being a sperm donor." Due to possible moral judgments from third parties, Alfred had not only chosen to donate semen as an anonymous donor, but he had also developed a particular way of telling people that he is a sperm donor, something that, according to him, makes them potentially more sympathetic toward his decision: "It is about telling people that you help others, like that some of it (semen) is used for sciences and some of it is used for donations. I also tell people stories about people who need help, like a lesbian couple I knew where both became pregnant in this way. Or that I have people in my family who had been trying to have kids for many years before they then were successful in this way and that they were really happy about it. It is these kinds of stories that I try to tell people."

Decisions such as involving one's family in the question of whether or not to become a sperm donor, like Jeppe and Anton did, or donating semen anonymously and developing particular ways of talking about being a donor that aim to avoid moral judgment, are all attempts by sperm donors to protect their families and loved ones from possible negative impacts. These practices are ways of accepting specific responsibilities as sperm donors, and thus constitute part of taking care of loved ones and families in a biomedical day and age. Biosocial relatedness demands that sperm donors consider the repercussions that their choice to become donors might have for their loved ones and families.

That sperm donors take care of their loved ones and families, by trying to protect them from outside interference from donor-conceived individuals and their families, became obvious in the way in which they talked about donor-conceived individuals. While they clearly did not regard donor-conceived individuals to be kin, since connections to them were "just biogenetic," as one donor formulated it, they did figure as an intrusive element that could disturb sperm donors' own family life. One dominant image that appeared repeatedly in sperm donors' talk about donor-conceived individuals was an incest scenario in which the unknown, biogenetically related offspring would disturb sperm donors' family life by falling in love with sperm donors' children, an image that is also part of media coverage about sperm donors in Denmark (Mohr 2013; Klotz and Mohr 2015). As discussed in chapter 2, Malthe, a father of two, married, and in his thirties, was one of the donors concerned about incest. In his narrative, he feared that his daughter would fall in love with someone who would turn out to have been conceived using his semen, a scenario that he positioned as "very, very awkward" and filling him with "negative thoughts." Noah, although not yet a father when I met him, was also concerned about one of his future children meeting a person who had been conceived using his semen and falling in love with them: "What I mostly think about in relation to fathering a bunch of children [*en masse børn*] or one's genetic material and stuff like that, is when I have my own children one day and they will meet someone (who is donor-conceived and genetically related to me) of their age and then they will fall in love with one another. That wouldn't be very good actually." Alfred also talked about his possible future daughter falling in love with someone to whom she is genetically related. We were talking about his thoughts about donor-conceived individuals when he said: "I keep thinking about this story, when you are out in town as a forty year old one evening with your soccer buddies and then you will see all those young people and you're wondering whether one of them could be (conceived with your semen), I mean that could actually happen, and if you have a real child then, a son or a daughter, and if she is out at night, she could actually run the risk of meeting her brother."

Besides figuring as part of incest scenarios, donor-conceived individuals also figured as potentially infringing on sperm donors' family life by making fatherhood claims and requesting financial support, despite the fact that Danish law protects sperm donors from such situations. For Haldor, the possibility of donor-conceived individuals claiming financial support thereby directly threatened the well-being of his children. He and I were talking about what kind of information he sought when becoming a sperm donor when he explained: "What I was mostly concerned about were judicial things in relation to donor children. I mean, I have my own children and I don't want to put them into a situation in which they would miss anything, and where I could be made responsible economically in regard to possible donor children. There are examples of that in other countries." Victor, a father of one, married, and in his thirties, had similar concerns and was glad to find out that there are measures in place in Denmark to guarantee that donor-conceived individuals and their families could not make whatever claims they thought reasonable: "They (the sperm bank) also explained to me that I couldn't be made responsible, you know, in the case that, one day, someone will find you and say: you have donated half of me. And that there was no possibility for that in Denmark, to confront a donor with that, requesting things, that was important to me because I don't think it is specifically reassuring to be met with claims like that, not just me but also my family." Magnus also took certain precautions to avoid possible claims from donor semen recipients and their families by telling women that they would have to concede some of their parental rights if they were to attempt to make him pay child support. When I asked him whether he was concerned about possible claims from donor semen recipients, since he was not protected by law in the same way as someone who donates semen through a sperm bank, he answered: "Well, that is just money."—"Just money?"—"Well, yes, that is not important for me. You could say that I am running a risk here and maybe I am. But I tell them, if they make any claims then I also want to regularly see the child, and that is definitely not what they want. So, I am not really concerned about that."

Another way in which the potential intrusion of donor-conceived individuals took form in sperm donors' narratives was their possibly high number in the sense that one donor's semen could potentially be used to conceive multiple children on a global scale. While current Danish legislation limits the number of families who can use the same donor's semen in Denmark to twelve (from the former twenty-five), international limits vary from as few as three children per donor in Hong Kong to as many as twenty-five per eight hundred thousand inhabitants as is the case in the United States and Canada (Nelson, Hertz, and Kramer 2016). With Danish donor semen being shipped to destinations around the globe, the number of offspring per donor could thus easily be one hundred and beyond. When I discussed the potentially high numbers of offspring with donors, it became clear that all of them had a personal limit of how many individuals should be conceived using their semen. While donors' personal limits varied, they all agreed that too high of a number of offspring was an overwhelming and at times even a threatening scenario. Thommy, an anonymous sperm donor, a father of one, in a long-term relationship, and in his thirties, for example, expressed his disapproval of "bombarding small societies with my semen." At the same time, he thought it would be better for the donors to know how many times their semen was used successfully so that they could prepare themselves and their families for the numbers of offspring. Emil, donating nonanonymously, held the same viewpoint and elaborated on why it made a difference if there were five, fifty, or even one hundred donor-conceived individuals per donor: "This of course makes a difference because you will have to consider them as individuals. I mean, they will all be different. Maybe they share some traits with me but they basically will all be different and you would have to meet them as individuals. And then it makes a huge difference whether it is only five, fifty, or one hundred. But I have no chance of knowing how many there will be, one hundred or fifty, or maybe even 1600. I hope it is not going to be 1600!" For Jeppe, who donated anonymously, the prospect of meeting high numbers of donor-conceived individuals would be too overwhelming, particularly when considering having a family at that time: "If I had to meet 120 donor children that would be absolutely insane. I could not do that. I mean, just consider if you had to use one day per child. And in twenty years' time when they have the right to know who you are, then you risk having all these people who want to get into contact with you. That is extreme. That would be totally out of control, especially when you are in a family situation."

Sperm donors are concerned about interference from donor-conceived individuals and experience themselves to be without real control over those individuals' impact on their future family life. Yet while sperm donors talked about donor-conceived individuals as threatening in these ways, something that should also be seen as part of the dominant kinship narrative in Denmark, a country in which kinship and kinship responsibilities are traditionally assigned to biogenetic connections, they nevertheless were also very clear that connections between them and donor-conceived individuals did not represent kinship and therefore did not bear the same responsibilities as relations to loved ones and family. Distancing themselves from donor-conceived individuals thus became a way of reclaiming their authority in matters of who counts as family and who does not, an attempt to deal with the transilience of biosocial relatedness by building wayward relations instead of kinship. Felix, for example, understood connections to donor-conceived individuals in the following way:

> Well, I don't think this bothers me. Of course, they are not my own children, because they are not in any way. But it is somehow more a part of me, I mean more than if they were just some random children. There is no emotional bond with them; it is just the biological bond in some way. But I mean, there still is some sort of bond, I don't know how I should describe this. But it doesn't really mean anything. I am looking forward to having a cup of coffee with them, if they want to meet me once or so, and talk about how their life has been. That is fine.

The image of meeting donor-conceived individuals for a cup of coffee and talking things over with them was prominent among all the donors I talked to. While most men had not been sperm donors long enough for donor-conceived individuals to actually contact them, Magnus, who donates privately and thus has direct contact with donor semen recipients, also arranges to get to know the children conceived with his semen. But he is also very clear that he does not want to build a family as a sperm donor. Explaining to me what contact between him and donor semen recipients looks like once the child is born, he said: "Well, I get an email once in a while and I also get pictures but that's usually it. I told them that I am curious to know more but I am not making demands, like if you don't send pictures then I won't participate. That's not how I am. I am simply the tool [*redskab*] so that all of this actually works out." When I then asked him whether he would also want to visit the children once they are older and he said yes, Magnus elaborated under what conditions that should happen: "My condition is that I am not building a family with them. I am simply there so that the children will get an answer to who fathered them. That's all."

Making these authoritative decisions about who is kin to them and who is not, and whom sperm donors regard as part of their family and whom they do not want to include in that circle of loved ones, sperm donors protect their family life from possible outside intrusion from donor-conceived individuals and their families. It is their way of caring about their life partners, their children, their parents, and their siblings. While sperm donors are clear that connections to donor-conceived individuals are only biogenetic and they therefore do not count as kinship or family, they are also aware of the context in which they make this claim, a context that traditionally equates biogenetic connections between people as kinship. Aware of the transilient character of these relations—it is not clear whether or not connections between donor-conceived individuals and sperm donors will come to matter as kinship in the future— sperm donors seek ways to honor the moral responsibility of participating in the creation of new life through sperm donation (and thus being biogenetically connected to donor-conceived individuals) on the one hand, while on the other hand taking care that this decision will not negatively influence what they perceive to be their family and loved ones. In other words, sperm donors participate in building wayward relations that exist alongside traditional notions of kinship while also being something different.

An important part of accepting one's responsibility as a sperm donor and caring for one's family and loved ones by protecting them from possible outside intrusion is sperm donors' decision to donate semen anonymously or nonanonymously. As became clear earlier in this chapter, sperm donors consider many things when deciding whether or not to donate semen anonymously, such as the social stigma connected to being a donor, the well-being of the yet unconceived child, and not least their own fears of being met with potential legal or economic repercussions. Yet whereas one might make the claim that the choice to donate semen anonymously is equivalent to being concerned about outside intrusion and the choice to donate semen nonanonymously is not, both choices are probably better understood as expressions of wanting to take care of one's family and loved ones, that is, while the decision to donate anonymously will have different consequences in regard to the likelihood of actually being contacted by donor-conceived individuals in the future, they are nevertheless both decisions that aim to care for family and loved ones by clearly defining who gets to be inside and outside of what sperm donors consider to be their family. Sperm donors who decide to donate semen anonymously are also most likely to argue that doing so provides them with the opportunity to protect their family life from outside intrusion, while sperm donors who decide to donate semen nonanonymously would make the same claim since donating semen nonanonymously gives them the chance to draw the line between family and nonfamily (Mohr 2015).

For William, in his twenties and in a long-term relationship, the possibility of donating semen anonymously was a precondition for signing up as a sperm donor. Partly also due to the agreement he has made with his partner that donating semen should not influence their private life, as became clear in chapter 2, donating anonymously was for him a definite choice to protect himself, his partner, and their future family life together from outside interference from possible donor-conceived individuals. With that decision, he took precautions against the potential for connections to donor-conceived individuals to matter as something more than just biogenetic connections:

> I am also an organ donor. If anything happens to me, if I happen to have a traffic accident, then I think it is wonderful that I can help others. But to possibly be contacted by some children in twenty years' time, I am afraid about, I am bad at being emotionally distanced. Some people are good at this, distancing themselves: I don't have anything to do with this. But I am afraid that I won't be able to do that. I think, in that situation, I will start to have, I don't think I could not have a relation to them. . . . I can just feel that I would not be able to close the door in their face and say: leave. They would probably come to fill more than I am maybe ready for.

As a consequence of these concerns, William was not only happy about being able to donate semen anonymously, he was also glad that he did not receive any information about how many children are conceived and born with the help of his semen. Talking about whether this lack of information might be frustrating, he said: "No, I don't think so. I don't feel that that is important to know. I mean, I am guessing that children will come out of this. I think, you would be a lot more committed if you received information each time a child is born, and you would then follow the whole thing a lot more closely and then I think it would be too difficult to put that behind you, I think then it would come to mean too much [*at fylde for meget*]."

While William had chosen to donate semen anonymously because he felt this was the best way to protect himself and his partner from possible intrusion, Oliver, in his twenties and single, thought that donating semen nonanonymously was the only ethical choice because it would give him the opportunity to provide donor-conceived individuals with the option to know who fathered them as well as providing him with the chance to define who is part of his family and who is not. For him, the choice for nonanonymity was thus a way of setting clear boundaries. When I asked him whether or not he would regard children being conceived with the help of his semen to be his own, he said: "Well, they are my children in some sense. But I cannot be a father for them and that is also why I think it is important to meet them, you know, to give them a chance to know who I am and to tell them that I cannot be a father for them." A little later, when he and I were talking about donor semen recipients, he reiterated this point by saying:

> My biggest reservation [*forbehold*] is that I cannot take responsibility for so many, I cannot, you know, involve myself in all those people's lives, and also not for those children in the future, I mean, I have friends to begin with and in twenty years' time I will have my own family. I cannot be a father for twenty-five children and that's why I cannot have a relation with those parents who have used my semen. I can offer to meet them for a cup of coffee, that I would like to do, but I cannot invite them to come to my fiftieth birthday or say that I will come to their birthdays. That I can't do because it would come at the expense [*på bekostning*] of my own family.

Taking care of one's family and loved ones means protecting them from outside interference, to make sure that being a sperm donor does not come at their expense, as Oliver formulates it. As his and William's stories show, decisions to donate semen anonymously or nonanonymously are two different ways of achieving the same goal, namely, taking care of families and loved ones by protecting them from outside interference. While for William being anonymous was a precondition of becoming a sperm donor in the first place, since for him it provides the distance between him and donor-conceived individuals that he deems necessary in order to be a donor, for Oliver donating semen nonanonymously is the only way of making sure that donor-conceived individuals will have a chance of understanding that they cannot be a part of his family. Whether sperm donors decide to be anonymous or not, their decision is part of taking responsibility for biosocial relatedness. They act upon a sense of responsibility that comes with being connected and relating to people through the use of reproductive technologies.

Sperm Donors' Biosocial Relatedness

Biosocial relatedness is about the kinds of responsibilities that come with relating and being connected to other people through the use of reproductive technologies. As I have argued throughout this chapter, by caring for donor-conceived individuals and donor semen recipients as well as by caring for their families and loved ones, sperm donors honor the kinds of responsibilities that come with biosocial relatedness. The kinds of responsibilities that biosocial relatedness demands from sperm donors in relation to donor-conceived individuals and donor semen recipients derive on the one hand from the biomedical value that is assigned to biogenetic connections between sperm donors and donor-conceived individuals as well as from the moral obligations that come with being biogenetically connected in a context in which these connections are understood to hold important information for the health and well-being of the yet unconceived child. To that end, sperm donors make themselves available to biomedical scrutiny and integrate the moral obligation of protecting future life as part of their self-image as reproductively responsible men.

On the other hand, sperm donors have special responsibilities in regard to donor-conceived individuals and recipients of donor semen in the sense that the mode of reproduction that connects them—sperm donation and donor insemination—carries with it certain moral implications in a societal and cultural context with normative assumptions about how reproduction is supposed to take place—via heterosexual intercourse—and what it is supposed to establish—kinship and family. To this end, sperm donors consider the moral permissibility of partaking in the conception of a child whom they will not raise themselves as well as the moral permissibility of sperm donor anonymity. Whatever sperm donors' reasoning looks like when considering these questions, they all aim at being responsible men.

The same desire to be responsible men is involved in sperm donors' contemplations about what kinds of responsibilities they have in regard to their families and loved ones. Here a sense of responsibility derives from the concern that their decision to donate semen will have repercussions for those whom they consider to be their family. In order to honor this responsibility, men seek ways of engaging as sperm donors that guarantee the protection of their family life from outside interference from donor-conceived individuals and their families, and to that end they clearly define who is part of their family and who is not (by donating semen either anonymously or nonanonymously), and they guard their loved ones from possible moral judgments about sperm donation by third parties.

In this sense, biosocial relatedness and the specific kinds of responsibilities it demands manifest themselves in particular practices and experiences of relating and being connected to people through the use of reproductive technologies. As the experiences of the men in this chapter show, biosocial relatedness is characterized by an uncertainty about how connections might come to matter in the future, something that could be called *transilience* (Konrad 2005). At the same time, being connected and relating to people through the use of reproductive technologies also encompasses modes of relating that integrate elements of kinship relatedness while also offering ways of relating that go beyond kinship and geneticization, ways of relating that could be referred to as *wayward relations* (Klotz 2014, 2016).

This inherent indeterminacy in terms of wayward and transilient relations that give biosocial relatedness its form leaves sperm donors with the task of finding ways in which they can live up to their own and others' expectations to act responsibly in a biomedical day and age. As has become clear throughout this chapter, the specific ways of organizing sperm donation in Denmark through legal and contractual regulations that describe sperm donors' responsibilities first and foremost in terms of biomedical registers and biopolitical valuations become important guiding principles when men consider what responsibility as a sperm donor actually means. However, sperm donors also need to feel that what they decide and what their engagements as sperm donors look like are right in a moral sense. In other words, they need to be able to experience themselves as men who act in a morally responsible way. Doing biosocial relatedness and thereby also remaking themselves as biosocial subjects, sperm donors assume positions as responsible men, men who know how to honor the kinds of responsibilities that come with relating and being connected to other people through the use of reproductive technologies. It is in this sense that sperm donors continuously re-create the experience of being the responsible men they would like to be, or, put differently, the enticement of gender as responsibility helps sperm donors to navigate the terrain of biosocial relatedness.

Chapter 5

THE LIMITS OF BIOSOCIAL SUBJECTIVATION

MALE SHAME AND
THE DISPLEASURE OF GENDER NORMATIVITY

Alfred had first heard about the possibility of becoming a sperm donor through one of his roommates, who had been donating semen for a while. In his twenties, attending university while also working, single with no children, and a donor for about a year when I met him, Alfred told me that becoming a sperm donor was partly due to this roommate: "We joked about it and he said that he had better semen quality than I did and that I should get mine tested to see if I was just as good as he was, stuff like that." Being teased by his roommate, Alfred took up the challenge and applied to become a donor at the same sperm bank with which his roommate had signed a contract: "I am a bit of a competitive person, and I wanted to be as good as he was [*jeg ville ikke står tilbage for min kammerat*]. I wouldn't have gone there if he hadn't provoked something within me." Once approved as a sperm donor, Alfred's competition with his roommate turned into a sort of sperm donor companionship, with regular jokes about semen quality and paying rent by providing semen samples. In addition, being a sperm donor had provided him with a different sense of male self-worth: "When you know that only a few guys actually make it (being a sperm donor) then you, it gives you somehow, not necessarily a feeling of pride, but it somehow gives you a push for your masculinity [*en skubber til ens mandighed*], that you are part of an elite, that you are one of them. And it is always good to know that you have good semen quality." At the same time, however, Alfred had also been provoked by the thought of having to masturbate at a sperm bank, something that he considers to be a rather private thing to do:

> . . . I was curious to hear how that was, and I was maybe also a little bit outraged about, maybe not outraged, but also curious about, do you just stand next to each other, do you just close a curtain, do you go into a room, because I thought that that would be a very strange situation. I mean, this is not, usually you think of your sperm, that is something that you only have with yourself or with your girlfriend, something intimate, and just leaving it at some random place, that is, well that was a strange thought somehow.

Alfred's uneasiness about masturbating at the sperm bank also related to a feeling of insecurity in regard to how to actually masturbate as a sperm donor. When I asked him if he remembered his first semen sample, he said:

> Yes, well, that felt rather unnatural [*unaturligt*]. I didn't know what I should do with myself in there: should I stand up, should I sit down, how was one to actually do this. Now it is more of a routine.—So, they (staff at the sperm bank) didn't say anything about what to do?—No, not more than that I should probably figure it out myself. You get your cup and then they tell you that you should place the cup on the counter when you're done and that this and this room is vacant. The rest is pretty much learning by doing. There is not a lot of information. But again, I probably didn't need that information either.

While his initial concern about the transgressive dynamic of being a sperm donor calmed somewhat once he had actually been to the sperm bank and developed a routine for providing semen samples on demand, being a sperm donor nevertheless remains a part of Alfred's everyday life that is a continuous source of concern for him. Never having talked with his parents about being a sperm donor, for example, Alfred is careful to keep the fact that he donates semen within a limited circle of friends: "That has to do with how other people might react. I mean, this is nothing that I will post on Facebook or anything like that. This is more private; also because it involves my body, this is a part of me that I am giving and that's also why only certain people should know about it." And Alfred has also experienced people reacting negatively to him being a sperm donor: "Nothing extreme, but you know, some said very bluntly [*meget direkte*]: well, that is your choice! Things like that. It is often women who react that way. Men are a bit more like: okay, I could do that (being a sperm donor) as well." In addition, even though

Alfred has found a routine for being able to provide semen on demand—usually on Mondays and Thursdays—and while he has likewise changed his eating habits to incorporate what he considers to be a healthier diet in order to provide samples with good quality, he also still feels anxious every time he goes to the sperm bank knowing that he could potentially meet someone he knows and feeling that his personal intimate space is transgressed somehow when being there:

> I mean, I can't talk on behalf of the other men, but there are these porn magazines and then they just place a bottle of disinfectant next to them. I mean, the reason no one uses this stuff is because everyone has to grab it, you know. No one sits there and goes through those magazines page by page. I mean, that could just as well not be there. I think their intention was that men would use the different things that are there, but the fact is that you're just trying to get through the whole thing as fast as possible.

This chapter explores the limits of biosocial subjectivation. While the previous chapters attended to the making of sperm donors as biosocial subjects through the enticement of gender, this chapter is concerned with the potential unmaking of biosocial subjects through situations of male shame. Situations of male shame might be understood as moments in which sperm donors have transgressive experiences as part of their performativity of gender, experiences of displeasure that discipline men to be good sperm donors while also potentially leading them to reconsider their decision to become donors. These kinds of situations are an everyday part of being a sperm donor, for example feeling embarrassed about donating semen, feeling inadequate for failing to deliver samples that pass quality assessments, feeling incapable due to being unable to achieve an erection on demand, feeling awkward while being at the sperm bank or when interacting with other donors, or feeling exposed and ashamed during physical exams or while being interviewed by sperm bank staff. In these kinds of situations, men are confronted with forms of moral reasoning and/or affective investments that they possibly experience as transgressive and unpleasant, moments in which their enjoyment of gender normativity is put to the test and that, as a consequence, bear the potential to disrupt the process of biosocial subjectivation while simultaneously also contributing to the remaking of sperm donors as biosocial subjects. As such, these moments of male shame are an integral part of being a sperm donor because they occur on a regular basis. Moments of male shame are important for sperm donors' performativity of gender and thus for their process of biosocial subjectivation; they mark the boundaries of what is acceptable and what is not. As became clear in the previous chapters, splotches of semen on the floor in donor rooms, embarrassing comments by friends and acquaintances, or visions of a disturbed future family life are all examples of how men make being a sperm donor a meaningful decision. Yet if such moments of male shame become too transgressive, or if there are too many of them, the displeasure of gender performativity that they might cause could be enough to make sperm donors reconsider their decision to donate semen. This chapter deals with this transgressive dynamic of male shame by exploring situations that arise in sperm donors' everyday life in which the making of the sperm donor might reach its limits.

Alfred was rather vocal about moments in his life as a sperm donor that caused embarrassment and shame for him. In particular, the circumstance of having to masturbate at the sperm bank and knowing that the frail boundaries of intimacy during these moments could be transgressed was of concern for him. As he put it, donating semen means that he gives a part of himself, and it is this sense of giving something of himself that defines the moments of male shame as he experiences them. These moments point to the vulnerability of his gendered self, moments in which his preferred way of being a man is at stake. Rather than experiencing indulgence and pleasure in gender normativity during these moments, Alfred just wants "to get through the whole thing as fast as possible." He situates being a sperm donor as a continuously transgressive experience that he has to be able to manage in order to continue as a donor. As the previous chapters have shown, sperm donors manage this continuous transgression successfully through particular forms of moral reasoning, affective investments, and ways of relating, and thus make themselves into biosocial subjects. Yet while Alfred's narrative was clearly about becoming a biosocial subject in this sense, it was also about the inherently transgressive dynamic that being a sperm donor involves. Alfred faces situations of potential embarrassment and shame continuously throughout his everyday life. Remarks or judgments about being a sperm donor from friends and relatives, even possible disapproval, cause contemplations about the moral permissibility of sperm donation; the possibility of meeting someone he knows at the sperm bank causes embarrassment about potentially being caught doing something that could be considered inappropriate; and having to touch the same magazines as other donors and using the same furniture as them provokes disgust. As such, all these moments hold the potential to undermine Alfred's decision to become a sperm donor. While they are an inevitable part of what it means to be a sperm donor, they also threaten the making of sperm donors as biosocial subjects and are thus defining moments for how biosociality takes hold in the lives of men who donate semen. This chapter explores these moments of male shame and their role as part of biosocial subjectivation.

The Indeterminacy of Biosocial Subjectivation, Male Shame, and Ethnographic Practice

The experience of transgression and male shame is nothing particular to being a sperm donor. As anthropological and sociological scholarship on reproductive biomedicine, particularly male infertility, shows, the use of reproductive technologies makes "individuals realize the boundaries of their subjectivity and personhood" (Mohr and Koch 2016: 94) and is thus always already also a transgressive experience. As research on the experiences of male infertility in Denmark shows, for example, having to subject oneself to semen quality tests, being evaluated, and undergoing fertility treatment makes men vulnerable and can lead them to feel less like men (Schmidt 1996; Tjørnhøj-Thomsen 1999, 2009), a finding that is supported by research on male infertility in other national and cultural contexts (Goldberg 2009; Inhorn 1996) and that also reflects the experiences of men with erectile dysfunction (Wentzell 2013b; Zhang 2015). But while men undergoing fertility treatment and men with erectile difficulties can utilize a health and healing discourse in order to relate to moments of male shame and the transgressive dynamics inherent to them, and can thus also restitute their masculine self-image through the use of (reproductive) biomedicine (Bell 2016; Wentzell 2013a), sperm donors cannot activate that kind of contextualization. They are not men who are identified as ill and in need of medical treatment in order to reproduce. Rather, sperm donors are men who embody reproductive masculinity in the sense that they are chosen precisely because they are able to provide semen samples of high quality on demand. Failing to do so makes it impossible for men to be sperm donors, and sperm donors cannot expect to receive biomedical help if they are not able to perform on demand. Sperm donors are simply expected to be highly reproductive at all times, and, as a consequence, their experiences of situations of male shame are also likely to be qualitatively different from those of men who are undergoing fertility treatment or who have to use medicine in order to achieve erections.

Exploring this qualitative difference, I want to approach situations of male shame as moments in which sperm donors experience transgression as part of how they do gender. Understood as such, the transgressive dynamics inherent to male shame connect to some of the conceptual thinking around biosocial subjectivation and the enticement of gender as I have introduced it in the first chapter. While my conceptualization of biosocial subjectivation with the help of scholarship on biosociality, biomedicalization, and biological citizenship (Clarke et al. 2010; Petryna 2002; Rabinow 1996; Rose 2007) focuses on the making of subjects with a sense of self in terms of biomedical registers and biopolitical valuations, and while I have argued that the enticement of gender secures the successful making of sperm donors as biosocial subjects through pleasurable experiences of gender normativity sustained by affective investments (Ahmed 2012), flows of affect (Fox and Alldred 2013), and the alluring power of gender (Butler 1993; Foucault 1990; Rubin 1975), the conceptualization of biosocial subjectivation also contains an element of indeterminacy that makes it into an always incomplete and fragile process of becoming. No sperm donor will ever be a perfect biosocial subject. Rather, biosocial subjectivity is under contestation at all times, and the transgressive experiences that situations of male shame contain are instances in which the inherent indeterminacy and incompleteness of biosocial subjectivation become apparent; in other words, the making of the sperm donor is also always already his potential unmaking.

This notion of biosocial subjectivation emerges from the scholarship on biological citizenship. For example, as Adriana Petryna makes clear in relation to survivors of the nuclear disaster in Chernobyl, the common sense these survivors embody not only makes them recognizable within a specific welfare system but also produces new kinds of vulnerabilities and thus likewise makes possible other ways of thinking of oneself and one's relation to the state and its welfare system (Petryna 2004). This element of indeterminacy is also important for the process of biosocial subjectivation that sperm donors undergo. Once men are recognizable as sperm donors and think of themselves in terms of biomedical registers and biopolitical valuations, new kinds of transgressions are possible and new kinds of vulnerabilities are created, for example when men feel inadequate because they cannot produce good enough semen samples. The transgressive potential of that particular experience is a consequence of becoming a sperm donor, a process of biosocial subjectivation as part of which doing masculinity right depends on one's ability to provide high quality semen samples.

In this sense, the kind of affective investments that becoming a sperm donor demands, and the flows of affect it depends upon, also produce the possibility of unmaking the sperm donor as a biosocial subject. As Sara Ahmed argues, while norms persist through our affective relations to them, norms can also be reformulated and undone precisely because we relate to them in an affective sense and therewith can also relate to them differently through affect and emotion (Ahmed 2012). And while flows of affect might be territorialized in specific ways (Fox and Alldred 2013) in order for men to be able to donate semen, they can also be reterritorialized through transgressive experiences and thus might cause men to think twice about whether being a sperm donor is something they want to commit themselves to. The performative character of biosocial subjectivation thus also always already contains the possibility for shifting boundaries and therewith also changes what men might deem acceptable. As Judith Butler argues, since gender has no authentic core it is always open to reformulation, that is, a defining characteristic of gender performativity is the reformulation of gender as a norm through doing it (Butler 1990, 1993, 2004), and in this sense the process of making the biosocial subject through the enticement of gender is never finished and therefore also open to being undone.

This inherent indeterminacy of biosocial subjectivation is exemplified in the transgressive experiences contained in situations of male shame. The transgressive dynamic of these situations might be said to be similar to transgressive (sexual) acts as Hastings Donnan and Fiona Magowan define them: "a modality of action in which the body responds through sensory and emotive experiences of interpersonal relations to produce transformative attitudes with the potential to affect social structures" (Donnan and Magowan 2009: 11). In this sense, the transgression that men can experience as part of being sperm donors in situations of male shame is an embodied form of awareness that personal boundaries are being transgressed, which might lead to *transformative attitudes*. This may happen during physical exams in which sperm donors have to expose their body to the gaze of a medical doctor, or when donors have problems maintaining an erection when asked to provide a semen sample. In these instances, they encounter the frailty of their gendered and sexualed self, an awareness that maintaining their own gender normativity may be at risk, and it is these kinds of experiences that might make them reconsider acting as sperm donors. At the same time, however, the transgressive experience in moments of male shame can also serve to discipline men to be good sperm donors, that is, the transgressive experience can likewise sustain the process of biosocial subjectivation that sperm donors undergo. As Georges Bataille argues, transgression "opens the door into what lies beyond the limits usually observed, but it maintains these limits just the same" (Bataille 1986: 67). In other words, just as the transgression of boundaries holds the potential to transform norms and our affective relations to them, it also reifies norms and the boundaries that protect them. In this sense, situations of male shame are potentially moments in which sperm donors' biosocial subjectivation is undone, while male shame also contributes to disciplining men into being good sperm donors (Graham, Mohr, and Bourne 2016; Mohr 2016a).

My understanding of this pivotal importance of moments of male shame in the everyday life of sperm donors was bound to experiencing moments of male shame myself as part of my ethnographic fieldwork. While the methodological framework of my fieldwork was inspired by accounts of the sensual situatedness of human existence (Classen and Howes 1996; Howes 2003; Stoller 1989; Pink 2009; Vannini, Waskul, and Gottschalk 2014) and by epistemological and methodological discussions about the embodied dimensions of fieldwork (Coffey 1999; Ellingson 2006; Mohr and Vetter 2014; Okely 2007; Turner 2000), and while my own way of engaging as an ethnographer took its point of departure in reflective accounts about the epistemological implications of fieldwork's erotic and sexual dimensions (Bain and Nash 2006; Bolton 1998; Detamore 2010; Kristiansen 2009; Kulick and Willson 1995; Lewin and Leap 1996; Mohr 2018; Mohr and Vetter 2017; Newton 1993), it was first by experiencing and sharing with my informants male shame and the transgressive dynamics it can cause that I understood what it might mean to be a sperm donor. Experiencing the transgressive dynamics of intimacy, shame, and embarrassment was in itself epistemologically important for me insofar as it provided me with an immediate understanding of sperm donors' process of biosocial subjectivation. Sharing male shame with them made empathic engagements with their everyday experiences as gendered subjects in a biomedical day and age possible. It allowed for "feeling into the other" (Bubandt and Willerslev 2015: 7), to understand biosocial subjectivation's indeterminacy due to the frailty of the gendered subject.

In addition, once I had shared male shame with my informants, I also began to realize how my own research produced moments of male shame for them. As such, my experience of male shame not only functioned as a reflexive moment that enabled the understanding of sperm donors' process of biosocial subjectivation, but likewise also pointed to how my ethnographic practice created moments in which men could potentially reconsider being sperm donors. Far from being innocent, my ethnographic practice relied on transgressing spaces of self and therewith had a lot in common with the dynamics that men face as sperm donors.

In the remainder of this chapter, I will attend to this transgressive dynamic inherent to situations of male shame as sperm donors experience them by comparing how situations of male shame play out at sperm banks and in the lives of sperm donors with how I created moments of male shame during interviews that made men reflect on their gender performativity. As I will argue throughout, situations of male shame highlight the incompleteness of sperm donors' biosocial subjectivation (and thus also its potential unmaking) through the unpleasant transgressive experience of gender performativity that moments of male shame contain.

The (Un)making of Sperm Donors as Biosocial Subjects

For sperm donors, medical checkups and examinations are a regular part of life. As mandated by regulations in Denmark, semen samples can only be released for sale once tests guarantee that a donor is not a carrier of a number of diseases (HTVL, HIV, hepatitis, chlamydia, syphilis, and gonorrhea). These tests occur every three months. In addition, donors have to undergo exams by a medical doctor on a regular basis. During interviews, men would talk about the tests as an added benefit of being a sperm donor, as they gave comfort through the knowledge that one is healthy. While men generally framed medical exams as part of this logic as well, they also said that exams can be boundary-breaking. During these exams, physicians examine the body of the donor for signs of diseases, deformations, or defects. One physician told me that he would look for bodily deformations and signs of sexually transmittable diseases or genetic disorders, all reasons to exclude men from the corps of sperm donors. According to this physician, webbed toes, for example, would lead to exclusion whereas a crooked or deformed penis would not. During interviews, men told me that the most uncomfortable part of these exams is the inspection of testicles, penis, and anus. As some men reported, physicians may also examine the rectum by inserting a finger. When I asked another physician about this practice, he said that it could be used to determine prostate cancer and the likelihood of receptive anal intercourse. As such, medical exams are very likely to contain situations of male shame because they directly connect to men's gendered and sexualed self-images.

For Noah, a donor for about a year, single, and in his twenties, this was certainly the case. He talked about his first physical exam as a sperm donor in the following way:

> That was fine. Well, it stank in there when I came in, but there were probably a bunch of people before me. It really smelled like dirty ass [*sur røv*], but there is nothing you can do about it. In many ways the whole thing is really boundary-breaking. I mean, not even at the military [*session*] did they check me in that way. They did not check, they did not mess with my genitals [*rodede med mine genitaler*]. But here, he had to check everything. He had to see whether there were signs of diseases and whether it looks normal. He even looked at my asshole [*røvhul*]. That was rather boundary-breaking. But I guess they have to do that.

When I asked Noah a little later whether there was anything that he did not like about being a sperm donor, he referred to the physical exams again and positioned them as something that could ultimately stop him from being a donor if they occurred too often: "I can live with the blood tests. Those are fine. I mean, I am already a blood donor anyway, so that doesn't bother me. If you were to ask me where my limit was, where I wouldn't feel like it (being a donor) anymore, then I would say that if I had to go through one of those exams every time or every other time, that I wouldn't do [*det gad jeg ikke*]. Then I would finish it as fast as possible."

While most other donors reflected on the medical exams in a similar way to Noah, the embarrassing and transgressive dynamic of the exams first became truly comprehensible to me after I had experienced for myself the shame and transgression they can cause. Only after I had experienced male shame myself during these exams was I able to understand their importance for what it means to be a sperm donor. The embodiment and sharing of male shame opened up the analytical possibility that the biosocial subject sperm donor could be undone by the very same practices and norms that make the good sperm donor. An entry from my field journal provides more details of the experience of male shame during medical exams, and how the transferal of that experience onto the ethnographer opens up an understanding of the processes of biosocial subjectivation as also a matter of gender performativity, that is, situations of male shame as sperm donors experience them are a continuous challenge to their gendered and sexualed self-images:

Petro, in his late teens, single, and just starting at university, is the donor-candidate who is supposed to undergo his initial interview as well as a physical exam today. He is in one of the donor rooms. Since there is not much space here, the donor rooms are in the middle and divide the laboratory from the waiting area. The examination room is separate. Nick, the physician responsible for conducting the interview and exam, as well as Charly, the lab technician, are waiting for Petro to finish.

When Petro arrived, Charly told him to produce a semen sample as well as a urine sample. Sitting in the waiting area, I can hear everything that goes on in the donor room: Petro opening his pants, urinating into the specimen cup, I can even hear how he goes through the pornographic magazines a little while later. This intimacy takes me by surprise and I feel embarrassed. I keep thinking that this situation must surely be stressful for Petro, knowing that three people are waiting for him to finish masturbating. A few minutes go by and, all of a sudden, Nick comes out of the examination room and says to Charly: "Well, I guess he is also busy producing a sample." Charly nods in agreement. The two strike up a conversation about Petro and the information that he provided in the medical and family history questionnaire. I am astonished that this conversation is going on, since it has to be obvious to Charly and Nick that Petro is very likely to overhear what they are saying. Nick then looks in the direction of the donor rooms and checks the time on the clock on the laboratory wall. He obviously wants Petro to finish. Nick and I go into the examination room and talk about his work. After a few minutes of conversation, I can hear a donor room door opening and Petro setting the specimen cups on the registration desk. Charly says "Good," and her intonation makes it sound as if she is belittling Petro and actually meant to say, "Well done my little boy."

The interview itself proceeds without any noteworthy events. Nick does not find anything wrong with Petro's medical history. When it is then time for the physical exam, Nick asks Petro to take off his shirt and first checks Petro's breathing and lungs with a stethoscope. Thereafter, Nick checks eyes, ears, throat, lymph nodes, shoulders, and stomach. He then asks Petro to take off his pants and explains that he needs to see the penis and testicles as well and that Petro would also have to retract his foreskin. I turn my gaze away from the examination. All I can hear is Petro opening and dropping his pants and then laughing shyly. Nick says: "Well, this is also part of the examination," while laughing embarrassed. I feel embarrassed as well and find myself unable to lift my head. The warm smell of body odor makes itself noticeable. Nick then asks Petro to put his pants back on and to sit down on the examination bench. He tests Petro's reflexes on elbow and knee. After also checking Petro's back, Nick asks Petro to lift his arms so he can check the armpit lymph nodes. Petro seems to be embarrassed again and says: "They are a little wet." "Don't worry," says Nick, "I need to wash my hands after the examination anyways." Once the examination is done, Nick tells Petro that everything is alright: "Everything is completely normal."

Situations like this are filled with transgressive dynamics. Most obviously, the physical exam in and by itself points to the vulnerable position in which sperm donors and donor candidates find themselves: they are being evaluated and checked for possible pathologies. At the same time, the setup of the examination—knowing that someone is waiting for your semen sample, overhearing conversations about your medical status, handing over specimen cups containing your warm semen and urine—produces compliance by invoking male shame or installing the possibility of it. While medical histories make up a large part of these situations, it is first and foremost exposing men's bodies to the medical gaze that marks the frailty of the male subject in these instances. For men wanting to become sperm donors, such a physical exam might be the very first time that they have to present their genitals and anus to a physician, especially if they are as young as Petro. While the female body is more likely to be exposed to comparable transgressive dynamics from an early age, men's exposure to the medical gaze is limited and normally does not involve exposing penis, testicles, and anus. Petro's embarrassment the moment he drops his pants indicates that being looked at and touched in this particular way is a transgressive experience for him. Silenced by having to accept being looked at, touched, and assessed, his shy laughter is an attempt to deal with this situation of male shame. Nick's reaction points to his institutional role as a physician, a medical expert who, due to his authority, is sanctified to look at and touch men's naked bodies, a practice normally not accepted as an everyday interaction between strangers. Verbalizing the fact that having to look at and touch Petro's penis and testicles is a necessary part of the examination reminds everyone present that this situation is a medical assessment and not an erotic moment. One man touching another man's genitals is made legitimate because it is positioned as part of a medical procedure. Simultaneously, the situation also points to what is at stake for donor-candidates like Petro, namely, whether they can become a donor or not. If Petro is accepted as a donor, he can leave the room with the confidence that nothing is wrong with him. He can be assured that he has what it takes to be a sperm donor. If he is not accepted, however, he will leave wondering what might be wrong with him.

I also experienced the transgression that is inherent to moments of male shame and embodied them in similar ways to how sperm donors described them to me during interviews. While I certainly had not been naïve about the bodily aspects of providing semen samples and undergoing a physical exam, I was nevertheless taken by surprise by the intensity of intimacy during this particular situation. Part of the transgression that I experienced as an ethnographer had to do with the sensual immediacy of masturbation at the sperm bank as well as with my immediate bodily reactions during the examination. Experiencing shame and embarrassment myself, and feeling the unease they cause in my own body, I finally understood what the process of biosocial subjectivation was about, and how the frailty of the masculine self makes itself noticeable to those present in these situations. While during interviews I had been able to understand donors' talk about boundary-breaking experiences intellectually, the experience of male shame in situations like the one described above made me understand being a sperm donor in a phenomenological sense.

That situations of male shame directly relate to sperm donors' gender performativity is also reflected in Alfred's earlier description of masturbating at the sperm bank as a "strange situation." As Alfred explained, masturbation, ejaculation, and semen are things that he considers private, and thus being a sperm donor for him is also about giving a part of himself. Hence, the transgressive dynamic of having to masturbate in a semipublic place like a sperm bank marks the boundaries of Alfred's gender normativity, something that would not necessarily be deemed transgressive as part of other social contexts, such as gay men's cruising culture, for example. Alfred's feeling of uneasiness and insecurity seemed furthermore to directly relate to his stipulation that the combination of doing something private—masturbating—in a place that is not private—the sperm bank—caused a transgression of what he would deem appropriate male behavior, a normative logic also voiced by other donors. This became obvious when he and I were talking about his choice of pornography when masturbating at the sperm bank, when he positioned sexual enjoyment as something that one should not indulge in at the sperm bank: "I don't think that I focus on the video that much. Usually I just click on one of the most popular videos on the homepage. Those are typically nothing too extreme, you know, just normal stuff. For those guys that like more crazy [*syrede*] things, they can search for other stuff. That's very easy to find. It's not like I have to see a new video every time I am there. That's not something I do there. That's something that I need to take care of [*pleje*] someplace else."

This kind of anxiety around the act of masturbation at the sperm bank and the sexual connotation of it was also prominent in other donors' narratives. Across the different experiences that men had with masturbating at sperm banks, this anxiety described both the normative boundaries of gender performativity and the possible transgression of these boundaries for sperm donors. In this sense, sexual indulgence, for example, was not deemed appropriate as part of donating semen, nor was possible excitement about the presence of other men and their bodily fluids (Mohr 2010, 2016a). Oliver, a donor for about a year, in his twenties and single, had a particular way of describing this normative boundary. Talking about the atmosphere at the sperm bank, he said:

> There is this special atmosphere when you donate sperm, if, for example, others are waiting (to get into the donor rooms). It is the same atmosphere as being at the urinals in a men's room, where you also know that there are other men, but you are not allowed to look into each other's eyes, you know. You only look at the floor and you don't talk to one another, the same atmosphere as in a men's room. You don't just stand there and look at another man's penis while he is taking a piss, you know, and you don't look at another man's sperm, this feeling, that whatever happens here is private.

For Mathias, also in his twenties, in a long-term relationship with no children, and a donor for about a year, the anxiety around having to masturbate at the sperm bank was directly connected to the possibility of being caught in the act. While he talked about being a sperm donor as something ordinary and nothing special, it was also clear that coming to the sperm bank and delivering semen samples was a transgressive experience for him. As with every donor I met, I asked him to describe the atmosphere at the sperm bank for me. When he talked about the donor rooms, he said:

> Well, I guess you could compare them to a guest bathroom. There is a little bench with a magazine stand in front of you, a little sink next to you, and then there are magazines of course, and that's it. There is nothing fancy about it. Music is playing, you know, in order to drown

out everything else. When you enter the room the one thing you have to remember though is to lock the door and switch on the light. When you switch on the light, the red lamp on the outside will light up so that everyone knows the room is occupied. That is the most important thing to remember: to switch on the light so that people outside know it is occupied.

I wanted to know why that would be the most important thing to remember: "Well, in that way, in case you forgot to lock the door, no one will just walk in on you all of a sudden while you are sitting there. With the light on and the lamp lit up, well, then they will not even try to get into the room." Switching on the light and thereby activating a little red lamp that signals that a donor room is occupied is the most important thing to remember as a sperm donor. It is this routine that protects Mathias from the ultimate transgression: being exposed to a gazing audience and being made vulnerable by someone laying eyes on his enticed body. While it is hard to say whether Mathias would stop being a sperm donor if he was ever walked in on when masturbating at the sperm bank, having measures such as the red lamps that secure intimate privacy at the sperm bank certainly makes it easier for sperm banks to recruit men as donors.

Staff at sperm banks are aware of the transgressive potential that these moments of male shame hold for sperm donors. The potential of being exposed while masturbating was an unbearable thought for all donors I talked to, an imagined and ever-present possibility connected to embarrassment and male shame. The red lamp functions as a device that helps everyone involved to minimize moments of male shame, and the importance of such devices becomes clear in situations in which they do not function properly, when they break down. These kinds of breakdowns are calculated into the daily routines at sperm banks. As became clear during observations and while talking to sperm bank staff, staff members paid attention to which donor rooms were occupied. In instances in which the red signal lamp did not work, staff would make up for failing mechanisms by other means. A leading lab technician told me, for example, that she would keep track herself of how many donor rooms were occupied and would ask new arriving donors to wait until a certain room was available in instances in which the signal lamps did not work. While the signal lamps are visible to both staff and donors, lab staff can thus also keep track of donors by other means. At sperm banks where donors have to fill out a short questionnaire upon arrival, for example, sperm bank staff know how many donor rooms are occupied at any given moment purely by counting the number of arrival questionnaires still not assigned to a specimen cup. In addition, donors themselves are very cautious about opening doors. As Lærke, a lab technician with many years of experience, told me: "Most of them know very well not to open doors that are closed. So, sometimes they will come back to the desk even though no one is in the rooms just because the doors are closed." Sometimes, however, even this precautionary measure does not prevent situations of male shame from occurring. Though I never observed them myself, staff reported that situations in which donors try to open doors to rooms that are occupied occur now and then. Bearing in mind sperm donors' anxiety about being caught masturbating, it is not hard to imagine what kind of shameful situations these events might produce.

Moments of male shame such as these not only threaten the successful making of sperm donors as biosocial subjects. They also help to reestablish the normative boundaries within which sperm donors' biosocial subjectivation occurs. The transgression inherent to moments of male shame makes sperm donors as biosocial subjects by disciplining them to be good donors while also potentially unmaking sperm donors as biosocial subjects by exposing them to the displeasure of gender performativity. In donor candidate interviews, for example, references to an uncomfortable conversation about masturbation and other sexual practices are made in order to communicate to donor candidates the importance of sticking to the ejaculatory regimen in place at sperm banks (Graham, Mohr, and Bourne 2016). Donor candidates are told that if their samples were to fail quality assessments repeatedly, they would have to undergo a mandatory talk about whether or not they adhere to the established abstinence rule or whether some other factor in their intimate sexual life hinders them from providing good-quality samples. While at first it startled me that sperm bank staff seemed to be deliberately creating situations of male shame as part of their interactions with donors, once I realized the necessity of male shame and the transgression it implies for the making of good sperm donors, the disciplining effect of these situations was hard to miss.

Situations of male shame in which this dynamic between transgression and disciplining becomes rather obvious can be found in the procedures that ensue when donors drop off their samples. In order to ensure that donors comply with the rule of abstaining from ejaculations for at least forty-eight hours before delivering a semen sample, sperm banks require men to recount when they had their last ejaculation. While these moments are potentially embarrassing for men, they also ensure that they stick to the rules and thus guarantee the making of sperm donors as biosocial subjects. However, the transgressive dynamics of these moments of male shame might also lead men to reconsider their decision to become sperm donors. An entry from my field journal captures just how transgressive it can be for some men to be forced to quantify and verbalize when they had their last ejaculation:

The donor who is here to deliver his first semen sample comes back from the donor rooms. He places the specimen cup on the counter. Lærke takes the cup and asks him when he had his last ejaculation. The donor seems surprised by the question and says that he wouldn't know exactly when that had been. He seems even more confused when Lærke explains that she would need a very precise estimate. "The precise moment?" the man asks now almost frightened. "As precise as possible," Lærke replies. After a moment of silence and reflection he says: "Sixty hours." Lærke asks whether that meant that it had been on Sunday or Saturday. "Saturday," the man says, now with a visible expression of embarrassment on his face. "Saturday morning or afternoon?" Lærke asks, forcing him to be even more precise. He nods and says that Saturday afternoon would be right. Once he has left, I turn to Lærke and ask her whether she considers the embarrassment that donors might feel in situations like this. She agrees that it is very likely to feel awkward having to put a time and date on your last ejaculation. "But as a donor you have to stick to the agreements made, and this is one of them," she explains.

The transgressive dynamic inherent to situations like this one is easy to recognize. Whereas this moment of embarrassment seems to be a matter of sticking to the rules for staff working at the sperm bank, for donors it is very likely to also provoke male shame in the sense that having to verbalize when one last reached an orgasm opens up the masculine self to vulnerability. Giving a precise date and time for the last ejaculation is not only about knowing when something happened, but also opens up the possibility of a qualitative judgment about donors' intimate and sexual life. By putting a precise number on the hours since their last ejaculation, men enter a space in which they are forced to reflect on the when and how of their sexual and intimate life while also entering into relationships in which an outside evaluation of their sexual engagements seems likely, since knowing when you last ejaculated might also lead to considerations about whether that is too long or too short a time period to be considered acceptable in a normative sense. Occasional comments by sperm bank staff about donors' hours of abstinence—"That is surely a lot of hours!" or "Are you sure it has been that long?"—indicate that these evaluations do take place. Thus, whereas asking donors about their last ejaculation is very much a measure of reassurance for staff that contractual relations are respected, for donors it installs an outside gaze on something that they consider rather intimate and private. As Alfred's, Oliver's, and Mathias's uneasiness about masturbation at the sperm bank attests, having your masculine self exposed can be a transgressive experience that is likely to produce male shame. Yet while these deliberate moments of male shame hold transgressive potential and thus also might run the risk of making men not want to be sperm donors after all, they also help to make the good sperm donor since they force men to stick to the ejaculatory regimen in place at sperm banks. A certain degree of transgression—exposing men to minimal amounts of male shame—thus minimizes the likelihood of noncompliance. Through the invocation of male shame, men are disciplined and made into biosocial subjects.

This fine balance between too much transgression and just enough transgression in order for men to discipline themselves to be good donors is very important in interactions between donors and staff. Considering the uneasiness with which most donors talked about having to masturbate at the sperm bank, whether or not staff find the right way to approach sperm donors is critical. Lucas, in his twenties, single, and a donor for about a year, said the following about his interactions with staff at the sperm bank:

> Of course you say hi to the lab technicians and stuff like that, but these are not conversations between friends, also because I think that discretion is very important. So, there is nothing beyond "Hi" and "Good-bye" and so on. There is nothing more than that. It's not as if you sat down for a casual conversation [*hyggesnak*] together. I mean, I am actually a very talkative guy, but there, you don't sit down and have a friendly conversation. They also have work to do. I really like that there is discretion about the whole thing and I also like that you greet one another, but that is all.

For Alfred, discretion also included not being recognizable to other donors at the sperm bank. When I asked him what he thought about the atmosphere at the sperm bank, he said:

> It is just the way it is supposed to be. It should not be too personal. One should not be on a first-name basis. There is this special thing

about what one does there. The professional boundaries should not be taken down, for example in: "Hi, how are you doing today. Let me take you down to the room," or "Why don't you let me take your jacket," and stuff like that. It feels good to walk with a hoodie over your head, if you know what I mean. Not that I do that, but, you know, you pass by one another there. Actually, there should be another staircase that you could use on the way out, that would be the optimal setup. Because you don't feel like meeting the guys that are on their way out and you don't feel like seeing those men that have just been in those rooms. In that sense it would probably be better if you could go out a different way than the one you came in.

The moments of male shame as sperm donors encounter them at the sperm bank are sidelined by moments of male shame that they experience because of being a sperm donor even when they are not at the sperm bank. Most obviously, these moments might occur when men are exposed as sperm donors in contexts in which they do not feel comfortable with others knowing about it. Alfred, for example, actually met a colleague at the sperm bank and therewith had to face the possibility that people other than those he trusts and confides in would now know that he is a sperm donor. Talking about meeting his colleague, he said: "One time I met someone there that I know, somebody that I work with and that was a really strange situation because you normally have this professional relation to one another at work and now all of a sudden you know something about the other person that, now you have this secret." When I asked him whether that made it more difficult to control who actually knows that he is a sperm donor, he added: "Yes, in that situation it moves into another area, you know. And you don't know what people's reactions will be. You don't know what their prejudices are. You just don't know what will happen." Victor, married and a father of one, and a sperm donor for well over a year when I met him, was also concerned that colleagues or business partners would find out that he is a sperm donor. While he repeatedly said that he does not treat being a sperm donor as a secret, he was worried about having to justify his decision to donate semen if friends, colleagues, or business partners were to find out about it. Talking about what he would deem most important for being a sperm donor, he said: "Well, as I said before, that there is anonymity. That is very important because of the work that I do. That is very important to me personally. Not that I think that people necessarily would have problems with it, but for me personally it is very important that there is anonymity."

In addition to these moments of male shame that are due to other people knowing that one is a sperm donor, being a sperm donor also has repercussions for men's intimate and sexual lives. While men learn how to live with the ejaculatory regimen in place at sperm banks, as chapter 3 showed, being a sperm donor might also provoke moments of male shame in men's intimate relations with partners, girlfriends, and lovers. For William, in his twenties, in a long-term relationship, and a sperm donor for about a year, being a sperm donor compromises his duties as a sexual partner, as became clear in chapter 2. While he works hard not to let being a sperm donor influence his intimate relations with his partner, he cannot always live up to that promise and, as a consequence, ends up in situations in which his sexual performance is compromised. "Sometimes I have money on my mind," as he put it, a reflection during sex with his partner that compromises his intimate life. In addition, he talked about missing his personal sexual freedom now that he is a sperm donor. Pointing out to me that masturbation had always been important to him, he told me that as a sperm donor he misses the freedom to just enjoy himself when he feels like it, an experience that undermines his masculine self-image: "You know, that feeling that you just want to give into it when you feel like it. I mean, maybe it is also healthy to live more like celibacy but sometimes it just sucks you know. It is just like eating chocolate when you are not allowed to, then you crave it even more. And that I can feel now. I really miss doing it when I feel like it. At the same time though, this also gives me more fun when I finally can (masturbate). So, I am missing it, but not more than I am still a donor." In his description of how he misses being able to just give in, William points precisely to the possibility of no longer wanting to be a sperm donor if he had to miss out on more than he currently does. At the same time, he also says that not being able to enjoy himself has not yet reached the point where he has actually considered stopping donating, or as he put it: "I am missing it, but not more than I am still a donor."

A similar contemplation characterizes Alfred's sex life since he became a sperm donor. Whereas being a sperm donor undermines William's enjoyment of himself during masturbation, for Alfred the element of male shame was more pronounced in the sense that he talked about feeling embarrassed about being unable to perform properly during sexual intercourse due to being a sperm donor. When he and I were talking about the repercussions of being a sperm donor for his sexual life, Alfred said:

You are supposed to abstain, you know, you should not have had emission [*sædafgang*] during the last seventy-two hours, and if you are in such a rhythm, where you do it twice a week, that means that the only time you do it is when you are there. And when you have done that for three weeks, then the only time that you did it was there (at the sperm bank). And then you just want to get it over with, so you do it really fast, and then you leave and don't do it for another three days, until you come up there again, and then you just do it fast. And I can feel that this, when I am together with a girl, then you don't last as long. So, I keep thinking about that, I mean, this is embarrassing, to ejaculate too early because you don't get to practice it, since the only time you get to do it, you do it as fast as possible because you don't feel like being at the sperm bank.

Here, Alfred positions premature ejaculation during intercourse as an embarrassing experience, a moment of male shame in which his gender performativity becomes unpleasant. Routinized masturbation as a sperm donor undermines his sexual performance as a man. Being able to control his sexual life in order to produce semen samples, Alfred lives up to his obligations as a donor. Yet doing so compromises his obligation as a sexual partner, a lover, a man who knows how to pleasure women. He cannot control his orgasms any longer and ejaculates too early. Thus, being a sperm donor and being forced to routinized masturbation provokes moments of male shame in Alfred's life, moments in which his gender performativity is put to the test and that therewith also might compromise his future commitment as a sperm donor. While the experience of male shame had not yet deterred him from being a sperm donor when I interviewed him, the possibility that his process of biosocial subjectivation as a sperm donor might be undone through these kinds of moments of male shame is an inherent possibility of his sperm donor livelihood.

Talking to men about these kinds of issues during interviews, I forced them to reflect on their ways of being men. Whether or not men were aware of this interview dynamic, situations of male shame arose nonetheless. Because different people handle questions about matters they deem private and intimate very differently, donors met me and my questions with a range of approaches. Some men were assured of themselves as men and turned the transgressive dynamic of the conversation around to make me feel like an emasculated jerk who got off on hearing other men talk about masturbation. In one instance, homophobic remarks after I had come out during the interview as gay were made by an interviewee in what seemed like a demarcation of hegemonic masculinity. In another situation, an interviewee offered to show me how he masturbated if I really wanted to know. Yet more often than not, men would simply respond to the questions by accepting their transgressive dynamics. With the help of two interview experiences, I want to exemplify how questions about masturbation and sex life in particular created a series of effects that can be understood as situations of male shame, situations in which men were made to reflect on their gender performativity and especially their possible shortcomings in terms of being sexually active men.

Oscar, in his thirties and working a regular job with steady hours, had been a sperm donor for about two years when I met him, and usually donated semen three times a week. He was single and had no children. When I asked him how often he masturbates, he answered: "Well, that depends, when I am going to the sperm bank, then it is typically Monday, Wednesday, Friday, or Monday, Thursday and Saturday." Our conversation continued with him telling me about his workdays and how he organizes donating semen as part of his work schedule. Oscar described himself as a person who easily falls into habits and a repetitious everyday life. When I asked him how he would describe his sex life, he seemed embarrassed and tried to downplay his embarrassment by laughing: "There is not a lot to say [laughing], it would be great if there was more to say, but there isn't, so... I mean, it's fine the way it is." A little later I asked: "How often do you have sex then?" and he answered: "Ehm, well, I can say, actually quite seldom, well, I can actually go half a year without sex, especially when I am a donor, right. I think the first year and a half, maybe I had sex, I don't know, three or four times or something like that, so, not that often." When I asked if he had set himself a maximum period for being a donor, he replied:

> Well, I have thought about setting a limit, also because I am an A-person, and once in a while I need, I need to be shaken up a little because otherwise I fall into the same old tracks. So, I have thought about how much time I should spend doing this (being a sperm donor). Right now I have been doing this for almost two years, minus the break. So maybe another year or two and then I think it is time to try something else. I mean, it also takes up a lot of time, more or less a whole day, right, because if it is on a day where I have to work, I usually work in the evening, around two in the afternoon, then you can go and donate and then to work. And then that was more or less my day, and there are many days that go like this. At some point something new has to happen, you have to do something else.

Oscar's narrative reveals how he complies perfectly as a good donor: his sexual activity consists only of masturbating at the sperm bank—Monday, Wednesday, Friday—enabling the sperm bank to obtain semen samples that will pass quality assessments every time. At the same time, his narrative also points to the transgressive character of my questions. Probing him repeatedly, I forced the experience of male shame, which, in his case, centers on the fact that his sexual activity is limited to masturbation at the sperm bank and culminates in his acknowledgment that there are many days in his life on which he only goes to work and masturbates at the sperm bank. It is here that Oscar is forced to take a reflective stance on his self-image as a man, a situation in which he has to face what for him might be an embarrassing situation: the shameful acknowledgment that he might not live up to normative ideals of manhood. Taking Oscar's embarrassment into consideration and reflecting on the normative framework surrounding masturbation in Western Europe, which marks men who only masturbate as failed men, as well as acknowledging Oscar's resignation about his life course, his answers can be understood as an experience of male shame produced by the interview situation and my mode of inquiry. Seen as part of his everyday life as a sperm donor, this situation of having to reflect on his gender performativity might be reason to reconsider being a donor, or as Oscar himself put it: "At some point something new has to happen."

In my interview with Emil, a married man in his thirties and a father of two, being confronted with intrusive questions also invoked a situation of male shame, but this shameful encounter was handled very differently. As with all other men, my way of asking questions forced a reflection on masculine self-images. Yet while Oscar seemed to accept the intrusion, Emil took a more authoritative approach and brushed off a possible questioning of his masculine self-image. While also being affected by the production of male shame, Emil did not accept it as a valid contestation of his masculine self-image. At the time when I met Emil, he had been married for many years and had been a sperm donor for about two. Like most other donors, he went to the sperm bank twice a week. Talking about masturbation, he positioned it as something that he only did if he had nothing better at hand: "It is a means to an end, really. When I have not seen my wife for about two weeks I might consider it, other than that it is not really interesting." At the same time, Emil found masturbating at the sperm bank difficult. He had never gotten used to it, as he was not able to relax at the sperm bank. Acknowledging this difficulty, he said: "You can hear them (sperm bank staff) talk when you're in there (in the donor room). And it might very well be that they are only talking about a new bicycle, but they are nevertheless right outside and that is a mood killer to be honest. So, it takes longer because I am out of my comfort zone." For Emil, being a sperm donor meant that he had to face himself when being outside of his comfort zone, as he puts it. He is confronted with the possibility of being unable to deliver a semen sample twice a week, which would mean coming out of the donor room having failed to accomplish what everyone at the sperm bank expects of him. Being a sperm donor and being faced with my interview questions forced Emil to confront this shortcoming, this masculine flaw, in a context in which being able to deliver semen on demand is the most important requirement. In addition, my questions, it seemed, incited Emil to react to a normative ideal about what an active sex life should look like, which he felt was inadequate. When I asked him how he would describe his sex life, he said brusquely:

> Normal I think, very traditional. You know, I think when you look at all this talk and public debate about sex, you cannot watch a TV show any longer without having to talk about this and that, you know, almost as if when you don't do it four times a day and anally and who knows what else, then you are almost not normal any longer. Listen, I am almost 40 years old and married and have a good and reasonable [*fornuftig*] marriage with my wife. So, I think it (my sex life) is alright.

Being asked questions about masturbation and about his sex life, Emil seemed to feel probed to such a degree that he felt outside of his comfort zone. Just as having to provide a semen sample on demand puts him out of his comfort zone, so too did my questions. I confronted him with his continuous experience of male shame in regard to having difficulties masturbating at the sperm bank while at the same time forcing him to take a reflective stance on his performance as a husband and a man faced with norms about what kind of sex life a man should have. Situated at the limits of what he deems appropriate and acceptable, Emil nevertheless stands by his decision to be a sperm donor—at least for the time being.

Sperm Donors' Limits of Biosocial Subjectivation

Situations of male shame are inherent to the lives of sperm donors. Understood as moments in which men have transgressive experiences as part of their gender performativity, male shame contributes to the making of sperm donors as biosocial subjects while also containing the potential to disrupt sperm donors' process of biosocial subjectivation. Situations of male shame make sperm donors as biosocial subjects insofar as they discipline men to live up to their contractual obligations—donating semen once or twice a week, living a healthy life, sticking to the ejaculatory regimen—and thus are pivotal in making men into good sperm donors. In this sense, situations of male shame mark the normative boundaries for what is deemed acceptable behavior and remind men of their duties as sperm donors.

On the other hand, situations of male shame have the potential to unmake sperm donors as biosocial subjects since the transgression inherent to them may lead men to question their decision to become donors. Exposing men to shameful and embarrassing moments in which their gender performativity becomes unpleasant due to transgressions of their personal boundaries (for example invasive medical exams, disgusting experiences in donor rooms, or anxiety about masturbation and sexual performance), situations of male shame also already always contain the potential that men might reconsider being sperm donors and thus may disrupt the process of biosocial subjectivation. As such, situations of male shame put men's gender normativity to the test through the transgression of what sperm donors personally deem acceptable as gendered subjects and thus point to the repercussions of being a sperm donor for sperm donors' self-images as men.

As I have argued throughout this chapter, understood as such, situations of male shame point to the limits of biosocial subjectivation, to its indeterminacy and incompleteness, and therewith also to its potential unmaking. While the making of sperm donors as biosocial subjects relies on the enticement of gender—the enjoyment of gender normativity as sperm donors identify and remake themselves as men in terms of biomedical registers and biopolitical valuations—the unmaking of sperm donors as biosocial subjects is already always a possibility because the enticement of gender does not have an original gendered subject. Rather, the performative effects of the enticement of gender create new ways of identifying in terms of gender and therewith also new kinds of vulnerabilities and unforeseen possibilities of undoing gender. In other words, while men might enjoy being sperm donors because it provides them with the possibility to experience themselves as the men they want to be, they also become different men throughout this process and may thus also develop different (affective) relations to norms and, as a consequence, might also stop enjoying themselves as sperm donors. As the stories of the men in this chapter show, being a sperm donor is a continuous transgressive experience. Situations of male shame point to the omnipresent potentiality of transgressing gender normativity. They force men to reflect on their engagements as sperm donors and they force men to meet themselves as gendered subjects, to face the frailty of their masculine selves.

In this way, situations of male shame might be understood as the queer moments of biosocial subjectivation. While the alluring power of gender might make men adhere to the normative ideals of reproductive masculinity insofar as men remake themselves as men in terms of biomedical registers and biopolitical valuations, the transgressive experiences this process of becoming entails also bear the possibility of men reflecting on their preferred way of being men. Situations of male shame not only contain the potential for men to rethink their decision to be sperm donors. These situations also have the capacity to make men think differently about themselves as men. Male shame not only points to the limits of biosocial subjectivation, it also points to the limits of its inherent gender normativity. While the men in this and the other chapters certainly were sperm donors in a normative sense, insofar as they lived up to what is expected of them as sperm donors, their stories are also evidence of the potential reflective engagements with gender normativity that biosocial subjectivation as an incomplete process encourages. While for some men thinking of themselves in terms of biomedical registers and biopolitical valuations supports rather traditional notions of masculinity, for others the performative effects of biosocial subjectivation open up reformulations of gender norms. And although donors such as Alfred and Emil were good donors in the sense that they delivered semen samples on demand, the continuous transgression of their gendered sense of self as part of being sperm donors also made them critical of the normative frameworks of their ways of being men. Sperm donors are probably misunderstood as queer activists, yet the queer seed inherent to their livelihood as sperm donors might just be enough to remake their lives as men.

CONCLUSION
BIOSOCIAL SUBJECTIVATION RECONSIDERED

An everyday life that includes the provision of semen samples for purposes of reproductive donation through regular masturbation at a sperm bank is an experience limited to only a few men, even on a global scale. Danish sperm banks advertise an availability of semen from between three hundred and one thousand donors in online catalogues. Considering that not all men who were sperm donors in Denmark are included in these numbers, and taking into account that sperm banking in Denmark has been a business for well over fifty years, an educated guess would be that between twenty-five thousand and thirty-five thousand men have donated semen at a sperm bank in Denmark at some point in their life, meaning that only about 0.8 to 1.2 percent of all Danish men have been sperm donors, given current estimates of how many men there are in Denmark.

Yet while the number of men who actually are sperm donors is limited, their experiences can tell us a lot about what it means to live an everyday life in a biomedical day and age. Sperm donors' lives are microcosmoses of what could be called the biosociality (Rabinow 1996) of gender and sexuality in the sense that sperm donors live their gendered and sexualed lives in terms of biomedical registers and biopolitical valuations. Once men are accepted as sperm donors at Danish sperm banks, all aspects of their lives—their self-images, moral contemplations, intimate experiences, and social relations—become intertwined with the material, social, and political aspects of sperm donation. Sperm donors are not simply providing semen samples on a regular basis. Rather, they live sociality remade through the generative force of reproductive biomedicine.

As I have argued throughout this book, being a sperm donor can be understood as a process of biosocial subjectivation, that is, the becoming of subjects in terms of biomedical registers and biopolitical valuations. In order to be sperm donors, men need to fit a particular biomedical profile: first and foremost, men's semen samples need to contain at least 200 million sperm cells per milliliter. Considering that the average Danish man's semen sample is estimated to contain only about 40 to 50 million sperm cells per milliliter (Jørgensen et al. 2012), sperm donors are a selected few among reproductive men. In addition, medical exams, blood work, and genetic tests as well as evaluations of men's social suitability further define who gets to be a sperm donor. Through an assessment of men's biomedical profiles as well as their biopolitical commitments (Burghardt and Tote 2010; Graham, Mohr, and Bourne 2016; Mohr 2010; Mohr and Høyer 2012), sperm banks thus select men according to their dedication to reproductive futurity (Edelman 2004). While these tests and evaluations for some may only seem like a way of guaranteeing the safety of recipients of donor semen and their children, as I have argued throughout this book, the making of sperm donors in this sense might also be comprehended as part of a particular way of becoming a person. As the previous chapters have shown, sperm donors are men whose gendered, moral, affective, sexual, and relational lives are remade in light of biosociality's performative effects.

The making of sperm donors as biosocial subjects can be conceptualized through what I have called the enticement of gender. As I have understood it in this book, the enticement of gender describes an incitement to gender as a lustful praxis, a continuous (re)making of the gendered self through an enjoyment of gender normativity. While becoming a sperm donor means to be subjected to rigorous testing and evaluation, and while being a sperm donor infringes on men's intimate lives through the regulation and control of their sexual habits, becoming a sperm donor nevertheless also opens a space in which men can experience themselves as the men they want to be. Their preferred ways of being a man in a normative sense are actualized through their engagements as sperm donors, recommitting themselves to the reproductive endeavor of sperm donation. As such, the enticement of gender involves men's embodied (common) sense of self (Novas and Rose 2000; Petryna 2004), their regimes of living and moral reasoning (Collier and Lakoff 2005), their affective investments (Ahmed 2012), and flows of affect (Fox and Alldred 2013). Through the enticement of gender, sperm donors learn to be affected in such a way that their preferred way of doing masculinity becomes the enticing normative ideal for who they want to be as men. Sperm donors learn to think of themselves as men in terms of biomedical registers and biopolitical valuations.

The stories of men such as Malthe, Thommy, Magnus, and Alfred, whose portraits were points of departure for the previous chapters, as well as all the other men's experiences as they are reflected in the preceding pages of this book, are witness to this process of biosocial subjectivation as the enticing and performative power of gender. Rather than simply being a tale about motivations and attitudes to which sperm donors' lives are commonly reduced in much of the scientific literature, this book has been an attempt to provide an understanding of and insights into what men's lives look like when producing a semen sample on demand for reproductive donation two or three times a week has become an unquestioned part of how they live their lives. As such, this book is not a truth claim about what it means to be a sperm donor. Rather, it is a window into a contemporary form of sociality that, when engaged with on its own terms, promises to tell us more about how lives are reformulated through (reproductive) biomedicine.

One of the men I interviewed who left a permanent impression on me because of his ordinariness in terms of being a sperm donor was Oscar. As became clear in the previous chapter, Oscar complies perfectly with the terms of being a sperm donor, since his only sexual activity consists of masturbating at the sperm bank, which he does three times a week. In addition, he does not engage in what could be defined as risk behavior, either sexually or in any other way, and thus lives his life according to what is expected of him as a good sperm donor. Oscar was in his thirties and had been a sperm donor for about two years when I met him. Single and without children, Oscar's life mainly revolves around work, physical training, and donating semen. Describing his lifestyle to me, he said:

> My lifestyle? Well, I don't know. I don't do much. I should probably do more than I do. Well, what do I do, what do I spend my time on. Well, I train a bit and then I donate once in a while and then I go to work, and I am also together with my family and friends. I guess pretty usual.—But do you have any hobbies?—No, not really. I train quite a bit and I ride my bike if the weather allows for it. But besides that I don't have any hobbies. If I didn't work that much I might have a hobby.

Oscar's life is predominantly organized around his work schedule and his commitment as a sperm donor. He stops by the sperm bank on his way to work—either Mondays, Wednesdays, and Fridays or Mondays, Thursdays, and Saturdays—and heads home from work just to have the same routine the following day. This way of life has become ordinary for him, Oscar's own normalcy. Reflecting about this circumstance, he said that he would probably try something new in a year or two since he had a tendency to fall into routines. Yet, besides having a daily life that enabled him to be a steady provider of semen, Oscar also took a moral vantage point from which donating semen is a good thing, since it helps people in need, and something that should not be motivated by financial needs and thus compared it to donating blood and being an organ donor:

> The first time I thought about this (donating semen) was when I was still a student. We were a bunch of guys who talked about it, you know, because you could earn some money. But I don't think that one should do it because of money. So, a few years back I thought about it again and speculated for about a year on whether to do it or not. And then I just thought: Okay, I'm just gonna do it.—What was the deciding factor this time around?—Well, I have asked myself the same thing and I think it's for the same reason that I am a blood and organ donor. It falls into the same category. I just think that this is a good thing to do. I mean, this is so easy for me to do, and if it can help someone then I think it is a good thing to do [*en fin ting at gøre*].

Throughout the interview, this moral reasoning on Oscar's behalf surfaced again and again with him positioning donating semen as something that one should do, if possible, since it helps other people, and that one should not do for financial reasons: "There shouldn't be too much money. I don't think people should do this because of money. It shouldn't be economically attractive. It's about ethics." This kind of moral reasoning about the goodness of sperm donation to the point of positioning it as a matter of ethics mirrors Danish sperm banks' preferred rhetoric of sperm donation as a good deed. Oscar has internalized this moral standpoint, positioning himself as part of a moral order in which he becomes recognizable as and identifies himself as a man who does good deeds. This kind of moral reasoning also extended to Oscar's decision to donate semen as a nonanonymous donor, which he committed himself to out of consideration for the well-being of donor-conceived individuals: "I am not anonymous because I thought that if I was a donor-child then I would like to have an opportunity to find out who I am. If you really want to know that but have no way of getting that (information), that must be frustrating. So, I think people have the right to know if they want to find out about it." In this all-encompassing sense, Oscar is the perfect sperm donor: he donates semen for the right reasons, he adheres to all the rules and provides semen samples three times a week, and he is concerned about the well-being of donor-conceived individuals. In other words, Oscar's life is that of a biosocial subject in the sense that he is biomedically available and biopolitically responsible. He lives biosociality.

At the same time, Oscar's life is also characterized by the inherent indeterminacy of biosocial subjectivation as I have explored it in the previous chapter. At different points in the interview with Oscar, it became clear that being a sperm donor for him also involved a continuous transgression of his personal boundaries, moments in which he felt ashamed or embarrassed, causing him to possibly rethink being a sperm donor. These moments included his uneasiness about masturbating at the sperm bank and handing over his semen samples to staff at the laboratory, his feeling of shame when having to undress during physical exams, and his embarrassment about being a sperm donor in regard to his family, friends, and acquaintances. More importantly, his story also pointed to the inherent unmaking of biosocial subjectivation through the performative effects of becoming a biosocial subject, namely, the dullness of being the perfect sperm donor. As became clear in the last chapter, Oscar's reflection about his sex life—"There is not a lot to say [laughing], it would be great if there was more to say, but there isn't"—marked a point of realization that, as Oscar himself termed it, "at some point something new has to happen." Complying perfectly as a sperm donor comes at a price: men's sense of self, their regimes of living, their affective investments, and their social relations are remade in terms of biosociality and thus can also, as in Oscar's case, become too normative to be enjoyable any longer. While the process of biosocial subjectivation as the enticing and alluring power of gender helps to make good sperm donors, it also potentially unmakes the biosocial subject.

The chapters of this book have explored this dynamic of biosocial subjectivation. Each one of them was dedicated to the nuances of becoming a biosocial subject by exploring men's experiences with being a sperm donor and donating semen in Denmark. In chapter 2, "Regimes of Living," Malthe's contemplations about keeping being a sperm donor a secret from his wife and children and regarding this decision as an act of care as a caring father and responsible husband opened the analysis of the process of biosocial subjectivation through an exploration of men's situated forms of moral reasoning. What emerged in this chapter was that sperm donors legitimate their partaking in sperm donation by assuming recognizable and acceptable positions within a gendered moral order. Remaking themselves as loving sons, caring fathers, and/or responsible husbands through the enticement of gender, men can justify being a sperm donor as a good deed, as something that is morally permissible. As such, becoming a biosocial subject as a sperm donor requires men to align their own moral convictions with public attitudes toward sperm donation and not least with the biopolitical objective of reproductive donation as a whole. Finding ways of living their lives ethically, sperm donors engage in intellectual reflections about what is good and what is not, and what they deem acceptable and what they do not deem acceptable. Assuming gendered subject positions such as the loving son, the caring father, and/or the responsible husband thus clearly is a reflective process of moral becoming in which being recognizable as part of a specific gendered moral order helps men to come to terms with being a sperm donor. Yet negotiating the moral permissibility of sperm donation and one's partaking in it is also a matter of feeling what is right to do. Sperm donors need not only to reflect on the rightness of things; they also need to embody becoming a sperm donor as a morally acceptable decision. To that end, the enticement of gender makes men claim positions as loving sons, caring fathers, and/or responsible husbands because it provides them with the experience of being good men. The enticement of gender makes biosocial subjects through the alluring power of normatively doing gender.

In chapter 3, "Affective Investments," it was Thommy's reflections on having to abstain from ejaculation for up to seventy-two hours before delivering a semen sample at the sperm bank and his characterization of this requirement as a challenge around which he would have to organize all of his other activities that was the starting point for an analysis of the process of biosocial subjectivation by attending to men's masturbatory practices at sperm banks and the affective investments that providing semen samples requires. The chapter highlighted that sperm donors' process of biosocial subjectivation involves men's masturbatory practices, since it is through them that sperm donors incorporate biomedical registers and biopolitical valuations into their ways of being a man. By being a sperm donor, men develop affective relations through masturbation to the norms of reproductive masculinity as they are enforced at sperm banks: providing high quality semen samples on demand for purposes of reproductive donation. Training themselves to provide semen samples, sperm donors are able to experience themselves in accordance with a normative ideal of masculinity as part of which high sperm counts and the ability to ejaculate right when needed constitute the normative boundaries of doing gender right. Through men's masturbatory routines, flows of affect are territorialized in such a way that men are able to provide semen samples on demand. They remake themselves as good sperm donors through the entice-ment of gender, since it is successful masturbation that reassures men that they have what it takes to be good sperm donors. A con-tinuous invocation of gender normativity as an enticing experience through masturbation makes men into sperm donors and thus also into biosocial subjects.

In chapter 4, "Biosocial Relatedness," Magnus's decision to do-nate semen as part of private arrangements with women whom he meets online, after having been a sperm donor at a sperm bank for many years, and his critique of sperm banks' business practices, which deny sperm donors the right to know how many children are conceived and born with the help of their semen, led to an analysis of biosocial subjectivation as a matter of relatedness by exploring sperm donors' ways of determining what responsibilities they have toward donor-conceived individuals, donor semen recipients, and not least their own families and loved ones. The chapter showed that this process, while also being about kinship, is more concerned with the question of what partaking in a particular mode of repro-duction—sperm donation and donor insemination—demands from sperm donors than with the question of who is kin to whom. As I argued, sperm donors' ways of honoring their connections to do-nor-conceived individuals and their ways of relating to donor semen recipients as well as protecting their own families and loved ones are an expression of biosocial relatedness. I understood biosocial relat-edness as particular kinds of responsibilities resulting from relating and being connected to other people through the use of reproduc-tive technologies. As such, biosocial relatedness as a particular way of relating to one another in a biomedical day and age is concerned with the uncertainties that arise when the mode of reproduction one partakes in creates connections between and modes of relating to people that do not necessarily have an established social script and therefore also do not have established norms for what respon-sibilities come with these connections and ways of relating. In this sense, biosocial relatedness is characterized by transilient and way-ward dynamics, that is, ways of relating and being connected to peo-ple that are not predetermined as to how they will come to matter in the future, even though they are similar to and simultaneously more than kinship relations. As I pointed out in the chapter, when navigating biosocial relatedness in this sense, sperm donors use the value ascribed to them as men with certain biomedical characteristics and biopolitical commitments as one way to determine what responsibilities they have. Another way is to rely on feeling that what they decide and what they do as sperm donors is right in a moral sense, or, put differently, they remake themselves into responsible men by assuming responsibilities as sperm donors. The enticement of gender thus makes sperm donors biosocial subjects by helping them to make sense of biosocial relatedness through the performativity of gender as responsibility.

In chapter 5, "The Limits of Biosocial Subjectivation," Alfred's considerations of being a sperm donor as something that makes him feel good about himself because it supports his male ego while also being a continuous source of concern, shame, and embarrassment in his daily life due to its boundary-breaking dynamics and its taboo status paved the way for an analysis of biosocial subjectivation as an always already incomplete and indeterminate process by delving into situations of male shame as sperm donors experience them. The chapter illustrated how situations of male shame are defined by transgressive experiences inherent to gender performativity and that they are unavoidable for sperm donors. Male shame makes sperm donors in the sense that it contributes to the disciplining of men to be good sperm donors by making them adhere to the rules and regulations in place at sperm banks. At the same time though, situations of male shame also contain the possibility of unmaking the sperm donor as a biosocial subject in that too much transgression can lead men to reconsider being a sperm donor. Biosocial subjectivation as the enticement of gender does not build on an original subject that is reformed through biosociality. Rather, biosocial subjectivation as the enticement of gender is performative in the sense that the subject itself is constantly being (re)made and finds its form in the (shifting) normative boundaries of sperm donor livelihood, and as such, the potential unmaking of the biosocial subject is always already contained in the process of biosocial subjectivation itself. Becoming sperm donors, men are (re)made as men in terms of biosocial registers and biopolitical valuations, and thus the performative effects of this process lead to new ways of identifying oneself and thereby also to new kinds of vulnerabilities. Situations of male shame actualize this dynamic of biosocial subjectivation as sperm donors undergo it, by making the frailty of the masculine self visible.

How the nuances of biosocial subjectivation, as they are explored in each of the preceding chapters, play out in sperm donors' lives is likely to depend on each man's life circumstances. As the reflections and contemplations of Danish sperm donors show, the personal experience of being a sperm donor is probably never one and the same for all men who donate semen. However, as the insights into the everyday lives of Danish sperm donors throughout this book also make clear, and as the earlier portrait of Oscar shows, being a sperm donor involves particular ways of moral reasoning, specific affective investments, and certain ways of connecting and relating to others that are shared by sperm donors across their different life circumstances. Whatever men's individual normative understandings of being a man might be, once they are sperm donors, they are enticed by gender to remake themselves as men in terms of biomedical registers and biopolitical valuations.

It is in this sense that the lives of sperm donors are epistemologically interesting, since they weave together the gendered and sexualed norms of the era of reproductive biomedicine as easily as they do. While sperm donors are certainly not the only ones whose lives are touched by reproductive biomedicine, and while their experiences are certainly different from the ones egg donors, infertile men, surrogates, or women undergoing IVF make, their lives are also typical of and simultaneously unique for sociality in a biomedical day and age in the sense that sperm donors donate semen on a regular basis for years at a time, two or three times a week, while being biomedically assessed and checked continuously, even after having stopped actively donating semen, without necessarily experiencing it as invasive or understanding it as a biotechnological intervention in their bodies, without being diagnosed and treated, and without risking their health. Sperm donors are men whose lives are ordinarily biosocial in that all aspects of their lives are reformulated through the normative logics of reproductive biomedicine, without men necessarily considering it problematic. They not only regard themselves as highly reproductive men; they also think of themselves as good men because of their commitment to reproduction as the ultimate moral deed. And they not only identify as men in this sense; they also embody this normativity in their ways of being a man.

As such, this book is certainly not about the kind of political activism and/or normative subversion that scholarship on biosociality often is concerned with. Sperm donors' process of biosocial subjectivation is not one of political critique or social upheaval. This book is not about the objectifying, commodifying, or subjugating dynamics of reproductive biomedicine that scholarship on the development, uses, and politics of reproductive technologies frequently attends to. The lives of sperm donors are not lives corrupted or violently changed by the intervention of reproductive biomedicine. Rather, this book is about the ordinariness of biosociality and about men's enjoyment of its performative dimensions made possible through sperm donation. The experiences of Danish sperm donors as represented in this book reflect how biosociality becomes a "a prime locus of identity" (Rabinow 1999: 13) through an enjoyment of its normative ideals as the enticement of gender.

In these terms, the insights into the lives of Danish sperm donors that this book provides are important if biosociality in its ordinariness is to be understood adequately. As the chapters of this book show, while being a sperm donor requires a lot of work from men, in that their everyday life is remade by becoming a sperm donor, and while that surely contains transgressive dynamics revealing men's vulnerable sides, biosocial normalcy is first and foremost (re)established through pleasurable experiences by creating affective relations to biosociality's normativity that allow for positive identifications as men. Biosocial subjectivation as the enticement of gender means the continuous lustful experiences of gender normativity, and it is in this way that biosociality becomes the new ordinary in sperm donors' lives. For an analytics of biosociality, this means following the self-evident sides of biosocial subjectivation and its interconnection with gender performativity, interrogating that which seems to give itself and which incites and entices. It is precisely attention to how a life in terms of biomedical registers and biopolitical valuations comes to be ordinary that promises to provide an understanding of how biosociality takes shape, and the interconnectedness of biosocial subjectivation and gender performativity is a central empirical and analytical object to study this process.

For an analytics of gender, the lives of Danish sperm donors highlight the importance of gender normativity as a lustful experience for the reproduction of gendered lifeworlds, while also pointing to the radical potential of (biosocial) normalcy's performative effects to undo those lifeworlds. The enjoyment of gender normativity is important for how men make their engagements as sperm donors meaningful. Gender thus provides a normative guideline for how they make decisions, while also being an affective relation in and through which men feel that what they do is right. This means that for sperm donors, the experience of being in sync with gender norms or doing gender right is a matter of positive self-identification, or put differently, sperm donors are men who simply like to be men. Living gender normativity—sperm donors' preferred ways of being a man—makes their lives as sperm donors enjoyable, no matter the regulative and controlling dimensions that being a sperm donor involves.

Yet while the lives of Danish sperm donors are particular, the enticement of gender in this sense is not. Rather, the enticement of gender can also be understood as making gender effective as a category of social differentiation, or, in other words, the differentiating effects of gender are bound to the enjoyment of gender normativity insofar as doing gender right (in whatever normative sense) provides pleasure and satisfaction for some while installing a sense of failure and domination in others. If gender is to be taken seriously in this sense, wanting to change the differentiating effects of gender as they persist today would require changing how people relate to gender. It would require people to learn to be affected in such a way that forms of gender normativity that do not produce differentiating effects (or that produce fewer of them) are enticing for them. And as the lives of Danish sperm donors show, this process will probably be most effective if a new normalcy can constitute itself through positive experiences of gender normativity.

At the same time, however, the lives of sperm donors are also witness to the fundamental radical potential of biosocial normalcy. As especially the previous chapter on the limits of biosocial subjectivation shows, being a sperm donor contains transgressive experiences that open the possibility for a different kind of future. The situations of male shame that sperm donors experience are not only instances in which they might reconsider being a sperm donor. They are potentially also instances in which men reflect on their preferred ways of being a man, their enjoyment of gender normativity, and, not least, the production of gender normativity in their own lives through what they do. In addition, the ordinariness of being a sperm donor has performative effects in and by itself that create new sensibilities and new vulnerabilities that open up for different relations to gender. While sperm donors might experience a boost in masculinity through successful masturbation and high sperm counts, they are also vulnerable when they cannot get an erection or when their samples do not pass quality assessments. And being vulnerable in this way might make men reconsider the normative ideals of masculinity that they aspire to as sperm donors. In this sense, (biosocial) normalcy holds the promise of undoing gender as we know it.

For an analytics of kinship and relatedness in a biomedical day and age, the lives of sperm donors hold the promise to unburden sociological and anthropological analysis of kinship and relatedness of its embeddedness in its own normative dimensions. While the lives of Danish sperm donors are certainly about kinship—providing semen for the conception of children in a cultural context that defines one's relations to these children as kinship, while oneself and the organizational context one finds oneself in does not, undoubtedly forces one to consider kinship—they are also not about kinship in the sense that men who donate semen have responsibilities as sperm donors. Their participation in sperm donation connects them and makes them relate to people in a way that is more about the moral and social challenges of relating and being connected to people through the use of reproductive technologies than about the social and moral dimensions of kinship. Reproductive technologies are generative in their own way by connecting people and relating them to one another through a particular mode of establishing connections and relating people to one another. They connect people without necessarily being about kinship, and they thus also produce other kinds of sociality than kinship. Thinking biosociality in this sense promises to help see and analytically cross ethnography's normative boundaries when attending to kinship and relatedness.

If one is interested in more practical questions in regard to working with sperm donors or organizing a sperm donation program, the lives of Danish sperm donors point to the necessity of considering the effects that becoming a sperm donor has and to be aware of the consequences of living a life as part of which thinking of oneself in terms of biomedical registers and biopolitical valuations has become normal. Being a sperm donor is about more than simply delivering a semen sample once or twice a week. It is a process of moral and gendered becoming. Sperm donors not only decide whether they can morally justify being a sperm donor or not. They remake themselves as men and therewith also their social and relational lives. Decisions about consent and anonymity are thus not only one-time questions or questions that only regard the sperm donors themselves. They are questions that men might have changing attitudes toward the longer they are sperm donors, and questions that might impact how they engage with loved ones, families, friends, and colleagues. Being a sperm donor is not only a matter of being motivated by monetary incentives or wanting to help people. It is a matter of taking a stand on the question of what is deemed a legitimate way of conceiving children.

Taking the lives of sperm donors seriously in this sense would demand integration of the ongoing reflective process of being a sperm donor and thus the making of moral and gendered selves into the organizational logic of sperm donation programs. Practically speaking, this could, for example, take the form of consent procedures that integrate men's possibly changing attitudes toward the moral permissibility of sperm donation. It could also mean that sperm donors are actively involved in a reflective process about the implications of donating semen through the sperm donation program they are part of. Here sperm banks could, for example, consider donors' own concerns about what happens with their semen, their thoughts about who uses their samples and how many children are born by means of them, and their contemplations about and possible reservations about donor insemination. Last, but not least, integrating men's process of moral and gendered becoming into the organization of sperm donation programs could also mean conducting the program in light of men's possible sexual inhibitions and gender role concerns. While situations of male shame certainly help to discipline men to be good sperm donors, enticement rather than transgression promises to make for more pleasant experiences as a sperm donor.

The process of biosocial subjectivation as the enticement of gender as I have explored it throughout this book is primarily an account of the lives of Danish sperm donors. However, since Danish sperm donors are a group of men whose lives are remade through the generative force of reproductive biomedicine, their experiences also reflect how masculinity and male sexuality take shape in terms of biosociality. Danish sperm donors and their experiences make us understand how reproductive biomedicine takes hold in men's lives, how men come to think of themselves in terms of biomedical registers and biopolitical valuations. When men become sperm donors, reproductive biomedicine's generative force interweaves with their lives and their ways of being a man with a profound perplexing subtlety, so subtle that when asked directly in interviews whether their life changed after becoming a sperm donor, men would outright dismiss any kind of impact of being a sperm donor on their life and self-perception. It is through this subtlety in which sperm donation, as a particular part of reproductive biomedicine, makes its way into the lives and bodies of men that fascinates me. As an ethnographer,

I am intrigued by the extraordinary; but I am even more intrigued by what goes unnoticed because it seems so mundane and ordinary, and the analysis of biosocial subjectivation as the enticement of gender put forward in this book is meant to provide an insight into how profound the mundane and ordinary can be.

BIBLIOGRAPHY

Adrian, Stine. 2006. "Nye skabelsesberetninger om æg, sæd og embryoner. Et etnografisk studie af skabelser på sædbanker og fertilitetsklinikker." Linköpings Universitet, Filosofiska Fakulteten.

———. 2010. "Sperm Stories: Policies and Practices of Sperm Banking in Denmark and Sweden." *European Journal of Women's Studies* 17, no. 4: 393–411.

———. 2015. "Psychological IVF: Conceptualizing Emotional Choreography in a Fertility Clinic." *Distinktion: Journal of Social Theory* 16, no. 3: 302–317.

Ahmed, Sara. 2012. *The Cultural Politics of Emotion.* New York: Routledge.

———. 2014. *Willful Subjects.* Durham: Duke University Press.

Alldred, Pam, and Nick J Fox. 2015. "The Sexuality-Assemblages of Young Men: A New Materialist Analysis." *Sexualities* 18, no. 8: 905–920.

Almeling, Rene. 2006. "'Why Do You Want to Be a Donor?': Gender and the Production of Altruism in Egg and Sperm Donation." *New Genetics and Society* 25, no. 2: 143–157.

———. 2007. "Selling Genes, Selling Gender: Egg Agencies, Sperm Banks, and the Medical Market in Genetic Material." *American Sociological Review* 72, no. 3: 319–340.

———. 2009. "Gender and the Value of Bodily Goods: Commodification in Egg and Sperm Donation." *Law and Contemporary Problems* 72, no. 3: 37–58.

———. 2011. *Sex Cells: The Medical Market for Eggs and Sperm.* Berkeley: University of California Press.

Bain, Alison L., and Catherine J. Nash. 2006. "Undressing the Researcher: Feminism, Embodiment and Sexuality at a Queer Bathhouse Event." *Area* 38, no. 1: 99–106.

Barney, Sandra. 2005. "Accessing Medicalized Donor Sperm in the US and Britain: An Historical Narrative." *Sexualities* 8, no. 2: 205–220.

Bataille, Georges. 1986. *Erotism: Death and Sensuality.* San Francisco: City Lights Books.

Baumeister-Frenzel, Katja, Michi Knecht, Markus Langenstrass, and Matthias Schöbe. 2010. "Gespräche mit Spendern." In *Samenbanken—Samenspender: ethnographische und historische Perspektiven auf Männlichkeiten in der Reproduktionsmedizin,* ed. Michi Knecht, Anna Frederike Heinitz, Scout Burghardt, and Sebastian Mohr, 81–112. Berlin: Lit Verlag.

Bay, Björn, Peter B. Larsen, Ulrik Schiøler Kesmodel, and Hans Jakob Ingerslev. 2014. "Danish Sperm Donors Across Three Decades: Motivations and Attitudes." *Fertility and Sterility* 101, no. 1: 252–257.

Beauvoir, Simone de. 1972. *The Second Sex.* Harmondsworth: Penguin.

Bell, Ann V. 2016. "'I Don't Consider a Cup Performance; I Consider It a Test': Masculinity and the Medicalisation of Infertility." *Sociology of Health & Illness* 38, no. 5: 706–720.

Birch, Kean, and David Tyfield. 2012. "Theorizing the Bioeconomy: Biovalue, Biocapital, Bioeconomics or . . . What?" *Science, Technology & Human Values* 38, no. 3: 229–327.

Birenbaum-Carmeli, Daphna, and Marcia C. Inhorn. 2009. "Masculinity and Marginality: Palestinian Men's Struggles with Infertility in Israel and Lebanon." *Journal of Middle East Women's Studies* 5, no. 2: 23–52.

Bolton, Ralph. 1998. "Mapping Terra Incognita: Sex Research for AIDS Prevention—An Urgent Agenda for the 1990s." In *Culture, Society and Sexuality. A Reader,* ed. Richard Parker, 434–456. London: Routledege.

Bourdieu, Pierre. 1990. *The Logic of Practice.* Stanford: Standford University Press.

———. 2001. *Masculine Domination.* Cambridge: Polity.

Brubaker, Sarah Jane, and Heather E. Dillaway. 2009. "Medicalization, Natural Childbirth and Birthing Experiences." *Sociology Compass* 3, no. 1: 31–48.

Bubandt, Nils, and Rane Willerslev. 2015. "The Dark Side of Empathy: Mimesis, Deception, and the Magic of Alterity." *Comparative Studies in Society and History* 57, no. 1: 5–34.

Burghardt, Scout, and Kerstin Tote. 2010. "Zwischen Risikovermeidung, Normalisierung und Markt. Spenderauswahl und matching in Samenbanken." In *Samenbanken—Samenspender: ethnographische und historische Perspektiven auf Männlichkeiten in der Reproduktionsmedizin,* ed. Michi Knecht, Anna Frederike Heinitz, Scout Burghardt, and Sebastian Mohr, 142–162. Berlin: Lit Verlag.

Butler, Judith. 1986. "Sex and Gender in Simone de Beauvoir's Second Sex." *Yale French Studies* 72: 35–49.

———. 1990. *Gender Trouble: Feminism and the Subversion of Identity.* New York: Routledge.

———. 1993. *Bodies That Matter: On the Discursive Limits of Sex.* New York: Routledge.

———. 2004. *Undoing Gender.* New York: Routledge.

———. 2015. *Senses of the Subject.* New York: Fordham University Press.

Calhaz-Jorge, C., C. De Geyter, M. S. Kupka, J. de Mouzon, K. Erb, E. Mocanu, T. Motrenko, G. Scaravelli, C. Wyns, and V. Goossens. 2017. "Assisted Reproductive Technology in Europe, 2013: Results Generated from European Registers by ESHRE." *Human Reproduction* 32, no. 10: 1957–1973.

Carrigan, Tim, Bob Connell, and John Lee. 1985. "Toward a New Sociology of Masculinity." *Theory and Society* 14, no. 5: 551–604.

Carsten, Janet. 1995. "The Substance of Kinship and the Heat of the Hearth: Feeding, Personhood, and Relatedness Among Malays in Pulau Langkawi." *American Ethnologist* 22, no. 2: 223–241.

———. 2004. *After Kinship.* Cambridge: Cambridge University Press.

———, ed. 2000. *Cultures of Relatedness: New Approaches to the Study of Kinship.* Cambridge: Cambridge University Press.

Clarke, Adele E., and Virginia L. Olesen. 1999. "Revising, Diffracting, Acting." In *Revisioning Women, Health, and Healing: Feminist, Cultural, and Technoscience Perspectives,* ed. Adele E. Clarke and Virginia L. Olesen, 3–48. New York: Routledge.

Clarke, Adele E., Janet K. Shim, Laura Mamo, Jennifer Ruth Fosket, and Jennifer R. Fishman. 2003. "Biomedicalization: Technoscientific Transformations of Health, Illness, and U.S. Biomedicine." *American Sociological Review* 68, no. 2: 161–194.

Clarke, Adele E., Laura Mamo, Ruth Jennifer Fosket, Jennifer Fishman, and Janet K. Shim, eds. 2010. *Biomedicalization: Technoscience, Health, and Illness in the U.S.* Durham: Duke University Press.

Classen, Constance, and David Howes. 1996. "Making Sense of Culture: Anthropology as a Sensual Experience." *Etnofoor* 9, no. 2: 86–96.

Coffey, Amanda. 1999. *The Ethnographic Self: Fieldwork and the Representation of Identity.* London: Sage.

Cohen, Carl I. 1993. "The Biomedicalization of Psychiatry: A Critical Overview." *Community Mental Health Journal* 29, no. 6: 509–521.

Collier, Stephen J., and Andrew Lakoff. 2005. "On Regimes of Living." In *Global Assemblages: Technology, Politics, and Ethics as Anthropological Problems,* ed. Aihwa Ong and Stephen J. Collier, 22–39. Malden: Blackwell.

Connell, Raewyn W. 1985. "Theorising Gender." *Sociology* 19, no. 2: 260–272.

———. 1987. *Gender and Power: Society, the Person and Sexual Politics.* Cambridge: Polity Press.

———. 1995. *Masculinities.* Cambridge: Polity Press.

———. 2009. *Gender: In World Perspective.* Cambridge: Polity Press.

Connell, Raewyn W., and James W. Messerschmidt. 2005. "Hegemonic Masculinity: Rethinking the Concept." *Gender and Society* 19, no. 6: 829–859.

Conrad, Peter. 1975. "The Discovery of Hyperkinesis: Notes on the Medicalization of Deviant Behavior." *Social Problems* 23, no. 1: 12–21.

———. 1992. "Medicalization and Social Control." *Annual Review of Sociology* 18, no. 1: 209–232.

———. 2007. *The Medicalization of Society: On the Transformation of Human Conditions into Treatable Disorders.* Baltimore: The Johns Hopkins University Press.

Daniels, Cynthia R. 1997. "Between Fathers and Fetuses: The Social Construction of Male Reproduction and the Politics of Fetal Harm." *Signs* 22, no. 3: 579–616.

———. 2006. *Exposing Men: The Science and Politics of Male Reproduction.* Oxford: Oxford University Press.

Daniels, Cynthia R., and Janet Golden. 2004. "Procreative Compounds: Popular Eugenics, Artificial Insemination and the Rise of the American Sperm Banking Industry." *Journal of Social History* 38, no. 1: 5–27.

Daniels, Cynthia R., and Erin Heidt-Forsythe. 2012. "Gendered Eugenics and the Problematic of Free Market Reproductive Technologies: Sperm and Egg Donation in the United States." *Signs* 37, no. 3: 719–747.

Daniels, Ken R., and D.J. Hall. 1997. "Semen Donor Recruitment Strategies—A Non-Payment Based Approach." *Human Reproduction* 12, no. 10: 2330–2335.

Deleuze, Gilles, and Félix Guattari. 2013. *Anti-Oedipus: Capitalism and Schizophrenia.* London: Bloomsbury Academic.

Detamore, Mathias. 2010. "Queer(y)ing the Ethics of Research Methods: Towards a Politics of Intimacy in Researcher/Researched Relations." In *Queer Methods and Methodologies. Intersecting Queer Theories and Social Science Research,* ed. Kath Browne and Catherine J. Nash, 167–182. Farnham: Ashgate.

Donnan, Hastings, and Fiona Magowan. 2009. "Sexual Transgression, Social Order and the Self." In *Transgressive Sex: Subversion and Control in Erotic Encounters,* ed. Hastings Donnan and Fiona Magowan, 1–24. New York: Berghahn Books.

Earp, Brian D., Anders Sandberg, and Julian Savulescu. 2015. "The Medicalization of Love." *Cambridge Quarterly of Healthcare Ethics* 24, no. 3: 323–336.

Edelman, Lee. 2004. *No Future: Queer Theory and the Death Drive.* Durham: Duke University Press.

Edwards, Jeanette, Sarah Franklin, Eric Hirsch, Frances Price, and Marilyn Strathern, eds. 1993. *Technologies of Procreation. Kinship in the Age of Assisted Reproduction.* Manchester: Manchester University Press.

Ellingson, Laura L. 2006. "Embodied Knowledge: Writing Researchers' Bodies Into Qualitative Health Research." *Qualitative Health Research* 16, no. 2: 298–310.

Estes, Carroll L., and Elizabeth A. Binney. 1989. "The Biomedicalization of Aging: Dangers and Dilemmas." *The Gerontologist* 29, no. 5: 587–596.

Fertilitetsselskab, Dansk. 2017. Årsrapport 2016. København: Dansk Fertilitetsselskab.

Finkler, Kaja. 2000. *Experiencing the New Genetics: Family and Kinship on the Medical Frontier.* Philadelphia: University of Pennsylvania Press.

———. 2001. "The Kin in the Gene: The Medicalization of Family and Kinship in American Society." *Current Anthropology* 42, no. 2: 235–263.

Flower, Michael J., and Deborah Heath. 1993. "Micro-Anatomo Politics: Mapping the Human Genome Project." *Culture, Medicine and Psychiatry* 17, no. 1: 27–41.

Foucault, Michel. 1990. *The History of Sexuality. Volume 1: An Introduction.* New York: Vintage Books.

Fox, Nick J., and Pam Alldred. 2013. "The Sexuality-Assemblage: Desire, Affect, Anti-Humanism." *The Sociological Review* 61, no. 4: 769–789.

Franklin, Sarah. 1997. *Embodied Progress: A Cultural Account of Assisted Conception.* New York: Routledge.

———. 2013. *Biological Relatives: IVF, Stem Cells, and the Future of Kinship.* Durham: Duke University Press.

Franklin, Sarah, and Maureen McNeil. 1988. "Reproductive Futures: Recent Literature and Current Feminist Debates on Reproductive Technologies." *Feminist Studies* 14, no. 3: 545–560.

French, Shaun, and James Kneale. 2012. "Speculating on Careless Lives." *Journal of Cultural Economy* 5, no. 4: 391–406.

Garlick, Steve. 2014. "The Biopolitics of Masturbation: Masculinity, Complexity, and Security." *Body & Society* 20, no. 2: 44–67.

Geertz, Clifford. 2000. *The Interpretation of Cultures.* New York: Basic Books.

Germon, Jennifer. 2009. *Gender: A Genealogy of an Idea.* New York: Palgrave Macmillan.

Gibbon, Sahra. 2007. *Breast Cancer Genes and the Gendering of Knowledge: Science and Citizenship in the Cultural Context of the "New" Genetics.* New York: Palgrave.

Gibbon, Sahra, and Carlos Novas, eds. 2008. *Biosocialities, Genetics and the Social Sciences: Making Biologies and Identities.* New York: Routledge.

Gilcher-Holey, Ingrid. 2004. "Modelle, moderner' Weiblichkeit. Diskussionen im akademischen Milieu Heidelbergs um 1900." In *Marianne Weber. Beiträge zu Werk und Person,* ed. Bärbel Meurer, 29–58. Tübingen: Mohr Siebeck.

Goldberg, Helene. 2009. "The Sex in the Sperm: Male Infertility and Its Challenges to Masculinity in an Israeli-Jewish Context." In *Reconceiving the Second Sex: Men, Masculinity, and Reproduction,* ed. Marcia C. Inhorn, Tine Tjørnhøj-Thomsen, Helene Goldberg, and Maruska la Cour Mosegaard, 203–225. New York, Oxford: Berghahn Books.

———. 2010. "The Man in the Sperm: Kinship and Fatherhood in Light of Male Infertility in Israel." In *Kin, Gene, Community: Reproductive Technologies Among Jewish Israelis,* ed. Daphna Birenbaum-Carmeli and Yoram S. Carmeli, 84–106. New York: Berghahn.

Goldie, Terry. 2014. *The Man Who Invented Gender: Engaging the Ideas of John Money.* Vancouver: UBC Press.

Graham, Susanna. 2012. "Choosing Single Motherhood? Single Women Negotiating the Nuclear Family Ideal." In *Families—Beyond the Nuclear Ideal,* ed. Daniel Cutas and Sarah Chan, 97–109. London: Bloomsbury Academic.

Graham, Susanna, Sebastian Mohr, and Kate Bourne. 2016. "Regulating the 'Good' Donor: The Expectations and Experiences of Sperm Donors in Denmark and Victoria, Australia." In *Regulating Reproductive Donation,* ed. Susan Golombok, Rosamund Scott, John B. Appleby, Martin Richards, and Stephen Wilkinson, 207–231. Cambridge: Cambridge University Press.

Hall, Lesley A. 1992. "Forbidden by God, Despised by Men: Masturbation, Medical Warnings, Moral Panic, and Manhood in Great Britain, 1850–1950." *Journal of the History of Sexuality* 2, no. 3: 365–387.

Hammarberg, Karin, Louise Johnson, Kate Bourne, Jane Fisher, and Maggie Kirkman. 2014. "Proposed Legislative Change Mandating Retrospective Release of Identifying Information: Consultation with Donors and Government Response." *Human Reproduction* 29, no. 2: 286–292.

Han, Clara, and Veena Das. 2015. "Introduction: A Concept Note." In *Living and Dying in the Contemporary World,* ed. Clara Han and Veena Das, 1–37. Oakland: University of California Press.

Haraway, Donna. 1988. "Situated Knowledges: The Science Question in Feminism and the Privilege of Partial Perspective." *Feminist Studies* 14, no. 3: 575–599.

———. 1991. *Simians, Cyborgs, and Women: The Reinvention of Nature.* London: Free Association Books.

Hearn, Jeff. 2014. "Sexualities, Organizations and Organization Sexualities: Future Scenarios and the Impact of Socio-Technologies (a Transnational Perspective from the Global 'North')." *Organization* 21, no. 3: 400–420.

Heath, Deborah, Rayna Rapp, and Karen-Sue Taussig. 2004. "Genetic Citizenship." In *A Companion to the Anthropology of Politics,* ed. David Nugent and Joan Vincent, 152–167. Malden: Blackwell.

Heinitz, Anna Frederike, and Rickmer Roscher. 2010. "The Making of German Sperm. Überlegungen zum Zusammenhang von Spermakonsivierung, Männlichkeiten und Nationalsozialismus." In *Samenbanken—Samenspender. Ethnographische und historische Perspektiven auf Männlichkeiten in der Reproduktionsmedizin,* ed. Michi Knecht, Anna Frederike Heinitz, Scout Burghardt, and Sebastian Mohr, 29–67. Münster, Berlin: Lit Verlag.

Hoeyer, Klaus. 2007. "Person, Patent and Property: A Critique of the Commodification Hypothesis." *BioSocieties* 2, no. 3: 327–348.

———. 2009. "Tradable Body Parts? How Bone and Recycled Prosthetic Devices Acquire a Price Without Forming a 'Market'." *BioSocieties* 4, no. 2–3: 239–256.

———. 2010. "An Anthropological Analysis of European Union (EU) Health Governance as Biopolitics: The Case of the EU Cells and Tissue Directive." *Social Science & Medicine* 70, no. 12: 1867–1873.

———. 2013. *Exchanging Human Bodily Material: Rethinking Bodies and Markets.* Dordrecht: Springer.

Holy, Ladislav. 1996. *Anthropological Perspectives on Kinship.* Chicago: Pluto Press.

Howes, David. 2003. *Sensual Relations: Engaging the Senses in Culture and Social Theory.* Ann Arbor: University of Michigan Press.

Ingold, Tim, and Gisli Palsson, eds. 2013. *Biosocial Becomings: Integrating Social and Biological Anthropology.* Cambridge: Cambridge University Press.

Inhorn, Marcia C. 1996. *Infertility and Patriarchy: The Cultural Politics of Gender and Family Life in Egypt.* Philadelphia: University of Pennsylvania Press.

————. 2006. "'He Won't Be My Son': Middle Eastern Men's Discourses of Adoption and Gamete Donation." *Medical Anthropology Quarterly* 20, no. 1: 94–120.

————. 2012. *The New Arab Man: Emergent Masculinities, Technologies, and Islam in the Middle East.* Princeton: Princeton University Press.

Inhorn, Marcia C., Tine Tjørnhøj-Thomsen, Helene Goldberg, and Maruska la Cour Mosegaard, eds. 2009. *Reconceiving the Second Sex. Men, Masculinity, and Reproduction.* New York, Oxford: Berghahn Books.

Jasanoff, Sheila, ed. 2011. *Reframing Rights: Bioconstitutionalism in the Genetic Age.* Cambridge: MIT Press.

Justitsministeriet. 1953. Betænkning om en sælrig lovgivning om kunstig befrugtning. København.

Jørgensen, Niels, Ulla Nordström Joensen, Tina Kold Jensen, Martin Blomberg Jensen, Kristian Almstrup, Inge Ahlmann Olesen, Anders Juul, Anna Maria Andersson, Elisabeth Carlsen, Jørgen Holm Petersen, Jorma Toppari, and Niels E. Skakkebæk. 2012. "Human Semen Quality in the New Millennium: A Prospective Cross-Sectional Population-Based Study of 4867 Men." *BMJ Open* 2, no. 4: e000990.

Kampf, Antje. 2013. "Tales of Healthy Men: Male Reproductive Bodies in Biomedicine from 'Lebensborn' to Sperm Banks." *Health:* 17, no. 1: 20–36.

Kirkman, Maggie. 2004. "Saviours and Satyrs: Ambivalence in Narrative Meanings of Sperm Provision." *Culture, Health & Sexuality* 6, no. 4: 319–334.

Kirkman, Maggie, Kate Bourne, Jane Fisher, Louise Johnson, and Karin Hammarberg. 2014. "Gamete Donors' Expectations and Experiences of Contact with Their Donor Offspring." *Human Reproduction* 29, no. 4: 731–738.

Klotz, Maren. 2014. *[K]information: Gamete Donation and Kinship Knowledge in Germany and Britain.* Frankfurt: Campus.

————. 2016. "Wayward Relations: Novel Searches of the Donor-Conceived for Genetic Kinship." *Medical Anthropology* 35, no. 1: 45–57.

Klotz, Maren, and Sebastian Mohr. 2015. "(Un-)Geordnete Verhältnisse: mediale Repräsentationen und Praktiken von Samenspende." *Kulturen. Zeitschrift für Kulturwissenschaften* 19, no. 2: 53–68.

Knecht, Michi, Anna Frederike Heinitz, Scout Burghardt, and Sebastian Mohr, eds. 2010. *Samenbanken—Samenspender. Ethnographische und historische Perspektiven auf Männlichkeiten in der Reproduktionsmedizin, Berliner Blätter. Ethnograpische und ethnologische Beiträge.* Münster, Berlin: Lit Verlag.

Koch, Lene. 1989. Ønskebørn: kvinder of reagensglasbefrugtning. Charlottenlund: Rosinante.

Koch, Lene, and Janine Morgall. 1987. "Towards a Feminist Assessment of Reproductive Technology." *Acta Sociologica* 30, no. 2: 173–191.

Konrad, Monica. 2005. *Nameless Relations: Anonymity, Melanesia and Reproductive Gift Exchange Between British Ova Donors and Recipients.* New York: Berghahn Books.

Kristiansen, Ingvill. 2009. "Managing Sexual Advances in Vanuatu." In *Transgressive Sex: Subversion and Control in Erotic Encounters*, ed. Hastings Donnan and Fiona Magowan, 235–252. New York: Berghahn.

Kroløkke, Charlotte. 2009. "Click a Donor: Viking Masculinity on the Line." *Journal of Consumer Culture* 9, no. 1: 7–30.

Kulick, Don, and Margaret Willson, eds. 1995. *Taboo: Sex, Identity and Erotic Subjectivity in Anthropological Fieldwork.* Routledge: New York.

Laqueur, Thomas Walter. 2003. *Solitary Sex: A Cultural History of Masturbation.* New York: Zone Books.

Larsen, Lars Thorup. 2015. "The Problematization of Fertility Treatment: Biopolitics and IVF Policy in Denmark." *Distinktion: Journal of Social Theory* 16, no. 3: 318–336.

Latour, Bruno. 1993. *We Have Never Been Modern.* Cambridge: Harvard University Press.

Layne, Linda L. 2013. "'Creepy,' 'Freaky,' and 'Strange': How the 'Uncanny' Can Illuminate the Experience of Single Mothers by Choice and Lesbian Couples Who Buy 'Dad'." *Journal of Consumer Culture* 13, no. 2: 140–159.

Lewin, Ellen, and William Leap, eds. 1996. *Out in the Field: Reflections of Lesbian and Gay Anthropologists.* Urbana: University of Illinois Press.

Mamo, Laura. 2005. "Biomedicalizing Kinship: Sperm Banks and the Creation of Affinity-Ties." *Science as Culture* 14, no. 3: 237–264.

———. 2007. *Queering Reproduction: Achieving Pregnancy in the Age of Technoscience.* Durham: Duke University Press.

Martin, Emily. 2001. *The Woman in the Body. A Cultural Analysis of Reproduction.* Boston: Beacon Press.

Medrano, Jose V., Ana M. Martínez-Arroyo, Jose M. Míguez, Inmaculada Moreno, Sebastián Martínez, Alicia Quiñonero, Patricia Díaz-Gimeno, Ana I. Marqués-Marí, Antonio Pellicer, Jose Remohí, and Carlos Simón. 2016. "Human Somatic Cells Subjected to Genetic Induction with Six Germ Line-Related Factors Display Meiotic Germ Cell-Like Features." *Scientific Reports* 6: 24956.

Meloni, Maurizio, Simon Williams, and Paul Martin. 2016. "The Biosocial: Sociological Themes and Issues." *The Sociological Review Monographs* 64, no. 1: 7–25.

Mohr, Sebastian. 2010. "What Does One Wear to a Sperm Bank? Negotiations of Sexuality in Sperm Donation." *kuckuck. notizen zur alltagskultur* 25, no. 2: 36–42.

———. 2013. "Ordnede forhold. Sæddonorer og sæddonation i danske medier." *Kritik* 209: 72–83.

———. 2014. "Beyond Motivation: On What It Means to Be a Sperm Donor in Denmark." *Anthropology & Medicine* 21, no. 2: 162–173.

———. 2015. "Living Kinship Trouble: Danish Sperm Donors' Narratives of Relatedness." *Medical Anthropology* 34, no. 5: 470–484.

———. 2016a. "Containing Sperm—Managing Legitimacy: Lust, Disgust, and Hybridity at Danish Sperm Banks." *Journal of Contemporary Ethnography* 45, no. 3: 319–342.

———. 2016b. "Donating Semen in Denmark." In *The Routledge Handbook of Medical Anthropology*, ed. Lenore Manderson, Elizabeth Cartwright and Anita Hardon, 63–67. New York: Routledge.

———. 2018. "When Bodies Talk—Indulging Ethnography." In *Sex: Ethnographic Encounters*, ed. Richard Martin and Dieter Haller, 15–25. New York: Bloomsbury.

Mohr, Sebastian, and Klaus Høyer. 2012. "Den gode sædcelle. . . En antropologisk analyse af arbejdet med sædkvalitet." *Kultur og klasse* 40, no. 113: 45–61.

Mohr, Sebastian, and Lene Koch. 2016. "Transforming Social Contracts: The Social and Cultural History of IVF in Denmark." *Reproductive Biomedicine & Society Online* 2: 88–96.

Mohr, Sebastian, and Andrea Vetter. 2014. "Körpererfahrung in der Feldforschung." In *Methoden der Kulturanthropologie*, ed. Christine Bischoff, Walter Leimgruber, and Karoline Oehme-Jüngling, 101–116. Bern: Haupt.

Mohr, Sebastian, and Andrea Vetter. 2017. "Eindringliche Begegnungen: von körperlichem Erleben und Feldforschung." In *Kulturen der Sinne: Zugänge zur Sensualität der sozialen Welt*, ed. Karl Braun, Claus-Marco Dietrich, Thomas Hengartner, and Bernhard Tschofen, 191–198. Würzburg: Königshausen & Neumann.

Moore, Lisa Jean. 2008. *Sperm Counts: Overcome by Man's Most Precious Fluid*. New York, London: New York University Press.

Moore, Lisa Jean, and Matthew A. Schmidt. 1999. "On the Construction of Male Differences: Marketing Variations in Technosemen." *Men and Masculinities* 1, no. 4: 331–351.

Moore, Lisa Jean, and Heidi Durkin. 2006. "The Leaky Male Body: Forensics and the Construction of the Sexual Suspect." In *Medicalized Masculinities*, ed. Dana Rosenfeld and Christoper A. Faircloth, 65–88. Philadelphia: Temple University Press.

Nelson, Margaret K., Rosanna Hertz, and Wendy Kramer. 2016. "Gamete Donor Anonymity and Limits on Numbers of Offspring: The Views of Three Stakeholders." *Journal of Law and the Biosciences* 3, no. 1: 39–67.

Newton, Esther. 1993. "My Best Informant's Dress: The Erotic Equation in Fieldwork." *Cultural Anthropology* 8, no. 1: 3–23.

Nordqvist, Petra. 2013. "Bringing Kinship into Being: Connectedness, Donor Conception and Lesbian Parenthood." *Sociology* 48, no. 2: 268–283.

Novas, Carlos, and Nikolas Rose. 2000. "Genetic Risk and the Birth of the Somatic Individual." *Economy and Society* 29, no. 4: 485–513.

Okely, Judith. 2007. "Fieldwork Embodied." *The Sociological Review* 55, no. 65–79.

Ombelet, Willem, and Johan van Robays. 2010. "History of Human Artificial Insemination." In *Artificial Insemination: An Update*, ed. Willem Ombelet and Herman Tournaye, 1–5. Wetteren: Universa Press.

Ortner, Sherry B. 1972. "Is Female to Male as Nature Is to Culture?" *Feminist Studies* 1, no. 2: 5–31.

Palsson, Gisli. 2012. "Decode Me! Anthropology and Personal Genomics." *Current Anthropology* 53, no. S5: S185–S195.

Pálsson, Gísli, and Kristín HarÐardóttir. 2002. "For Whom the Cell Tolls: Debates About Biomedicine." *Current Anthropology* 43, no. 2: 271–301.

Petersen, Margit Anne, Lotte Stig Nørgaard, and Janine M. Traulsen. 2015. "Pursuing Pleasures of Productivity: University Students' Use of Prescription Stimulants for Enhancement and the Moral Uncertainty of Making Work Fun." *Culture, Medicine, and Psychiatry* 39, no. 4: 665–679.

Petersen, Michael Nebeling. 2013. "To Belong to the Living—om queer slægtskab og reproduktiv futurisme." *Kvinder, Køn og Forskning* 2013, no. 1: 10–24.

Petryna, Adriana. 2002. *Life Exposed: Biological Citizens after Chernobyl.* Princeton: Princeton University Press.

———. 2004. "Biological Citizenship: The Science and Politics of Chernobyl-Exposed Populations." *Osiris* 19: 250–265.

Pink, Sarah. 2009. *Doing Sensory Ethnography.* London: Sage.

Proff.dk. 2017. "Regnskabstal 2016." https://www.proff.dk/.

Präg, Patrick, and Melinda C. Mills. 2017. "Assisted Reproductive Technology in Europe: Usage and Regulation in the Context of Cross-Border Reproductive Care." In *Childlessness in Europe: Contexts, Causes, and Consequences,* ed. Michaela Kreyenfeld and Dirk Konietzka, 289–309. Cham: Springer International Publishing.

Rabinow, Paul. 1994. "The Third Culture." *History of the Human Sciences* 7, no. 2: 53–64.

———. 1996. "Artificiality and Enlightenment: From Sociobiology to Biosociality." In *Essays on the Anthropology of Reason,* 91–111. Princeton: Princeton University Press.

———. 1999. *French DNA: Trouble in Purgatory.* Chicago: The University of Chicago Press.

———. 2008. "Afterword. Concept Work." In *Biosocialities, Genetics and the Social Sciences: Making Biologies and Identities,* ed. Sahra Gibbon and Carlos Novas, 188–192. London: Routledge.

Rabinow, Paul, and Nikolas Rose. 2006. "Biopower Today." *BioSocieties* 1, no. 2: 195–217.

Rafalovich, Adam. 2013. "Attention Deficit-Hyperactivity Disorder as the Medicalization of Childhood: Challenges from and for Sociology." *Sociology Compass* 7, no. 5: 343–354.

Rapp, Rayna. 1988. "Moral Pioneers: Women, Men and Fetuses on a Frontier of Reproductive Technology." *Women & Health* 14, no. 1–2: 101–116.

———. 1999. *Testing Women, Testing the Fetus: The Social Impact of Amniocentesis in America.* London: Routledge.

Richards, Martin. 2008. "Artificial Insemination and Eugenics: Celibate Motherhood, Eutelegenesis and Germinal Choice." *Studies in History and Philosophy of Biological and Biomedical Sciences* 39, no. 2: 211–221.

————. 2010. "Reading the Runes of My Genome: A Personal Exploration of Retail Genetics." *New Genetics and Society* 29, no. 3: 291–310.

Riggs, Damien W. 2008. "Lesbian Mothers, Gay Male Sperm Donors, and Community: Ensuring the Wellbeing of Children and Families." *Health Sociology Review* 17, no. 3: 226–234.

————. 2009. "The Health and Well-Being Implications of Emotion Work Undertaken by Gay Sperm Donors." *Feminism & Psychology* 19, no. 4: 517–533.

Riggs, Damien W., and Laura Russell. 2011. "Characteristics of Men Willing to Act as Sperm Donors in the Context of Identity-Release Legislation." *Human Reproduction* 26, no. 1: 266–272.

Riggs, Damien W., and Brett Scholz. 2011. "The Value and Meaning Attached to Genetic Relatedness Among Australian Sperm Donors." *New Genetics and Society* 30, no. 1: 41–58.

Riska, Elianne. 2010. "Gender and Medicalization and Biomedicalization Theories." In *Biomedicalization: Technoscience, Health, and Illness in the U.S.*, ed. Adele E. Clarke, Laura Mamo, Jennifer Ruth Fosket, Jennifer Fishman, and Janet K. Shim, 147–170. Durham: Duke University Press.

Rose, Nikolas. 2001. "The Politics of Life Itself." *Theory, Culture & Society* 18, no. 6: 1–30.

————. 2007. *The Politics of Life Itself: Biomedicine, Power, and Subjectivity in the Twenty-First Century.* Princeton: Princeton University Press.

Rose, Nikolas, and Carlos Novas. 2005. "Biological Citizenship." In *Global Assemblages: Technology, Politics, and Ethics as Anthropological Problems*, ed. Aihwa Ong and Stephen J. Collier, 439–463. Malden: Blackwell.

Rosenfeld, Dana, and Christopher A. Faircloth, eds. 2006. *Medicalized Masculinities.* Philadelphia: Temple University Press.

Rosewarne, Lauren. 2014. *Masturbation in Pop Culture: Screen, Society, Self.* London: Lexington Books.

Rubin, Gayle. 1975. "The Traffic in Women: Notes on the 'Political Economy' of Sex." In *Toward an Anthropology of Women*, ed. Rayna R. Reiter, 157–210. New York: Monthly Review Press.

————. 1984. "Thinking Sex: Notes for a Radical Theory of the Politics of Sexuality." In *Pleasure and Danger: Exploring Female Sexuality*, ed. Carole S. Vance, 267–319. New York: Routledge & Kegan Paul.

————. 2011. *Deviations: A Gayle Rubin Reader.* Durham: Duke University Press.

Ruestow, Edward G. 1983. "Images and Ideas: Leeuwenhoek's Perception of the Spermatozoa." *Journal of the History of Biology* 16, no. 2: 185–224.

Scheper-Hughes, Nacy, and Loïc Wacquant. 2006. *Commodifying Bodies.* London: Sage Publications.

Schmidt, Lone. 1996. *Psykosociale konsekvenser af infertilitet og behandling.* København: Foreningen af Danske Lægestuderendes Forlag.

Schneider, Kristina. 2010. "Das öffentliche Bild des Samenspenders in Fernsehserien und im Film." In *Samenbanken—Samenspender. Ethnographische und historische Perspektiven auf Männlichkeiten in der Reproduktionsmedizin,* ed. Michi Knecht, Anna Frederike Heinitz, Scout Burghardt, and Sebastian Mohr, 68–80. Berlin: LIT Verlag.

Schramm, Katharina, David Skinner, and Richard Rottenburg, eds. 2012. *Identity Politics and the New Genetics: Re/Creating Categories of Difference and Belonging.* New York: Berghahn.

Sharp, Lesley A. 2000. "The Commodification of the Body and Its Parts." *Annual Review of Anthropology* 29: 287–328.

Sherman, Jerome. 1980. "Historical Synopsis of Human Semen Cryobanking." In *Human Artifical Insemination and Semen Preservation,* ed. Georges David and Wendel S. Price, 95–105. New York: Plenum Press.

Simmel, Georg, ed. 1985. *Schriften zur Philosophie und Soziologie der Geschlechter.* Frankfurt am Main: Suhrkamp.

Simpson, Bob. 2004. "Impossible Gifts: Bodies, Buddhism and Bioethics in Contemporary Sri Lanka." *Journal of the Royal Anthropological Institute* 10, no. 4: 839–859.

Singy, Patrick. 2003. "Friction of the Genitals and Secularization of Morality." *Journal of the History of Sexuality* 12, no. 3: 345–364.

Speirs, Jennifer. 2007. "Secretly Connceted? Anonymous Semen Donation, Genetics and Meanings of Kinship." University of Edinburgh.

Speirs, Jennifer M. 2012. "Semen Donors' Curiosity About Donor Offspring and the Barriers to Their Knowing." *Human Fertility* 15, no. 2: 89–93.

Steiner, Camilla Blay. 2006. "'En eller anden forbindelse.' En etnografi om danske sæddonorer i et slægtskabsperspektiv." Institut for Antropologi, Københavns Universitet.

Stengers, Jean, and Anne van Neck. 2001. *Masturbation: The History of a Great Terror.* New York: Palgrave.Stolberg, Michael. 2000. "An Unmanly Vice: Self-Pollution, Anxiety, and the Body in the Eighteenth Century." *Social History of Medicine* 13, no. 1: 1–22.

———. 2003. "The Crime of Onan and the Laws of Nature: Religious and Medical Discourses on Masturbation in the Late Seventeenth and Early Eighteenth Centuries." *Paedagogica Historica* 39, no. 6: 701–717.

Stoller, Paul, ed. 1989. *The Taste of Ethnographic Things: The Senses in Anthropology.* Philadelphia: University of Pennsylvania Press.

Strathern, Marilyn. 1992. *Reproducing the Future. Essays on Anthropology, Kinship and the New Reproductive Technologies.* Manchester: Manchester University Press.

———. 1995. *After Nature: English Kinship in the Late Twentieth Century.* Cambridge: Cambridge University Press.

Sundhedsstyrelsen. 2014. Humane væv og celler. Årsrapport 2013. København.

———. 2015. Humane væv og celler. Årsrapport 2014. København.

Swanson, Kara W. 2012. "Adultery by Doctor: Artificial Insemination, 1890–1945." *Chicago-Kent Law Review* 87, no. 2: 591–633.

Thompson, Charis. 2005. *Making Parents: The Ontological Choreography of Reproductive Technologies.* Cambridge: MIT Press.

Thomson, Michael. 2008. *Endowed: Regulating the Male Sexed Body.* New York: Routledge.

Tjørnhøj-Thomsen, Tine. 1999. "Tilblivelseshistorier. Barnløshed, slægtskab og forplantningsteknologi i Danmark." Insitut for Antropologi, Københavns Universitet.

———. 2009. "'It's a Bit Unmanly in a Way': Men and Infertility in Denmark." In *Reconceiving the Second Sex: Men, Masculinity, and Reproduction,* ed. Marcia C. Inhorn, Tine Tjørnhøj-Thomsen, Helene Goldberg, and Maruska la Cour Mosegaard, 226–252. New York, Oxford: Berghahn Books.

Trundle, Catherine, and Brydie Isobel Scott. 2013. "Elusive Genes: Nuclear Test Veterans' Experiences of Genetic Citizenship and Biomedical Refusal." *Medical Anthropology* 32, no. 6: 501–517.

Turner, Aaron. 2000. "Embodied Ethnography: Doing Culture." *Social Anthropology* 8, no. 1: 51–60.

Van den Broeck, U., M. Vandermeeren, D. Vanderschueren, P. Enzlin, K. Demyttenaere, and T. D'Hooghe. 2013. "A Systematic Review of Sperm Donors: Demographic Characteristics, Attitudes, Motives and Experiences of the Process of Sperm Donation." *Human Reproduction Update* 19, no. 1: 37–51.

Van Gennep, Arnold. 2004. *The Rites of Passage.* London: Routledge.

Vannini, Phillip, Dennis Waskul, and Simon Gottschalk. 2014. *The Senses in Self, Society, and Culture: A Sociology of the Senses.* New York: Routledge.

Vermeulen, Niki, Sakari Tamminen, and Andrew Webster, eds. 2012. *Bio-Objects: Life in the 21st Century.* Farnham: Ashgate.

Vertinsky, Patricia. 1991. "Old Age, Gender and Physical Activity: The Biomedicalization of Aging." *Journal of Sport History* 18, no. 1: 64–80.

Walby, Sylvia. 1989. "Theorising Patriarchy." *Sociology* 23, no. 2: 213–234.

Waldby, Catherine. 2002. "Biomedicine, Tissue Transfer and Intercorporeality." *Feminist Theory* 3, no. 3: 239–254.

Waldby, Catherine, Marsha Rosengarten, Carla Treloar, and Suzanne Fraser. 2004. "Blood and Bioidentity: Ideas About Self, Boundaries and Risk Among Blood Donors and People Living with Hepatitis C." *Social Science & Medicine* 59, no. 7: 1461–1471.

Weber, Marianne, ed. 1919. *Frauenfragen und Frauengedanken.* Tübingen: Mohr Siebeck.

Wentzell, Emily. 2013a. "Change and the Construction of Gendered Selfhood Among Mexican Men Experiencing Erectile Difficulty." *Ethos* 41, no. 1: 24–45.

———. 2013b. *Maturing Masculinities. Aging, Chronic Illness, and Viagra in Mexico.* Durham: Duke University Press.

West, Candace, and Don H. Zimmerman. 1987. "Doing Gender." *Gender and Society* 1, no. 2: 125–151.

———. 2009. "Accounting for Doing Gender." *Gender & Society* 23, no. 1: 112–122.

Williams, Raymond. 2011. "Culture is Ordinary." In *Cultural Theory: An Anthology,* ed. Imre Szeman and Timothy Kaposy, 53–59. Malden: Wiley-Blackwell.

Zhang, Everett Yuehong. 2015. *The Impotence Epidemic: Men's Medicine and Sexual Desire in Contemporary China.* Durham: Duke University Press.

Zola, Irving Kenneth. 1972. "Medicine as an Institution of Social Control." *The Sociological Review* 20, no. 4: 487–504.

INDEX

Fertility, Reproduction and Sexuality

GENERAL EDITORS:

Soraya Tremayne, Founding Director, Fertility and Reproduction Studies Group and Research Associate, Institute of Social and Cultural Anthropology, University of Oxford.

Marcia C. Inhorn, William K. Lanman, Jr. Professor of Anthropology and International Affairs, Yale University.

Philip Kreager, Director, Fertility and Reproduction Studies Group, and Research Associate, Institute of Social and Cultural Anthropology and Institute of Human Sciences, University of Oxford.